The Pusan International Film Festival, South Korean Cinema and Globalization

T0345729

TransAsia Screen Cultures
Edited by Koichi IWABUCHI and Chris BERRY

What is Asia? What does it mean to be Asian? Who thinks they are Asian? How is "Asian-ness" produced? In Asia's transnational public space, many kinds of crossborder connections proliferate, from corporate activities to citizen-to-citizen linkages, all shaped by media—from television series to action films, video piracy, and a variety of subcultures facilitated by internet sites and other computer-based cultures. Films are packaged at international film festivals and marketed by DVD companies as "Asian," while the descendants of migrants increasingly identify themselves as "Asian," then turn to "Asian" screen cultures to find themselves and their roots. As reliance on national frameworks becomes obsolete in many traditional disciplines, this series spotlights groundbreaking research on trans-border, screen-based cultures in Asia.

Other titles in the series:

The Chinese Exotic: Modern Diasporic Femininity, by Olivia Khoo

East Asian Pop Culture: Analysing the Korean Wave, edited by Chua Beng Huat and Koichi Iwabuchi

TV Drama in China, edited by Ying Zhu, Michael Keane, and Ruoyun Bai

Cultural Studies and Cultural Industries in Northeast Asia: What a Difference a Region Makes, edited by Chris Berry, Nicola Liscutin, and Jonathan D. Mackintosh

Horror to the Extreme: Changing Boundaries in Asian Cinema, edited by Jinhee Choi and Mitsuyo Wada-Marciano

Cinema at the City's Edge: Film and Urban Networks in East Asia, edited by Yomi Braester and James Tweedie

Korean Masculinities and Transcultural Consumption: Yonsama, Rain, Oldboy, K-Pop Idols, by Sun Jung

Japanese Cinema Goes Global: Filmworkers' Journeys, by Yoshiharu Tezuka

The Pusan International Film Festival, South Korean Cinema and Globalization

SooJeong Ahn

香港大學出版社
HONG KONG UNIVERSITY PRESS

Hong Kong University Press
14/F Hing Wai Centre
7 Tin Wan Praya Road
Aberdeen
Hong Kong

© Hong Kong University Press 2012

ISBN 978-988-8083-58-9 *(Hardback)*
ISBN 978-988-8083-59-6 *(Paperback)*

British Library Cataloguing-in-Publication Data
A catalogue record for this book is available from the British Library.

10   9   8   7   6   5   4   3   2   1

Printed and bound by Liang Yu Printing Factory Ltd. in Hong Kong, China

Contents

Note to Reader

All quotations from festival catalogs and newspaper reports in this book preserve original punctuation and spelling.[1]

In referencing (endnotes and bibliography), this book uses the Documentary-Note Chicago Manual Style.

All Korean names in this book have been romanized according to the Revised Romanization of Korean in 2000 by South Korea's Ministry of Culture and Tourism (e.g., *jaebol* not *chaebol*). Moreover, wherever possible, names of Korean film professionals (director, actor, and producer, etc.) and film titles follow the system used in *Korean Film Database Book from 2000 to 2006*, published by the KOFIC in 2006.[2] Korean names are presented in Korean style, i.e., surname first, given name last, except in cases where individual authors have chosen to transliterate their name in Western form (i.e., surname last). This general rule of thumb encompasses the presentation of Chinese and Japanese names as well.

All English translations, including comments, quotations and interviews taken from Korean-language material, are my own unless otherwise specified.

Abbreviations

AAFA	Association of Asian Film Archives
AFA	Asian Film Academy
AFCNet	Asian Film Commissions Network
AFIC	Asian Film Industry Center
AFIN	Asian Film Industry Network
AFM	Asian Film Market / American Film Market
APEC	Asian-Pacific Economic Cooperation
ASEAN	Association of Southeast Asian Nations
ASEM	Asia-Europe Meeting
BEXCO	Busan Exhibition and Convention Center
BFC	Busan Film Commission
BIFCOM	Busan International Film Commission and Industry Showcase
DMB	Digital Multimedia Broadcasting
EDN	European Documentary Network
EFM	European Film Market
EFP	European Film Promotion
EU	European Union
FESPACO	Panafrican Film Festival of Ouagadougou
FIAF	Fédération Internationale des Archives du Film (International Federation of Film Archives)
FIAPF	Fédération Internationale des Associations de Producteurs de Films (International Federation of Film Producers Associations)
FILMART	Hong Kong International Film and Television Market
IFFR	International Film Festival Rotterdam
IMF	International Monetary Fund
JIFF	Jeonju International Film Festival
HAF	Hong Kong-Asia Film Financing Forum
HBF	Hubert Bals Fund
HKIFF	Hong Kong International Film Festival
KAFA	Korean Academy of Film Arts
KF-MAP	Korean Film-Making Assistant Project

KMPPC   Korean Motion Picture Promotion Corporation
KOFA   Korean Film Archive
KOFIC   Korean Film Council
MIFED   International Film and Multimedia Market
MoMA   Museum of Modern Art
MPAA   Motion Picture Association of America
NDIF   New Directors In Focus
NETPAC   Network for the Promotion of Asian Cinema
NHK   Nihon Hōsō Kyōkai (Japanese National Broadcasting Corporation)
PiFan   Puchon International Film Festival
PIFF   Pusan International Film Festival
PPP   Pusan Promotion Plan
PRC   People's Republic of China (Mainland China)
SeNef   Seoul Net and Film Festival
TIFF   Tokyo International Film Festival
TIFFCOM Content Market at the TIFF
UN   United Nations
UNESCO   United Nations Educational, Scientific and Cultural Organization
WTO   World Trade Organization

Introduction

Film Festivals between the National and the Regional in the Age of Globalization

This book examines an international film festival in South Korea, the Pusan International Film Festival (PIFF), between the years 1996 and 2005.[1] The purpose of this research is to elucidate how an individual film festival in a non-Western country has worked to position itself within the rapidly changing global film economy, and identifies a series of self-definition processes it used to differentiate itself from its regional counterparts, such as the Hong Kong and Tokyo film festivals. Furthermore, this project also reflects the complexities brought about by the rapid transformation of the South Korean film industry, which has striven to reach out to the global film market since the late 1990s.

Over the past two decades there has been a significant proliferation of new film festivals around the world. Despite the growing interest and importance of film festivals as a scholarly topic, research on film festivals has tended to focus on high-profile European festivals, such as Cannes, Venice, and Berlin.[2] Little primary empirical research has been conducted to date on the subject of non-Western film festivals. As a result, the existing scholarship on this topic has largely failed to comprehensively acknowledge the different social and cultural contexts of non-Western film festivals. In addition, it is worth noting that while the exhibition of new titles of world cinema has long been seen as a key to obtaining a high profile for major festivals in the West, it is surprising that the relationship between non-Western film festivals and their role in exhibiting and supporting the production of world cinema has rarely been explored in film studies.

In this book, I aim to address these gaps by specifically focusing on the PIFF, which, since its inception in 1996, has rapidly emerged in the global film market as the single most significant showcase of Asian cinema. The hypothesis of this study is that the PIFF's regional approach towards East Asia, synergized by the global visibility of South Korean cinema, displays a distinct agenda and sociocultural context different from that of Euro-American film festivals.

Moreover, the PIFF's vital role in linking with its national and regional film industries will be established as the first step to discovering the unexplored roles and functions that festivals play in the global film economy. In addition to the roles conventionally associated with film festivals, namely exhibition and distribution, this book uncovers the significant role festivals play in production by investigating the Pusan Promotion Plan (PPP), a project market run alongside the PIFF.[3] It is my contention that the PIFF provides a unique discursive site through which to understand the tensions and negotiations among cultural and economic forces locally, regionally, and globally.

The PIFF, Korea's first international film festival, is held annually in Pusan, a southeastern port and the second largest city in Korea. With a focus on Asian cinema, the PIFF has achieved enormous success since its inauguration on September 13, 1996, attracting huge local audiences—around 180,000 visitors per year—and receiving positive critical response from foreign participants.[4] Building upon this unanticipated success, the PIFF has become the leading international film festival in Asia, even surpassing the Hong Kong International Film Festival (HKIFF), which for the previous twenty years had been the prime viewing forum for the latest Asian films.[5]

It is widely believed that the PIFF's success coincides with an increased global interest in South Korean cinema.[6] The international recognition of Korean cinema has mainly been achieved through the festival circuit in the West and the remarkable growth of the national film industry since the 1990s.[7] Consequently, the evolution of the PIFF seems to be closely inter-related with the status of Korean cinema in the global economy.

Alongside the importance of the PIFF's intimate links with the national film industry, the festival's self-determined conceptualization and manipulation of an Asian identity in order to approach the global market provides a distinctive case study, as this systematic regional approach has not been evident in any other film festival. While the PIFF has acted as a key institution and agency for the promotion of Korean cinema, it has also attempted to brand Pusan's festival image more broadly as a showcase for Asian cinema in order to survive in a highly competitive global film market. I seek to explore this ambivalent combination of regional and national politics brought about by global forces.

The PIFF's unique regionalization strategy and its complex relationship with Korean and Asian cinema require serious consideration and raise important questions. As home to the first international-scale film festival in the history of South Korea, how and why was Pusan chosen as the host city from among other possible candidates? Why did the PIFF have to conceptualize a regional identity and actively build up industrial regional networks? How have the PIFF and the Korean film industry inter-related over the past decade? Why did the PIFF establish the PPP, a project market, and try to brand its products in the name of Asian cinema? Finally, how does the successful establishment of the PIFF help us understand the various facets of interaction among local, national, regional, and global forces? These specific research questions will be addressed in the following chapters.

This book seeks to shed new light on the worldwide phenomenon of film festivals by bringing the discussion of film festivals into a non-Western context. A proviso is necessary, however. By using the term "non-Western" here, I do not intend to lend credence to the binary division of the West versus the non-West. Countless scholars in cultural and media studies have pointed out the problems of this dichotomy. As Stuart Hall has argued, terms such as "the West," "the non-West," or "the Rest" are historically constructed notions embedded within global power relations.[8] Indeed, an irreflexive "West versus non-West" divide is too simple a way of approaching the issue. At the same time, however, this concept can still be used as a methodological tool to question such assumptions rather than to accompany and reinforce them. Thus, being aware of the problematic nature of this term, I will critically employ the notion of the "non-West" in this book to challenge and complicate the binary oppositions often produced in discourse surrounding film festivals. By concentrating on one film festival in a non-Western region, I will address the limits of previous accounts of film festivals and draw attention to hitherto unexplored aspects of this subject.

More than this, the reason I focus on the PIFF is not only because of the lack of previous work on non-Western film festivals, but also because it reflects wider changes both in Korean society and East Asia more generally. As will be argued in the following chapter, research on the PIFF also reveals the recent trend of film festivals that have begun to brand and promote world films via the festival circuit within the changing global cultural economy. For example, the emergence and development of the PIFF in the global film market is also related to the rise of non-American international film festivals in many parts of the world since the 1990s. Overall, my prime concern in this book is to show how the PIFF stands out from the wider panorama of film festivals, both in Asia and worldwide.

As this book cannot aim to address all aspects of film festivals, it targets instead topics which are the most urgently required in researching this subject: namely, the festival's vital links with film industries and its unique positioning at national and regional levels. In this regard, the PIFF can be more broadly seen as a representative case study of film festivals in Asia, as it demonstrates changing regional responses to economic and cultural globalization. At the same time, however, it stands out for its self-determined construction of regional identity and its distinctive ties to the fast-growing Korean film industry. The value of this research lies in its analysis of the diverse sides of contemporary film festivals, such as their economic viability and relations to national and regional film industries, through considering both typical and unique aspects of the PIFF.

Critical Self-Positioning

This study initially evolved out of my own personal experience working at the PIFF. Having been employed by this organization between 1998 and 2002, following a career in the film industry, my knowledge of the PIFF and Korean cinema was already extensive before starting this research. Given the insider knowledge gleaned through my industrial experience, film festivals were for me neither glamorous events nor sites of cinematic fantasy. Rather, the film festival required highly intensive physical labor and continuous responses to contemporary political, economic, and social changes at local, regional, and global levels.

Furthermore, despite the consistent emphasis on Asian identity as a key instrument to promote the festival, it was apparent to me that the PIFF also self-consciously considered itself a significant agent in promoting Korean cinema to the Western film market, in particular since the late 1990s. These complex and contradictory aspects of the festival prompted me to develop this research and enabled me to discover a theoretical framework for these personal interests. As I then began to position myself as a detached researcher by keeping a distance from the PIFF, my initial questions regarding the festival gradually evolved into more fundamental inquiries: What are the ultimate goals of film festival studies? What has been gained by film festival studies? What is a film festival? This book seeks to address these basic questions. By closely examining how the PIFF and the Korean film industry have coped with the impact of globalization within the specific Korean and East Asian context, this study seeks to take some first steps in understanding the complexities of film festivals, not only in East Asia but also the rest of the world.

The global phenomenon of film festivals is interlinked with multiple fields, from national cinemas, world cities, spatiality and temporality, to cultural industries and branding culture. Hence, this subject cannot be approached through one single dominant methodology. As Julian Stringer points out, "[m]ulti-dimensional phenomena can only be approached via a diversity of different viewpoints, using a variety of critical resources and research methodologies."[9] In the case of the PIFF, the use of an interdisciplinary approach helps disentangle the complex relationship between the national and regional film industries in the specific sociopolitical context of Korea and East Asia.

My research combines ethnographic investigation—including interviews, participation observation, and archival research—with textual analysis of primary materials. Through this, I seek to address a crucial gap in the existing largely theoretical scholarship on film festivals: a lack of empirically verified research methodologies. Rather than being fixed and self-contained, this book aims to follow the diverse, rapidly changing festival landscape by creatively employing a mobile, flexible, and interdisciplinary approach that draws upon writings on film festivals,

Korean cinema, East Asian studies, area studies, and cultural studies. In so doing, I am aware of the differing perspectives between Western and Korean literatures in examining the film festival phenomenon. In this respect, it is both a challenge and a benefit to be looking at a single non-Western film festival, as this means developing the debate on film festivals through a new critical paradigm.

In this research, ethnography is mainly composed of interviews between 2003 and 2007, and participation observation conducted during the fieldwork in Pusan for four months between September and December in 2005. This was during the tenth anniversary of the PIFF, as I will discuss in the final chapter. Rather than sketching a wide range of different people, my interviews focused on selected film professionals and were arranged to take an in-depth look at interviewees.[10] Personal one-to-one interviews were conducted in places such as Seoul and Pusan in South Korea, along with London, Paris, and Karlovy Vary.

There are three categories of interviewees in this book: international critics in academic journals and industrial magazines; professionals associated with the Korean film industry; as well as festival organizers and workers. The second group included Korean film journalists and those involved in policy making such as the general secretary of the Korean Film Council (KOFIC). However, due to fast shifts in the Korean film industry when conducting this research, the position of each interviewee often overlapped. For example, film director Park Kwang-su was interviewed not only as a former organizer of the PIFF but also as a founder of the Busan Film Commission (BFC). Therefore, this division was fundamentally intended to interpret each interviewee's attitude and perspective towards the Korean film industry and the PIFF.

It can be argued that "institutional ethnography" was used in arranging and interpreting those interviews. As Dorothy E. Smith discusses, institutional ethnography as practice is a method of inquiry that problematizes social relations at the local site of lived experience and that examines how textual sequences coordinate consciousness, actions, and ruling relations.[11] This methodology preserves their presence as subjects rather than objects. Thus, the interviewees recognize that researchers are in the same world as that which they are investigating. Such responses provide more opportunities "for opening up dimensions of the institutional regime that were not recognised at the outset of the project."[12] They are more willing to open up to people with shared understanding. For example, had I not been regarded as a former member of the local film community, it would have been very difficult as an outsider to understand fully the circumstances. However, at the same time, due to my position as a former "insider," it was also a challenge to deal with the interviewees' skepticism towards my relationship with the PIFF. For instance, some of them demanded off-the-record conversations during interviewing because they did not want their colleagues to hear about their opinions on the film industry and the PIFF.

Participation observation was conducted during the fieldwork in 2005. From the opening night to the closing party, key programs and sidebar events were examined in detail for the final chapter of this book. Among a number of special events to celebrate the PIFF's tenth anniversary, I paid particular attention to two: the PPP seminar titled "Advanced Window Marketing" on October 11 at the Paradise Hotel Pusan, and the international conference "Asia/Cinema/Network: Industry, Technology, and Film Culture" held from October 11 to 13 at the Westin Chosun Pusan Hotel.[13]

Finally, archival research was one of the important methodologies that I conducted. In this study, it was appropriate, as one of my priorities was to use primary rather than secondary sources. It allowed me to gain a sense of reality about this project and better understand the topic.

My position as former staff and my industry-related background also provided me with more opportunities to get access to materials "hidden" from the public.[14] When starting this research in 2002, there were no actual archives in the offices of film festival organizing committees, including the PIFF, and film companies in Korea (which will be illustrated in Chapter 3 when discussing retrospectives at festivals). This meant archival materials were dispersed in several places or not organized at all. For example, around August every year, all staff in the PIFF's branch office in Seoul make the move into its headquarters in Haeundae, Pusan to prepare for the event. Furthermore, until the PIFF decided to give up the festival venues in the Nampo-dong area in 2005, the Haeundae office had to move into Nampo-dong where the festival venues were located. Then the office had to move right back to Haeundae after the event. This meant that all the materials had to move around with the people who worked with them. In addition, researchers were not allowed to search the computers or bookshelves of film festival organizing committees. Therefore, in order to get the material that I wanted more effectively, it was necessary to establish and maintain an excellent relationship with staff, especially when I encountered sensitive materials that required professional handling or were confidential to outsiders.

Framing Film Festivals

Over the past two decades the number of film festivals has increased rapidly and become a global phenomenon. Their recent proliferation in non-Western regions deserves particular attention because it offers different contexts from existing prestigious film festivals in the West, such as Cannes, Berlin, and Venice. Despite its most visible emergence outside of the West in recent years, however, it is widely believed that the film festival is a Western invention.[15] Europe is considered the origins and "cradle" of film festivals. Apart from the Venice Film Festival under Mussolini in the 1930s, film festivals in Europe had been established within the specific European geopolitical situation during the war: Cannes in 1946, Edinburgh in 1947, and Berlin in 1951. The Berlin Film Festival, for example, was established as an outpost of postwar culture sanctioned by the occupying Allied forces in West Berlin, who were rebuilding it as a new cultural center.

In mapping film festivals in this region, however, it is important to point out how they are influenced by and closely tied to Hollywood in complicated ways. We see this not only from the fact that the Berlin Film Festival was initially supported by America, but also in the presence of Hollywood stars and glamour in Cannes.[16] Yet, for decades, Cannes has remained the most prestigious venue for the *auteur*, as a center of a new alliance against Hollywood products.

Outside western Europe, the Sundance Film Festival devoted to independent films was founded in 1978 in the United States. In Asia, the Hong Kong Film Festival has played an important role in showcasing Asian cinema to the West since 1977, while festivals in urban global cities such as Tokyo (1985), Singapore (1987), and Shanghai (1993) had been subsequently established. In the late 1990s, in particular, a cluster of international film festivals in South Korea had almost concurrently been launched in Pusan, Puchon, Seoul, and so forth.

While the origins of "major" film festivals are marked by urban regeneration projects after the Second World War and during the postwar period, it is distinctive that such events staged outside Europe have been organized under the forces of economic and cultural globalization since the 1990s. For example, the global emergence of film festivals in Asia, such as the Pusan and Singapore film festivals, is closely related with Asia's position in the international economy and the rise of "Asian cinema" in the global film industry since the 1990s.[17] In this context, mapping film festivals in East Asia, for example, is key to understanding the forces and transformation of ongoing globalization in the region. It is widely agreed that decentered cultural globalization has prompted the shift from an emphasis on center-periphery relations to a diffusion of cultural power. This point is particularly pertinent to the film festival phenomenon. As such events can be found scattered around the world, it raises the question of whether or not it is still possible to pinpoint exactly where its center is.[18] It also helps extend the boundary of the discussion of intraregional cultural flows and consumption in the region, as will be argued in this book.

With the proliferation of film festivals, the structure of the festival world has substantially transformed over the past two decades within a highly competitive global cultural economy. For instance, festivals vie with each other for the limited number of films produced in the annual festival calendar.[19] Furthermore, their functions in relation to the global film industry have become more influential and expansive at the levels of exhibition, distribution, and even production.

Despite its importance in global film culture and industry, little scholarly work on film festivals was produced until the 1990s, at a time when their worldwide proliferation was becoming increasingly visible. The majority of earlier studies have tended to focus on the high-profile major film festivals in Europe, mapping their relation to European and/or Hollywood cinema in the Euro-American context. Hence, film festivals outside of Europe and their precise role have rarely been explored. The absence of "other" voices in researching film festivals poses the question: can previous Euro-American-centered academic writing truly reflect the activities of the myriad other events across the world and the larger complexities of this global phenomenon? For instance, film festivals in East Asia, which have been actively interacting with their national and regional film industries, have never before been critically documented in a sustained way.

Earlier work on film festivals largely tended to focus on the issue of discovering new cinemas. In Britain, from the middle of the 1970s, there was a debate on film festivals among writings by Paul Willemen, Don Ranvaud, and Richard Allen in the film journal *Framework*.[20] Under the influence of the Pesaro Film Festival in Italy, which had introduced new cinema from Latin America, these critics began to recognize that film festivals provided opportunities to experience new cinemas originating from regions traditionally thought of as "the Other." While this debate was the first serious attempt to acknowledge the site of film festivals as a discursive location, this argument failed to further develop into a focused critical study of film festivals.

More recently, however, there has been a growing interest in film festivals, and it can be divided into three main areas based on the focus of this book. The first is concerned with the ways in which film festivals are framed by the idea of the national, while the second concerns the relationship between globalization and film festivals, particularly by focusing upon festival space—cities—with different levels. The third looks at film festivals from a regional rather than national perspective.

Film Festivals and the National

Historically, film festivals have been discussed predominantly in conjunction with the notion of the national. This is partly because the emergence of film festivals was closely aligned with regeneration projects focused on national levels in various European countries. Certainly, the origins of European film festivals such as Venice, Berlin, and Cannes clearly show that festivals were created on the basis of national developments.[21] It is widely believed that film festivals have served as "a kind of parliament of national cinema" or an Olympics of films, comprised of host and participant nations.[22] Does this mean that notions of the national still persist at film festivals despite the recent influx of transnational finance, technologies and the global circulation of media and transnational corporations?

Indeed, many scholars in film and media studies have tried to address this close but complex relationship between film festivals and the concept of the "national." Earlier critical attention to film festivals predominantly paid attention to the "discovery of new cinemas" at Western film festivals and allowed for the interpretation of new texts according to familiar paradigms of knowledge.

In his 1994 article, "Discovering Form, Inferring Meaning: New Cinemas and the Film Festival Circuit," Bill Nichols discusses the film festival experience and the interpretation of culturally unfamiliar films. Specifically looking at post-revolutionary Iranian films at the Toronto Film Festival, he claims that the film festival circuit places layers of new meaning on films through their festival circulation. What he attempts to explain is, to use his terminology, the processes of "discovery of the form" and "inferring [of] meaning" that occurs at festivals. As he notes:

> Films from nations not previously regarded as prominent film-producing countries receive praise for their ability to transcend local issues and provincial tastes while simultaneously providing a window onto a different culture. We are invited to receive such films as evidence of artistic maturity—the work of directors ready to take their place within an international fraternity of *auteur*—and of a distinctive national culture—work that remains distinct from Hollywood-based norms both in style and theme [...] Most forms of cinematic expressivity are minimally present. We find no magical realism, no expressionism, surrealism, collage, or bold figures of montage. Melodramatic intensities, or excess, are extremely rare, far from constituting the type of contrapuntal *system* found in Sirk or Fassbinder. Point-of-view dynamics are usually weak to nonexistent. The great majority of scenes unfold in a third-person, long-take, long-shot, minimally edited style. There is only limited use of music and even dialogue.[23]

This cross-cultural approach has been useful to explain how new texts circulate at film festivals. According to Nichols' account, film festivals become a crucial means of mediation in which new cinemas are encountered. Furthermore, he clearly recognizes the difficulties in acknowledging an unfamiliar culture at festivals. Being aware that the position of festival-goers ("white, Western, middle class") limits their understanding of the authenticity of "their" culture, he further points out that "the pursuit of intimate knowledge and authenticity is illusory."[24]

While Nichols explores the process of acknowledgement of new titles from (mostly, non-Western) "others" circulated at Western film festivals as aesthetic texts, this book is more concerned with how this particular process of discovery unfolds as a result of institutional intervention and can therefore be maneuvered at diverse levels. In other words, I focus on how a non-Western festival can engage with a self-conscious awareness in this "discovery of the form" and "inferring [of] meaning." What happens when a non-Western film festival showcases its own local films to local and global audiences? Will the process of discovery operate differently? Can non-Western festivals and audiences take up an active position in this process?

To answer these questions, Nichols' discussion needs to be further extended. What Nichols overlooks is that this process of interpretation of new texts at film festivals is dependent on a number of different contexts. In other words, as Julian Stringer points out, film festivals are *situated* sites.[25] In this context, Nichols' reading of the festival circuit leaves little room for explaining how films are shown at non-Western film festivals. This book attempts to address this problem by orienting the focus of the discussion in a different direction. It suggests that the cultural reception of specific films is dependent on a range of different contexts: different reception contexts, different exhibition circumstances, different interests, and different agendas. For instance, I suggest that the particular exhibition arrangements and subsequent reception histories of Korean cinema at its own film festival—the PIFF—in South Korea is different from that which is likely to be experienced at Cannes or Tokyo.

The process of discovering new cinemas at film festivals is also highlighted in an article by Dudley Andrew, who attempts to reconsider the widespread use of the term "new wave" in its relation to the European film festivals. He suggests "[c]ritics and festival programmers continue to invoke the term because the original New Wave inundated world cinema so decisively in the '60s that a total renewal of the art seemed imminent."[26] Differentiating the second set of new cinemas from the first new waves such as the French *Nouvelle Vague* in the 1960s, he claims that the canon formation of new cinemas at film festivals was a consequence of critics and programmers' desire to satisfy the needs of the European film festivals which sought to define new trends in cinema in order to show them to their audiences. He writes:

> As European art cinema was moribund, desperate festivals began looking elsewhere for signs of life. And life was found in what I call the Second Set of New Waves. By the early '80s, as if sucked into a vacuum, came films from places never before thought of as cinematically interesting or viable: Mainland China, Senegal, Mali, Ireland, Taiwan, and Iran. This second set of waves is distinct from those of the 1960s not only in their provenance but in the way they functioned in a greatly changed international system.[27]

On the one hand, Andrew's analysis of the meaning of new waves in film festivals in Europe after the 1980s seems to simply reconfirm that those prestigious contemporary film festivals have continued to "discover" new cinemas from "Other" parts of the world. For this reason, this argument needs to be repositioned in a non-Western context. On the other hand, this observation about a second set of "new waves" indicates that the concept of new cinemas, and discoveries thereof, has increasingly reinforced the idea of the national as an important marketing strategy. Despite the difference in approaching the film festival, obviously, both Nichols and Andrew look at film festivals within the national framework. Nichols also alludes to new films which are "discovered" by Western festivals, and therefore can be conceptualized as representative of distinct national cinemas.

In his 2002 book, *Screening China*, Yingjin Zhang critically analyzes Western influences on Chinese film production—the Fifth Generation films—through the international film festival circuit.[28] Zhang is critical of how the particular pattern of Western reception to Chinese cinema, especially through festival sites, has gradually determined national filmmaking trends in the People's Republic of China. He observes:

> As far as film audiences are concerned, western fascination with Chinese cinema may also be explained in so-called "poetic" or "aesthetic" terms [...] If we examine those Chinese films that have won major international awards in recent years, we see a narrative pattern gradually taking shape. From Zhang Yimou's *Red Sorghum* and *Ju Dou*, Ang Lee's *The Wedding Banquet* and *Eat Drink Man Woman*, to Chen Kaige's *Farewell My Concubine* and *Temptress Moon*, oriental *ars erotica* as a mystified entity is fixed at the very center of Western fascination.[29]

He further points out that these "favourable reviews at international film festivals" lead to the production of more "ethnographic" films, and that "the wide distribution of such films is translated into their availability for classroom use and therefore influences the agenda of film studies, which in turn reinforces the status of these films as a dominant genre."[30] This reception process, which includes garnishing awards at international film festivals, had a huge impact on local Chinese filmmaking, not least by establishing some Chinese film directors as "brand names" recognizable to consumers in the West. However, he argues, the success of Chinese cinema at international film festivals did not result in a boost for the local Chinese film industry. Highlighting the importance of festivals to film production and the context of cultural politics, Zhang succinctly outlines how targeting the international film festival circuit is a marketing strategy to effectively get into the global film market.

Viewed from this angle, further questions are raised in relation to the study of the PIFF: how is the recently growing interest in and popularity of Korean films different from that of Chinese cinema at Western film festivals? What parallels exist between the success of Korean cinema at the global film festivals and the case of Chinese cinema in the early 1990s? Is the spotlight on Korean cinema just another case of the "discovery" by the West of a national cinema that has reached so-called "artistic maturity"? Or is it rather the successful achievement of another refined type of "ethnographic approach"?

In attempting to answer these questions, it is worth looking at Chris Berry's writing on the relationship between Korean cinema and its international recognition through the film festival circuit. In his article "Introducing 'Mr. Monster': Kim Ki-Young and the Critical Economy of the Globalized Art-House Cinema," Berry discusses the function of the international film festival circuit and its critical standards. The premise of his argument is that the international film festival circuit operates on the basis of national cinemas and *auteurs*. He specifically looks at the case of Korean director Kim Ki-young, who received international recognition through the "Korean Retrospective" program at the PIFF in 1997. Pointing out that Korean cinema had previously not been able to establish its own distinctive image as a national cinema which would enable it to differentiate itself from Japanese and Chinese cinema, Berry attempts to interrogate how notions of "excess" and "violence" have impeded Korean cinema's international circulation. He suggests that for this circulation to increase it would be necessary for "a film or group of films to appear with characteristics which helped to establish a distinctive and appealing image as a new product, defined in national and *auteur* terms."[31]

What he proposes is that Kim Ki-young's films exhibit a potential ability to break into the international film world and thereby establish a distinctive image for Korean cinema, as his films show a different kind of excess acceptable to international audiences, what Berry calls "analytic excess."[32] According to Berry, Kim's unique, distinctive style fits the critical organization of the international art-house circuit, which seeks films by *auteur* directors with a noticeable style and national distinctiveness.[33] Berry's investigation of the relations between the international film festival circuit and specific Korean film texts, which had never previously been explored, allows us to further the discussion of film festivals and Korean cinema and effectively pinpoints the critical position of Korean cinema in the global art-house market in the 1990s.

This book takes Berry's argument in a slightly different direction. Although he presents the example of Kim Ki-young's reception at the PIFF, rather than at Western film festivals, his observations are based on the reception of Western audiences who participated in this event. Hence, the PIFF itself is not considered as the specific exhibition context within Berry's work. This means that culturally and locally specific arrangements, which can affect the reception of Kim's films in diverse ways, are ignored in his analysis. This question precisely indicates the difference between Berry's discussion and my approach in this book. This research is more concerned with understanding the PIFF, rather than Korean cinema itself. It explores how the PIFF attempts to frame the local, regional, and global reception of Korean cinema by using various institutional arrangements such as programming politics and promotional strategies. More specifically, I look at the PIFF as both a mediator of and a prime showcase for Korean cinema in the global market. In this context, the position of the PIFF in this research is related to Berry's argument about Korean cinema in a different but interlinked way. In his article, Berry states:

> For over a decade now, Korean filmmakers have targeted the film festival circuit, sending out retrospectives of new films in search of a "breakthrough" into the international film world. And for almost as long, international film critics have nominated Korean film as the next Asian cinema likely to make that breakthrough. But so far, it has not quite happened.[34]

A few years on after this observation was made, the situation has changed. A clear recognition of contemporary Korean cinema became globally visible in response to several works by Park Chan-wook, Kim Ki-duk and Hong Sang-soo among others. What I explore is how the PIFF is engaged with this newfound global attention on regional, national, and international levels.

In understanding the relationship between a national industry and its associated festival, Liz Czach's work on the Toronto Film Festival and the Canadian film industry is helpful.[35] Czach specifically argues that festival programming contributes to the formation of a national cinema by drawing on Pierre Bourdieu's idea of cultural capital—what she calls "critical capital"—by examining Canadian films at the Toronto Film Festival.[36] Her analysis offers opportunities to extend the discussion to other relevant factors that may influence the selection of particular national films, such as the role of festival programmers, awards and the premiere system, and the festival's inter-relation with its national film industry. I will explore these issues in detail as they relate to the PIFF in Chapter 3.

While Berry's argument in the abovementioned article is based on examining film festivals within a national framework, his recent analysis of Taiwanese cinema concerns the intersection of the national and the transnational. Although not discussing film festivals and Korean cinema specifically, Berry's reading of the "Taiwan Trilogy" is useful in understanding the complexities of the national and the transnational when researching the PIFF and the film festival phenomenon in general.[37] The point that Berry makes is that the national has not disappeared in the current post-national era but instead still exists within the forces of economic globalization. He claims that "our current era seems to feature *both* rising economic globalization and rising political nationalist tensions."[38] Berry argues that Hou Hsiao-hsien's "Taiwan Trilogy" invokes "a Chineseness that is trans-'national' in the sense of the nation-state, but national in the sense of a culture."[39] Reframing these films within the tensions operating within a national conjuncture, he suggests that the trilogy articulates a vision that accommodates a tension between both belongings. His argument beckons us toward a larger framework within which "the national is no

longer confined to the form of the territorial nation-state but is multiple, prolifer-
ating, contested, and overlapping."[40]

Modifying Berry's framework, I claim that film festivals can be a crucial means
to reveal the tension, contradiction, and negotiation between the global, the
regional, the national, and the local. Particularly, I focus upon the very relationship
between the regional and the national in terms of the strategic uses of the regional
and its tension with the national by specifically looking at the PIFF's case. Film
festivals have acted as a significant exhibition site for national cinemas and nationalistic agendas, and increasingly, their function has been multiplied and amplified
on the national level. At the same time, however, the regional, the global, and the
local are also permeated throughout the contemporary dynamics of film festivals
as they operate within the forces of economic globalization, as well as transnational finance and technologies. Within this context, I define the PIFF as a discursive space wherein the ambivalences of the relationship between the national and
regional appears in conjunction with the impact of economic and cultural globalization in this region. For example, regionalization and expansionism are distinctive modalities apparent in the PIFF that have accompanied the global spread of
film festivals over the past decade. Furthermore these two tendencies demonstrate
the PIFF's dual goals—one towards the establishment of a regional identity and
the other towards the promotion of the national film industry. Importantly, both
of these goals are closely related to the transformation of national and regional film
industries which have been searching for the "breakthrough" of their cultural products into the global film market.

In exploring the specific national context in this respect, Korean scholar Kim
Soyoung's argument on film festivals is significant in reading the phenomenon
encompassed by the rise of film festivals in Korea in the late 1990s. Kim explains
that the film festival phenomenon in Korea can be seen to have resulted from
"cinephilia and globalphilia via an emphasis on local politics."[41] In her analysis,
film festivals in Korea were widely seen as a key site of new social groups' cultural
practice, wherein political concerns gave way to cinematic ones.[42] More concretely,
she aligns the discussion of the film festival with the particular Korean context
to address the tensions that arose between ideological and cultural tendencies
invoked by *Segyehwa*, the official version of globalization and economic liberaliza-
tion launched with the establishment of the civil government in 1991.[43] As Kim
writes:

> The international-scale film festivals in particular thrive on the mani-
> fold manifestations of the global and the local and the national and
> the local. The local is a fragmented site contested by central and newly
> formed local governments. As noted above, the film festival provides a
> condensed space where different interests and ideologies all come into

play at the contested intersection of residual authoritarian and emergent democratic modes. The negotiations and compromises between
the state, the corporations, the intellectuals and the audiences betray
how the different social forces are contesting with one another in this
historical conjuncture.[44]

Kim's argument provides a crucial clue to understanding the cultural politics of
contemporary Korean society, especially to acknowledging the complicated structure of articulation working through the various film festivals, and to exploring the
issue of globalization in Korea. Her perceptive reflection on film festivals within
the historical, sociopolitical context of Korea pioneered a critical analysis of non-
Western film festivals that had not previously been systematically studied.

According to Kim, there are three categories of film festivals in South Korea:
festivals driven by a combination of the participation of the state, local governments, corporations, and intellectuals; corporate-sponsored festivals; and festivals
organized by activist groups. The focus of Kim's discussion in particular is on the
third category, namely, film festivals such as the Women's Film Festival, Human
Rights Film Festival, and the Queer Film Festival which have been organized by
both established and relatively new activist groups. Also, it is important to understand the implication of the shift in Korean society and cultural politics that
occurred in Korea between the 1980s and the 1990s, which was a crucial moment
for the nation in terms of its social formation and redefinition of self.

In a social formation where state intervention into every aspect of people's lives is still highly visible, even the second kind of festival needs
to compromise with the power of the state exerted through censorship and exhibition laws. The third kind of festival relatively is autono-
mous from the state and the corporate sector. Therefore, it provides an
interesting example of how the new social movement of the nineties
is taking tentative steps away from the preceding eighties social movement that was pivoted on the labour movement.[45]

Following her categorization and mapping of film festivals layered onto an understanding of Korean cultural politics in the 1990s, Kim aptly points out that the
importance of the PIFF lies in its geopolitics.[46] Overall, her argument about the
social status accorded to Korea between the 1980s and the 1990s is perceptive and
important to comprehensively understand the global phenomenon of film festivals
not only within Korea but also across the world. Furthermore, although her work
specifically deals with the different social/cultural realities in which Korean society
is rooted and their relations with film festivals in Korea, her critical analysis can
open up constructive discussion about diverse aspects of other film festivals that are
contradictory and in constant processes of negotiation with one another.

However, Kim's argument also poses some questions. The categorization that she originally developed needs to be updated and should be made to reflect the changing characteristics of film festivals at various levels. As there have been many subsequent rapid social, cultural, and political shifts in Korea since Kim's original investigation in the late 1990s, there are inherent limitations in her theory's ability to fully explain the current variety of film festivals with only these definitions and categorizations. For instance, the Women's Film Festival, which was a minor festival organized by feminist activists at the time of its launch in the 1990s, has more recently, and within the space of only a few short years, become one of the major festivals in the country and is firmly positioned in Korea with stable sponsorship from the corporate sector and positive support from the public. Despite receiving relatively less financial support, the Human Rights Film Festival has also differentiated itself from other local film festivals by focusing on human rights issues with a clear festival identity. The initial identities and sociopolitical aims of both film festivals seem to have become diluted over time, as they became increasingly well-established in Korea and well-received by audiences, funding bodies, and the media.

Despite these limitations, Kim's reading of film festivals has inspired this study to further develop her discussions within a larger context. Her innovative approach offers an accessible map to researchers navigating the complexities of film festivals in non-Western regions within many different sociocultural contexts. In looking at the PIFF from this perspective, this research does not limit its scope to Korea. Rather, to effectively elucidate the whole process of cultural globalization in this region, including Korea, the book is concerned with the PIFF in the East Asian context of historical, political, and cultural globalization.

Globalization and Film Festivals: Global Cities

Discourses on film festivals have been prompted by the rise of the global circulation of media and dramatic transformations of technology within global capitalism. Most of the work seems to rely on theories of globalization, in particular those of Arjun Appadurai, Manuel Castells, and Saskia Sassen, which focus on conceptions of global cultural flows, space of flows, and global cities respectively.

Although Appadurai's work does not directly speak to the phenomenon of film festivals in particular, his framework for exploring disjunctures and differences in the global cultural economy is useful in explaining the role of film festivals in the global economy. Appadurai argues that current global cultural flows "occur in and through the growing disjunctures among ethnoscapes, technoscapes, financescapes, mediascapes, and ideoscapes."[47] His account makes it clear that any discussion of film festivals should include an analysis of the disjunctures within and between these various "scapes," not to mention other facets and locations of social, technological, economic, cultural, and political operations. This framework also helps to explore the changing networks and productions in East Asia in their global and local interactions. For example, the PIFF's reliance on a strategy of regionalization for promoting the festival and positioning itself on the global stage is related to the political, economic, and cultural changes in the region wrought by disjunctures in the global economy, as theorized by Appadurai.

Amongst existing work on film festivals, Julian Stringer's arguments perceptively map out many of the key roles of film festivals on a global scale by considering the spatial relationships and organizational logics of festivals. His article, "Global Cities and the International Film Festival Economy," introduces a new perspective into the discourse surrounding film festivals. Identifying the important relation between cities and the international film festival circuit in a "global space economy," he argues that cities are nodal points on the festival circuit.[48] He redefines the widely-used term "international film festival circuit" by suggesting that it refers to "the existence of a socially produced space unto itself, a unique cultural arena that acts as a contact zone for the working-through of unevenly differentiated power relationships—not so much a parliament of national film industries as a series of diverse, sometimes competing, sometimes cooperating, public spheres."[49]

It is significant that Stringer contextualizes a critical link between international film festivals and global cities, as this account enables the previous debates surrounding film festivals, which largely relied on the notion of the national, to move into a new context—cities in the global space economy. He also outlines a common strategy amongst many festivals to market and project a city's own "festival image" within the global space economy.[50]

In explicating the logic of film festivals by focusing on "location," Stringer's emphasis on cities can be incorporated with Michael Curtin's notion of "media capital." Curtin argues how a specific location contributes to the operation of the media capital by facilitating: accumulation of the capital, creative migration, and forces of sociocultural variations.[51] According to Curtin, the spatial dynamics of media capital have played a structuring role in the film and media industries since the early twentieth century. He writes:

> Cities such as Cairo, Mumbai, and Hong Kong lie across significant cultural divides from their Hollywood counterparts, which helps to explain why producers in these cities have been able to sustain distinctive product lines and survive the onslaught of a much more powerful competitor.[52]

As he argues, the concept of media capital helps explain why some places become centers of cultural production and therefore tend to be more influential in shaping the emerging global system.[53] For instance, the logic of accumulation is useful in explaining that the film and media industry has tended to redeploy its creative resources and reshape its terrain of operations in order to survive competition and enhance profitability.[54] The dynamics of agglomeration can provide a useful framework to read the current trend in film festivals and cultural industries more broadly. Many contemporary film festivals are compelled to seek efficiencies through the extension of markets in order to survive, as will be seen in the tenth anniversary of the PIFF in Chapter 5.

While the PIFF has attempted to become a sustainable cultural cluster at the local and regional levels, it has also tried to broaden its roles and diversify its functions so as to effectively cope with the transformations of the global/local economy. For example, one of the significant new roles that festivals have begun to play in the global film industry is producing talents through various education programs such as the Asian Film Academy (AFA).[55] As the migration of creative labor to a place enhances its attraction to other talents (which, in this case, may include audiovisual industries), film festivals are reliant on creativity as a core resource and began to pay special attention to pools of labor.[56] Curtin describes: "patronage drew artists to specific locales and often kept them in place for much of their working lives, and they, in turn, passed their skills along to succeeding generations and to newly arrived migrants."[57] In this context, by establishing education programs, festivals can act as a powerful attraction to those who aspire to make films in the region and the world. Thus, in order to adapt to shifting global circumstances, each festival should maintain its infrastructure for organizational learning, even with massive infusions of capital or government subsidies.[58]

Moreover, in the case of the PIFF, the operation of media capital—specifically, forces of social variations such as government regulation and policies—has acted as an influential enabler that fostered the festival's growth in Pusan, South Korea, in the late 1990s. Within this context, I examine how the PIFF uses its particular location—the city of Pusan—geopolitically, economically, and culturally, and discuss how it has tried to link its distinctive festival image to the city's image in order to remain competitive in the global market.

Argument about the importance of cities as nodal points also enables us to include the larger context of a festival's cultural politics beyond the national framework. However, this does not mean that the film festival system no longer operates according to concepts of the national. As Stringer points out, hierarchical relations between the centers (major European festivals) and the peripheries (the rest of the festivals in "other" parts of the world) still exist and power relationships at contemporary film festival sites are reinforced in different ways.[59] This suggests that film festivals and notions of the national are interacting with each other in more complicated ways than previously imagined. Therefore, as this topic should be reconsidered from a new direction, I approach it by specifically investigating, across subsequent chapters, the institutional workings which frame the exhibition, reception, and production of films and their linkages with the national and regional film industries through a consideration of the PIFF's programming politics and film markets.

By drawing on globalization discourses of "spatial effect" and "cultural flow" from Castells and Appadurai, Janet Harbord attempts to conceptualize film festivals in the disjunctions between the festival as marketplace and as a forum of aesthetic evaluation. Harbord describes film festival sites as a mixture of temporality and spatiality, which creates added value for films and constructs them as examples of "material hybridity."[60] As she articulates:

> The "network" of global commerce creates linkages between sites, creating centres and peripheries, eclipsing other spaces altogether. More than the hybrid mixing of goods and cultures, the festival as marketplace provides an exemplary instance of how culture, and cultural flows, produce space as places of flows, in Castells's terms.[61]

Harbord's argument casts important questions on the discourse of film festivals. On the one hand, she underlines the significance of the spatial for understanding festival events wherein the conflicting and opposing values of commerce and art coexist. On the other hand, her contextualization of the temporal aspect of film festivals contributes to an explanation of how the hierarchical structure of the premiere system and cultural values are constituted. From this perspective, festivals effectively "enclave a film, seal it off from general release and, further, restrict it to circulation among and between festivals."[62]

In addition, for Harbord, film festivals can be perceived as a discursive but exclusive place which predominantly depends upon the particular mediating activities of journalism through which the meaning and value of film as text is reproduced at festival sites. Although Harbord's investigation of the role of journalism and media at festival sites, which up until now has been relatively overlooked, helps to extend the critical discussion to the cultural and industrial dimensions of festivals, her analysis on media and journalism needs to be further explored. As she does not precisely define the journalism and media activities she is referencing, it is not possible to distinguish their different roles at festivals. Their role in the process of adding value should be more specifically discussed. For instance, film critics who write for prestigious film journals and broadcasters who report on the appearance of Hollywood stars at festivals act as different kinds of mediators, constructing very different kinds of discourses. Additionally, with the growing importance and increasing visibility of journalists and media representatives at film festivals over recent years, a hierarchical categorization has been created for their accreditation,[63] and their activities seem to be more and more institutionally controlled and negotiated. Although Harbord emphasizes the close ties between texts circulated at festivals and the role of journalism and the media as producer and mediator, such a link is not explicitly established through empirical research in her writings. How do the media specifically interact with film industries at the festivals?

Importantly, the performance of film festival participation in industrial terms becomes a crucial practice in the global film industry. For industry professionals, including film critics, trade magazine journalists, and sales agents and distributors, the process of festival participation—from registration, traveling to, and attending exclusive screenings, parties, and press conferences to activities of negotiating, purchasing, and selling new titles—has become a significant part of industrial practice. Working practices in the industry are thus also very much shaped to follow the annual festival calendar. Although this book does not substantially discuss the role of journalism and media in film festivals, it attempts to reflect this industrial dimension of the film festival experience by carefully considering different voices from the global and local press at the PIFF.

Film Festivals and the Regional

> "PIFF continued to listen to Asia's voices and in turn provided the backdrop for Asian films to listen to one another. For the past ten years, PIFF has promoted Korean films across the world and elevated the international status of the harbour city of Busan. These achievements weren't made by the festival alone. Of course, PIFF was an Asian film festival, and its mainstay was the dynamic films and filmmakers of Asia. This is how the festival has unwavered for ten years, and this is why PIFF is as young and exuberant today as ever".[64]

On its tenth anniversary in 2002, the PIFF succinctly outlined and attempted to justify its ambivalent stance between Korean and Asian cinema. The above speech suggests how the PIFF sees itself: a crossover between Asian and Korean films. This observation provides the key to understanding contradictions and tensions in positioning the festival in national and regional contexts. Obviously, by making "Asian identity" a key concept to promote the festival, the PIFF fashioned itself as a regional "hub" that appealed to the global film market. Why has the PIFF tried to construct a regional identity so as to be a "hub" of Asian cinema? How do we account for the PIFF's regional approach in the increasingly competitive global economy? What does it mean in a wider context? Unlike the national perspective, the significance of regional frameworks in looking at film festivals has not been profoundly explored in film and media studies. The critical recognition of the regional tends to be vaguely implied and thus the critical concept of the regional, which is conflicting but interlinked with the national, needs to be more fully explored to understand the ongoing transformation within film festivals and cultural industries in Asia. In attempting to address these gaps and questions above, it is necessary to interrogate the development of the idea of the region in Asia and analyze how this process of conceptualization is related to the PIFF's efforts to build a regional hub to promote the festival.

The term "Asia" has been used ambiguously both as a geographical location and a symbolic destination. The fact that differences exist among Asian nations in social, political, economic, and cultural backgrounds, especially in language, ethnicity, and religion, is often overlooked in discussing the concept of Asia. Importantly, the definition of Asia can be read as "an artefact of Asian reaction to Western colonialism."[65] As Leo Ching notes:

> Asia is neither a cultural, religious or linguistic unity, nor a unified world. The principle of its identity lies outside itself, in relation to (an) Other. If one can ascribe to Asia any vague sense of unity, it is that which is excluded and objectified by the West in the service of its historical progress. Asia is, and can be one, only under the imperial eyes of the West.[66]

In the same vein, Ching suggests that Pan-Asianism must be understood as a historically constructed idea, which is "'invented' or 'imagined' in direct opposition to another putative unity of the West," rather than "a self-reflexive realization based on any genuine culture commonality."[67]

Koichi Iwabuchi also discusses Japanese cultural power in Asia and the Japanese discursive construction of Asia in relation to the rest of the Asian nations and the West. In suggesting there are difficulties in seeing Asia as a singular cultural geography, Iwabuchi asserts that the legacy of the "Asia is one" ideology was also pervasive in the Japanese media in the 1990s. He further states that "Asia is reimagined as a cultural space in which Japan is located in the implicit centre, playing the part of the conductor of Asian pop-musical cross-fertilization."[68] Japan reimagined Asia by means of its economic power and popular culture, such as animation and TV drama, which hit the rest of Asia including Taiwan, Hong Kong, and China in the early 1990s, as he discusses.

It is widely argued that recent regionalism and regionalization phenomena were driven by globalization. However, the debates on regionalism in relation to Asia tend to focus on particular economic, political, and security issues. Cultural aspects of regionalism in relation to globalization in Asia have been relatively neglected in academic discourses. Indeed, the concept of "the region" is helpful to explicate the complex relationship between the global and the local, which stand as an "ongoing cultural negotiation" rather than as a binary opposition.[69] In this respect, while regionalism has been driven by globalization as one of the key external forces that crosses the border of the nation-state, it is also "a response to and a dynamic behind globalisation."[70] In this sense, globalization and regionalization are "complementary processes."[71] Emphasizing the "constitutive" relationship between globalization and regionalization, Ching further suggests today's regionalist formations—commercialized popular culture—is radically different from earlier imperialistic high culture of the 1930s.[72] According to him, this shift in discussing Asianism has prompted some structural and historical changes in the ways Asia is perceived as "both a mode of production and a regime of discursive practice" in the Japanese imaginary.[73] As he explains:

> If the earlier Asianism was conditioned on the unequivocal difference between Asia and the West, where Asia existed as the absolute other to the increasingly colonized world system—its exterior—in today's Asianism that difference itself exists only as a commodity, a spectacle to be consumed in a globalized capitalist system precisely at the moment when exteriority is no longer imaginable."[74]

In the wake of this mass cultural Asianism, today's Asia has become a market and "Asianness" has become a commodity circulating globally through late capitalism, as he suggests.[75] Under conditions of globalizing market forces, both the nation and the region can be reified as brands at the same time as they operate—often at cross-purposes—as political and ideological forces.[76]

It is widely argued that decentered cultural globalization has prompted the shift from an emphasis on center-periphery relations to a diffusion of cultural power. This point is particularly important in accounting for Asian regionalism as this helps extend the boundary of the discussion of intraregional cultural flows and consumption in Asia. Referring to decentering globalization processes, Iwabuchi explains the rise of Japanese cultural power through which the Japanese conception of being "in but above" or "similar but superior to" the region is rearticulated.[77] While admitting the power asymmetry between Japan and other Asian nations, he claims that it may be wrong to simply consider Japanese spread of culture as unidirectional—a straightforward economic and cultural domination of Asia by Japan. Although it is uneven, transnational media and cultural flow in Asia becomes more multilateral, as he points out.[78] For example, it is a sense of coevalness that Taiwanese favorable consumption of Japanese popular culture is sustained by. Thus, it is important to consider such difference and rupture in consuming and perceiving Asian cultural products—between a sense of coevalness and a sense of nostalgia that Taiwanese drama invokes to Japanese audience, for instance—in properly understanding the regionalism in Asia.[79]

Indeed, it has become culture—popular and media culture, in particular—that transcends national borders and constitutes regional identity. Various approaches to the re-labeling of "Asia" are being carried out at a moment when, in the world at large, national borders are collapsing and increasingly giving way to transnational cultural flows. Within this context, the current emphasis on culture in East Asia closely relates with the logic of market functionalism or corporatism in constituting the concept of Asia as a region.⁸⁰ In other words, the economic role of culture in the construction of the region becomes normative goals in East Asia.⁸¹

Viewed from this angle, the PIFF's recent drive to be a representative of Asia shows how film festivals today tend to change their approaches to the global market. In this context, the PIFF's regionalization strategy requires particular recognition at multiple levels.

First, the PIFF's self-assertion of being a hub in the region was prompted by both the recent rapid growth of cultural industries and the economic-oriented globalization in South Korea. As argued by Kim Soyoung, the rise of film festivals in Korea in the 1990s is closely linked with the issue of globalization, *Segyehwa*. In addition to analyzing Korean cultural politics in the 1990s, Kim briefly delineates the development and promotion of a regional identity as a strategic concept of film festivals, using the PIFF's vision of an Asian identity as an example:

> Evoking its geographic proximity to the rest of Asia, Pusan claims the region as its main focus. The highlighted programme 'A Window on Asian Cinema' is an attempt to locate the city of Pusan as a new focus for Asian cinema in competition with the Hong Kong and Tokyo international film festivals. With rising interest in the Asian region, and North-East Asia in particular, Pusan selectively promotes Asian identity to reach out towards the global.⁸²

The particular regional identity promoted by this program—in competition with its regional counterparts, the HKIFF, for instance—has been strategically developed to promote Asian identity in a way that will enable it to reach globally. In this respect, it is global forces that have both promoted the regional identity and caused tensions between the regional and the national identity. Globalization in this particular sense seems to influence the trend of regionalization that is inter-related to the recent growth in cultural exchange at the regional level. For example, while national initiatives have resulted in the rapid growth of the Korean film industry, this in turn has led to the production of regional cultural developments such as *Hanryu* (the Korean Wave).⁸³

Second, the PIFF's regionalization presents its most dynamic link to globalization as its initiatives are driven by "the city." The festival combines a regional identity with the civic identity of Pusan and simultaneously attempts to integrate the festival image into the region of Asia. The festival's approach recognizes the multi-dimensional process of globalization while at the same time it reinforces ties with the national and local economy. In other words, as the following chapter will argue, PIFF's regionalization drive interacts with other approaches at the local and the national level on two fronts: urban regeneration and global networks.

It is important to note that rapid growth of modern Asian cities is linked with Asian regionalism. Iwabuchi stresses on the role of the globalized capitalist modernity which was significant in exploring the meaning of being Asian in the 1990s. According to him, it is between urban places, between global cities such as Tokyo, Seoul, Hong Kong, Taipei, and Shanghai that propelled today's Asian interconnections being forged by the flows of commercialized popular culture.[84] The emergence of the PIFF in the city of Pusan as a cultural, global city in a particular period of the 1990s in Asia can be explained in a similar context.

The PIFF has attempted to develop links between the urban image of Pusan and its festival identity as a hub of Asian cinema. To achieve this aim, the festival and the local community have established an efficient infrastructure to become an industrial base of Asian cinema. Significantly, PIFF has strategically established a pre-market PPP to attract transnational capital to invest in Asian cinema and to share information for participating in the production, distribution, and exhibition in the early stage of production. This effort reflects the pervasive trend of globalization, as Manuel Castells has described: the flow of transnational capital, or the flow of information in a highly technological society into a global space, namely global cities.[85] In this sense, the PIFF's urban regeneration project is interlinked with its global networks strategy which was simultaneously carried out. In order to differentiate itself from the Hong Kong and the Tokyo Film Festivals, the PIFF created new channels of finance and co-production for Asian films to access the global distribution circuit right after launching the festival. Propelled by the prominent development of regional film industries, the PPP has carved out a major network within Asia's rapidly rebounding film (co-)production sector.

In the wake of PPP's success, the Hong Kong and the Tokyo Film Festivals competitively established their own programs: the Hong Kong-Asia Film Financing Forum (HAF) and the Tokyo Film Creators' Forum. In short, the particular process of regional approach shown at the PIFF and Pusan corroborates the argument that globalization is a complex, dynamic coexistence of overlapping and contradictory modes at local, national, and regional levels.

Third, the PIFF's regionalization shows its inevitable contradiction in approaching the national and the global. Despite the deliberate elusion of the national, the festival's exploitation of the regional inherently reveals its national attachment. Ching situates the prevalence of regional discourse in Asia within global capitalism and brings the issue of contradiction whose nature exists within capitalism itself to explicate the complicated relations between the national and the regional. According to him, the contradiction is "between the immanent logic of capital and its historical manifestations, because of the processes of imperialism, colonialism, and decolonization, circumscribed it within the nation form."[86]

This observation also indicates the contradictory position where the PIFF stands. To put it differently, whilst Pusan and the PIFF both have long desired to position themselves beyond the nation-state of South Korea, and establish a regional identity to cross the national boundary, they have also deliberately attempted to boost the national film industry. The concept of Asia that the PIFF has struggled to establish was materialized through placing a priority on Asian films in programming and launching a pre-market PPP as a key instrument in making a festival brand image. However, this drive simultaneously faced a challenge in responding to the demand of the national film industry that had been growing and changing, as will be considered in the following chapters. As a result, the PIFF had to give a privileged position to national films in key programming sections and created an exclusive smaller section for national projects in the PPP.

Furthermore, the networks that PIFF has attempted to build may appear likely to degenerate into another form of nationalism or intra-Asian imperialism, reflecting ideas prevalent in Asia. According to Arif Dirlik, the economic success of East Asian nations is related to the growth of regional consciousness. Dirlik argues that this kind of regionalism is often accompanied by nationalism and he suggests that "claims to regional culture (be it Asia or East Asia) often serve national yearnings, where supposed national characteristics are projected upon entire regions and continents."[87] Indeed, since the 1990s it has been widely argued that throughout East Asia, a peculiar sense of "triumphalism" has been directed against the West "despite the 'internal antagonisms': the twenty-first century is 'ours'; 'we' are finally centred."[88]

As Julian Stringer points out, the historical backdrop of all major festivals suggests that film festivals may reinforce the continuation of the nation-state system.[89] The PIFF's regionalization strategy through the redevelopment of Pusan shows a different process and context from other major European festivals after the postwar period since the leading actor was the local initiative existing beyond nationally orchestrated propaganda. From this perspective, it is useful to consider how European cinema and European film festivals are inter-related, and how their relationship has affected the position of the regional in the global film culture.

Thomas Elsaesser explains European cinema's renewed global position and linkages with other parts of the world through the film festival circuit within the regional perspective. Elsaesser, who examined how film festivals operate as a competition system among nations to explain the international circulation of New British Cinema in the 1980s, attempts to reframe both the cultural and industrial dimensions of film festivals in European contexts. For Elsaesser, the film festival system is neither a form of Olympics nor a parliament of delegates to the United Nations, as he had once asserted. Instead, he claims that film festivals no longer operate upon "agreed, measurable standards of achievement."[90] He argues that although film festivals have always been recognized as fundamental to European cinema, their crucial relation with the author, national cinema, and hostility to Hollywood, which are the three most significant issues for a new understanding of European cinema, has rarely been investigated.[91]

Elsaesser tries to link the thriving festival circuit with the current status of European cinema faced by renewed competition from Hollywood and the challenges posed to national cinemas. He tries to challenge the existing binary perception of Hollywood as a cultural and economic threat to the European film industries by suggesting European cinema has always been in dialog with Hollywood even though the exchange of ideas has often been asymmetrical.[92] Despite his new approach to the relationship between Hollywood and Europe, however, he clearly admits that Hollywood, also referred as Europe's "bad other," still continues to occupy Europe's cultural imaginary. The contemporary cross-border collaboration in filmmaking in Europe such as the European Documentary Network (EDN) can be proof of shared economic concerns born of an "ingrained anti-Americanism" and designed to defy Hollywood's dominance.[93]

Apart from the regional perspective in festival context, one of the benefits of this approach is to help explain some background of the rise of non-American film festivals since the 1990s in terms of branding and promoting world films as an alternative network and a new alliance against Hollywood products. It is noticeable that Elsaesser attempts to look at festival networks to explain "the new topographies of cinema in Europe" by developing Bruno Latour's "actor-network-theory."[94] For him the significance of film festivals lies in when it is seen as a network (with nodes, flows, and exchanges). Viewed from this angle, it is in the non-Hollywood sector that film festival-aided distribution, marketing, exhibition, and even production have emerged as one of the most distinctive features of the global film industry since the 1990s.

For example, as I will discuss in Chapter 4 on the PPP, more festivals outside of America—notably in Europe and East Asia—have established film project and/or co-production markets for promoting and branding national/transnational films such as the co-production markets in the Berlin, Locarno, Rotterdam, and Hong Kong film festivals. In this context, it can be argued that the rise of non-American film festivals since the 1990s can be seen as a counter-movement in responding to the worldwide domination of US cultural products. These festivals located outside of Hollywood have been trying to brand their products as world cinema via film festival networks, "face to face" with Hollywood. Like Pusan, claiming strong regional identity, the Pan-African Film Festival of Ouagadougou (FESPACO) in Burkina Faso also reflects this aspect.[95]

Conclusion: Voices from Industry

So far, I have contextualized various academic discussions on film festivals, particularly from the national and the regional perspectives and sought to demonstrate there are complicated, ambivalent, and multi-layered factors in reading the rapid growth of film festivals in Asia in the light of decentering globalization. By examining the establishment and development of the PIFF between 1996 and 2005, this research aims to demonstrate how and why the PIFF has used its Asian identity as its most visible marketing strategy to differentiate itself from its counterparts, such as the Hong Kong and Tokyo film festivals. In conjunction with the festival's strong industrial drive within regional film industries, the book also considers the complexities brought by the rapid transformation of the South Korean film industry that has sought to reach out to the global film market since the late 1990s. As illustrated, in exploring the PIFF's evolution, its particular relationship with the Korean film industry that initially helped the festival rise to global prominence is crucial.

In closing, to illuminate this point, I will draw voices from industry. Aside from academic research, which is often late in reflecting what is currently going on in film industries, voices from industry are helpful in filling gaps which academic research can sometimes overlook. As a non-scholarly but insightful participant-observer account of festivals, the writings of Derek Elley deserve specific mention in order to highlight the politics of film festivals in the East Asian context.[96] In particular, his article "Korea, Beware! Ten Myths about the International Film Festival Circuit" poignantly reveals the current trend apparent in the Korean film industry when films have been spotlighted at global film festivals:[97]

> The hard reality of all this is that stories in South Korea's media about this or that film attending a festival and winning prizes, or laudatory reviews by specialised critics in foreign media, gives a false impression of South Korean cinema's international standing. [...] For filmmakers: concentrate on your home and regional markets and treat the festival circuit as a bonus, not as an end in itself (beware the Taiwan experience!). For sales companies: accept the most suitable—not necessarily the most "prestigious"—invitation for a film, and let word of mouth and your impressively organised industry do the rest. And for South Korean audiences: continue supporting your own cinema to give it a strong financial basis of its own, rather than be dependant on the shifting tastes and local concerns of festival programmers and foreign buyers. Western filmmaking has never looked East for "validation" and Korean cinema should not do the reverse. It's rich enough, inventive enough and exciting enough not to need it.[98]

Chapters

This book comprises five chapters. Chapter 1, "Why Pusan?: The Political Economy of a Film Festival" closely examines the PIFF's establishment in 1996 and its subsequent evolution across the following decade. The chapter seeks to demonstrate and understand how and why the PIFF has constructed and used its

Asian identity as its most visible marketing strategy, thus bringing to light a series of regional self-definition processes that the festival has used to differentiate itself from its regional counterparts in, for example, Hong Kong and Tokyo. While the first half considers the successful establishment of the PIFF in Pusan as the result of the motivated interests of different groups within the specific social, political, and economic context of South Korea, the second half of the chapter shows how the PIFF conceptualized and manipulated the notion of regionalization so as to be competitive in the rapidly changing global film market. In this chapter, I further explore the PIFF's subsequent changes and the evolution of its status and identity in relation to the local and global film industry by investigating two interlinked themes—the urban regeneration of the city of Pusan and an industrial drive to forge regional networks.

To further reveal the tensions between the national and the regional which appeared in the PIFF's formulation of regionalization, Chapter 2 and Chapter 3 specifically examine festival programming. Chapter 2, "Negotiating a Place between Korean Cinema and Asian Cinema: Programming Politics," analyzes contemporary Korean films within the Opening and Panorama sections, and argues that while PIFF sought to serve as a showcase for Asian cinema by strongly evoking an Asian identity, the festival equally strove to promote the national film industry by acting as a gateway to the global film market for those Korean films placed into prime sections.

Chapter 3, "Re-Imagining the Past: Programming Retrospectives," argues that similar to how the PIFF positioned contemporary Korean and Asian cinema in programming, it strategically exploited this section to promote the festival, and considers the mediation and negotiation that took place in the process of remapping classic Korean and Asian cinema. Focusing on three key Korean retrospectives—Korea's New Wave, Kim Ki-young and Shin Sang-Ok—as well as selected Asian retrospectives, I demonstrate how the PIFF sought to play a key role in sanctioning old films made in Korea as a legitimate agent of memory, while highlighting old Asian films in an attempt to justify its identity as a platform for Asian cinema. Both chapters therefore seek to illustrate how the programming of national and regional sections at PIFF is closely tied to the current political, economic, and social interests of the festival and how the festival has negotiated its position within the changing global/local festival landscape.

Chapter 4, "A Global Film Producer: The Pusan Promotion Plan," uncovers a new function of festivals and investigates a new kind of interrelationship between the film festival and the three main sections of the film industries—production, exhibition, and distribution. Focusing on the PPP, a project market in which new Asian feature film projects can seek co-financing and co-production partners, I argue that film festivals today have begun to play a new role in the global film industry as "producer" by actively engaging with the production process as well as exhibition and distribution. This chapter proposes that the PIFF's regionalization strategy was ultimately furthered and achieved by the PPP.

In Chapter 5, "Remapping Asian Cinema: The Tenth Anniversary in 2005," I examine the PIFF's ever-increasing scale and scope by considering this year as the key moment when the festival's development took a decisive turn by reinforcing its regional identity. I illustrate the PIFF's focus on Asian identity by investigating key special events and programs associated with the tenth anniversary festival on both industrial and critical levels. Whilst the Asian Film Industry Network (AFIN) and the Asian Film Market (AFM) show the way in which the festival accentuated its regional/industrial ties, special programs such as Asian Pantheon, Remapping Asian Auteur Cinema 1, and Special Screening for APEC Films further testify to the PIFF's desire to act as a critical hub in the Asia region. Paying particular attention to the AFA, a new education program which aimed to serve as a nodal point between the critical and industrial levels, I argue that the PIFF's strategic arrangement of diverse audience-friendly public events reflects the festival's awareness of its changing relationship with local audiences.

In conclusion, I summarize my findings and refocus attention on the relationship between the national and the regional. Then, I suggest research on the PIFF furthermore reflects on shifting dynamics of cultural industries in the region. Pondering on how the successful establishment of the PIFF helps us understand the various facets of interaction among local, national, regional, and global forces, this final chapter ends with a reflection on the prospects of the PIFF in a broader context.

1

Why Pusan?: The Political Economy of a Film Festival

The first annual PIFF was inaugurated on September 13, 1996 in Pusan, South Korea's second largest city. Since this first unanticipated, overwhelming, qualitative, and quantitative success, the PIFF has gone on, in a relatively short period of time, to become the leading international film festival in Asia,[1] even surpassing the Hong Kong International Film Festival (HKIFF), which for the previous twenty years had been a key platform for the latest Asian films.[2] Its rapid growth also threatened the position of the Tokyo International Film Festival, which has been categorized as an A-level festival.[3]

In this chapter I will examine the establishment and further development of PIFF in the light of globalization. The chapter is divided into two parts in order to effectively map out the intersections where the PIFF is located between the local, the national, and the regional in the global economy. Firstly, I will look at the political and economic factors behind the establishment of the PIFF in 1996 and examine how they were related to the transformation of the Korean film industry. To probe where and how the PIFF was established, I will identify some of the leading actors in the political, economic, and social situation in South Korea at the time. As the first international-scale film festival in the history of South Korea, how and why was Pusan chosen as the host city from among other possibilities in 1996? How did the PIFF reconcile the tension between the state and local authorities driven by a decentralization policy? How did the PIFF benefit from the particular conditions in Korea during this negotiation process? The first part will be devoted to addressing these questions within the specific local and national contexts.

The discussion of the second part in this chapter is positioned beyond the local and national frameworks. I will explore how the PIFF differentiated its identity and status as a platform of Asian cinema from its counterparts in East Asia, such as the film festivals in Tokyo and Hong Kong. How did the PIFF's regionalization strategies come about and how does the successful establishment of the PIFF help us understand the various facets of interaction between the local, the national, the regional, and the global? Developing our discussion in the introduction that explored why the PIFF has conceptualized a regional identity and used regionalization as a key tool in promoting the festival, this chapter will reveal that the PIFF's regionalization strategy incorporates the branding and redefining of its festival image and identity in conjunction with urban regeneration and global networks. Ultimately, the chapter aims to illustrate how the festival's regional approach is often at odds with other strategies at local and national levels.

Part 1: A Film Festival, Pusan, and South Korea: *The Local and The National*

As many commentators have noted, a film festival is more than a mere site for the screening of films. It is a place of business, of marketing within a specific system of "institutional assumptions, priorities, and constraints."[4] Each festival has a unique cultural policy background and organizers are motivated to establish it for specific reasons. For this reason, particularly in relation to the proliferation of globally scaled film festivals in South Korea, as Kim Soyoung aptly points out, investigating the establishment of film festivals in South Korea can cast a revealing light on Korean cultural politics in the 1990s.[5] In her influential article "'Cine-mania' or Cinephilia: Film Festivals and the Identity Question," Kim outlines four factors that have contributed to the rise of film festivals in South Korea. They consist of cine-mania, the Korean version of cinephilia; the enactment of a local self-government system; a shift in the site of Korean activism from the politico-economic to the cultural sphere; and the *Segyehwa* project as I noted in the previous chapter.[6] She further suggests that the prominence of international film festivals in Korea, such as PIFF, have emerged at a time of political and cultural rupture between two different periods. She explains that this phenomenon can be seen as resulting from "cinephilia and globalphilia via an emphasis on local politics."[7] In this regard, the in-depth examination of specific factors surrounding the establishment of the PIFF can effectively hold a mirror up to the larger transformations of Korean society in the mid-1990s.

International film festivals have appeared to bring national film cultures into the world cinema system, attracting foreign guests to cities and revenue to national film industries.[8] Julian Stringer argues that the growing importance of international film festivals should be understood in relation to the spatial economy of global cities in the highly competitive global economy. Stringer claims that international festivals have become a solid component of today's global city as they help to boost the local economy and "rejuvenate the value of urban space through the mobilization of global interests."[9] Moreover, to interrogate how each festival strategically positions itself within the uneven power differentiations of the global economy, he suggests that film festivals should be considered in their own locations, within their particular national context. As he states:

Pusan provides an interesting case study in that it has been self-consciously modelled (as a showcase for Asian cinema in the region) along the lines of the existing highly successful Hong Kong annual event. As Soyoung Kim has pointed out, Pusan is attempting to mobilize a sense of local identity around its festival as part of a wider initiative, on the part of Korea's newly inaugurated local governments, to challenge the legacy of the "Seoul Republic", or the heavy industrialization of Seoul which proceeded on the whim of the authoritarian, centralized government regime of the 1980s. As such, the festival has sought to attract financial investments to the city, its beaches, and the Pusan Yachting Centre in Haundae, away from the national capital, Seoul. As such an example suggests, a particularly important question concerns the status of international film festivals in postcolonial societies, and particularly in postcolonial global cities.[10]

This observation suggests that film festivals such as the PIFF, a non-Western one, can more clearly illustrate how film festivals interact with other political, social, and economic factors to build up a distinctive festival identity and to survive both local shifts and the increasingly competitive global economy. In other words, this view also demonstrates how forces of socio-cultural variation—one of the principles of the concept of media capital—such as particular political circumstances and government cultural policy in South Korea, reshaped the establishment and further strategies of a festival located in Pusan with global aspirations.[11]

The Korean Film Industry before the 1990s

The development of the Korean film industry is inseparable from the political, social, and economic situation of contemporary Korean society. Despite a history of colonization, war, and economic recovery, Korea—as a nation-state—has remained a "blank and unimagined space" for the West.[12] In a similar vein, Korean cinema was virtually unseen outside Korea until very recently. This was partly because the vast majority of Korea's early film footage was destroyed either during the period of Japanese colonization (1910–45) or the subsequent Korean War (1950–53). Censorship is another key factor that inhibited the local evolution of Korean cinema as well as its ability to garner global attention. During the Japanese occupation, censorship and economic restrictions on the film industry severely hampered indigenous film production.[13]

The Korean War divided the country into South and North Korea along the 38th parallel. Subsequent to the military coup in South Korea in 1961, the government of President Park Chung Hee fused severe political oppression with unrestrained economic growth. Until the 1980s, this right-wing military regime enforced a strict political and ideological agenda that stifled the film industry. For example, President Park introduced the 1962 Motion Picture Law to keep the film industry under tight control.[14] As a result, the industry developed slowly and exhibited a general lack of vitality during the 1970s and early 1980s, even though the regime founded the Korean Motion Picture Promotion Corporation (KMPPC) and the Korean Film Archive (KOFA) to revitalize the industry in the early 1970s. The Motion Picture Law was revised several times but government intervention continued to cripple film production.

Meanwhile, the post-war industrialization drive by the military regime was accompanied by heavy centralization in Seoul. This unbalanced regional policy was developed to mirror the Japanese strategy of concentrating resources on limited land in order to organize and manage industries within the space constraints presented by the geography of Korea.[15] In line with this strategy, the regime created industrial clusters mostly in the outskirts of Seoul and the southeastern provinces in the 1970s. Rapid economic growth was maintained by policies requiring the suppression of the most basic civil and labor rights. An opposition movement emerged, initially led by university students and intellectuals, which soon came to emphasize the *Minjung*, that is, working class Koreans.[16] After Park's assassination in 1979, the savage suppression of the Gwangju Uprising brought *Minjung* to the forefront of the opposition. Therefore, the Gwangju Uprising possesses potent historical meaning within South Korean society,[17] and Gwangju, the regional capital of the southwestern Honam province, came to signify "resistance" and left-wing politics.[18] (Conversely, Pusan, the regional capital of the Yeongnam province, became associated with privilege and right-wing politics in the popular imagination.)

It is also highly significant for the Korean film industry, as it is from this generation of students, those who were involved in or witnessed the uprising, that some of Korea's most influential contemporary film directors have emerged.[19] Park Kwang-su's *Chilsu and Mansu* (1988) and Jang Sun-woo's *A Petal* (1996), for example, reflect the political and social issues that dominated this period.

Throughout the 1980s, the government gradually eased the laws governing the production and release of films, partly in an attempt to bring the 1988 Olympic Games to Seoul. In 1988, the Film Act[20] finally abolished the quota system and established the "right to artistic freedom," by enabling a diverse range of films to be produced and by officially removing political censorship of film content.[21] Numerous small production companies thus began operating and creating films without official permission from the state. In these ways, the status of the Korean film industry has been enormously influenced by political and social turbulence in Korean society.

A History of Pusan

Mark Jancovich suggests that to fully understand a particular city, its character, history, and location "within the global relations of economic, political and cultural power" must be taken into account.[22] He states:

> The spatial organisation of social relations therefore means that one must be careful about how one envisions place. Instead of autonomous and authentic sites of meaning, every place is defined through its relation to other places. [...] The identities of places are therefore both mobile and multiple. They are inevitably composed of internal conflicts and contradictions, and hence there are competing meanings and definitions of any place as different social groups struggle over it. In other words, any place will be experienced differently by different social groups and will inevitably change over time.[23]

These observations indicate that to better understand the establishment of the PIFF in the Korean context, it is essential to scrutinize the diverse narratives surrounding Pusan. It also proves helpful to analyze how these narratives reflect Pusan's unique positioning within a web of political and socioeconomic relations and local, national and global factors. As a port city in the southern part of Korea, Pusan was, for centuries, not considered a culturally favored destination. While it has a politically privileged right-wing representation, as will be argued, it also has the flawed image often associated with a heavily industrialized port city. Bearing in mind the negative image and perception of the city, it is worth questioning how Pusan, as a post-colonial global city and a non-capital city in a divided nation, managed to host the first international film festival in Korea in 1996.

Historically, the geographic significance of Pusan has grown in importance along two dimensions: its relationship with the outside world, especially with neighboring Japan, and its relationship with its southwestern counterpart in Korea, Gwangju. Specifically, throughout the colonization period, Pusan emerged as an important place from the Japanese point of view and grew significantly in size as it became the gateway from both Japan and the Western world to Korea. In fact, as Pusan faces Japan, for centuries its geographical position inspired frequent attacks from the Japanese.[24] In contrast to Japan, which modernized rapidly during the nineteenth century, Korea sealed itself off from the rest of the world despite Western pressure to engage.[25] In 1876, however, the Japanese forced the Pusan port to open for trade. In 1904, Japan began building a railway north to transport troops to fight the Russians and it annexed Korea in 1910. During the next decade, the Japanese built wharfs and modernized the port to aid their northwards expansion. It was not until the end of the Pacific War in 1945 that Korea again achieved its independence.

The geopolitical importance of Pusan continued after Japan was defeated in the Second World War. In 1950, the Korean War broke out and Seoul was occupied by North Korean army. During the war, Pusan became the temporary South Korean capital and the last southern defensive position against North Korea. As the second largest city, with a population of over four million, Pusan was South Korea's principal port and continued to dominate the export trade, with more than half of all overseas shipments passing through it. It becomes apparent that as Pusan's role changed geographically, industrially, and strategically, the meanings associated with the city have also shifted.

However, although Pusan was the second largest city in the country and its geopolitical importance was growing, Seoul, the capital of Korea, has long been extremely central in every sector of Korean society. Korean sociologist Kang Myung-goo succinctly outlines the character of centralization in Korea:

> Historical experiences of powerful centralization, colonialism, and the state-led rapid economic growth, all have contributed to the enduring impact on the formation of a highly centralized state.[26]

It is most apparent how Pusan was perceived within this view when, for example, several meetings at the governmental level took place to discuss which city should host a planned new film festival in the early 1990s.[27] At those meetings, Pusan was not considered a potential candidate at all. Instead, Seoul and Jeju Island—Korea's most famous resort—were prioritized as potential candidates, mainly because of the potential benefits of investment and tourism. Under those conditions, several questions can be raised, such as: how was Pusan chosen from among other cities which may have initially been more obvious choices and which groups helped make this happen? In the following discussion, I will address these questions. I will look at the particular regional issues unique to Korea in conjunction with debates around the condensed localization and globalization drive (namely *Segyehwa*) at the time of the shift between the two regimes of the military and civilian governments.

A Transitional Vacuum Period: A Post-Industrialization Symptom and the PIFF

While understanding the historical and political backdrop of Pusan in the national context is vital to understanding the inauguration of the PIFF, it is also important to remember that the PIFF was launched and developed between two significantly different periods in the country's history. Kim Soyoung pays attention to this transitional period and attempts to explain the reasons that many film festivals suddenly emerged in Korea from the mid-1990s. As she points out, this was when Korean society was experiencing the politico-economic restructuring process driven by *Segyehwa*. There was also a rupture and aperture as "different interests and ideologies all came into play at the contested intersection of residual authoritarian and emergent democratic modes."[28] In the wake of the formerly powerful labor movement's decline during the 1980s, political and social activities faced a new climate in the 1990s. Furthermore, as she emphasizes, young people's desire for cinema had become a much discussed topic. Therefore, film festivals were widely seen as a key site of new social groups' cultural practice, as political concerns gave way to cinematic ones.[29] From this point of view, the late 1990s in Korea can be defined as a contested space and time.

Additionally, alongside the compressed industrialization and the subsequent drive towards globalization that occurred during this transition period, there was a pervasive pessimism in Korean society. This psychological and emotional mood was prevalent due to the bureaucratic governance system of the civilian government and the collapse of vital components of infrastructure such as the Seongsu Grand Bridge (1994) and the Sampung Department Store (1995) in downtown Seoul. This pessimism became even more widespread when the economic crisis followed.[30] In his article "Compressed Modernity and its Discontents: South Korean Society in Transition," Chang Kyung-sup states that in the wake of these collapses, "a grave society-wide pessimism" about renewed long-term economic and social development was haunting South Koreans at the time.[31] Chang further asserts that Koreans' sense of compressed modernity seemed to be a "sober awakening" to the ramifications of their miracle of achieving over a mere few decades what took Westerners two or three centuries.[32] One of the consequences of such a hurried economy-centered approach turns out to be an economic, political, and social system which was established only at severe costs and risks and which was highly prone to collapse. As he describes:

> The accident scenes described by witnesses reminded South Koreans of those *Die Hard*-type Hollywood movies. Additional shocking calamities, such as severe underground gas explosions, huge oil spills from stranded super tanks and train derailings, all on unprecedentedly large scales and within a short period, aggravated South Koreans' fear that their lives are under constant threat of fatal accidents of one kind or another.[33]

Moreover, intellectuals and grassroots citizens felt deeply betrayed by civilian governments as they had expected some clear transition from a military dictatorial political system to a civilian democratically-elected one. However, they were let down in their expectations as many undemocratic attitudes and practices plagued former "democracy fighters" once in government.[34] For example, in the cultural arena, due to the legacy of forced state-led modernization, indigenous or traditional culture had been neglected in favor of opening up venues for the importation of Western culture. Importantly, it was before Kim Young-sam's political bankruptcy and the national financial collapse that South Koreans began to feel the structural pitfalls and dangers of their economically driven compressed modernity.[35]

Therefore, it is evident that the PIFF developed at a crucial juncture. Its establishment came during a transitional and turbulent period for every sector of Korean society. This was just after an economic crisis, a change of government, and a collapse in buildings and self-confidence. Yet, it was also a time when the state-led drive towards economic globalization was in full flow and when more autonomy was being handed to local governments under a new policy of self-governance.

During this transitional period, it was far from clear that the establishment of the PIFF would be a popular move on a national and local level. Importantly, however, as stated above, the political and social focus moved on to the cultural sector. In addition, local governments were keen to host cultural events as a means of strengthening a sense of local identity. The shift from pessimism about national politics towards optimism within the local community was encouraged by the local media as well as by municipal governments. For example, ahead of the inauguration of the PIFF in Pusan, the local press conveyed a powerful sense of optimism and encouraged local communities to pay attention to this new cultural event. As Jancovich claims, "the local press is central to the production of local 'imagined communities' as much as the national press is central to the 'imagined communities' of the nation."[36] Thus, a turnaround which had been driven by the upsurge of local enthusiasm triggered the inauguration of this cultural event in the community. In other words, the PIFF grew out of a desire among the local community for wider recognition of Pusan. It was a branding exercise, promoted by the municipal government, the local media, and of course, the festival organizers.

The First International Cultural Event in Pusan

While the establishment of PIFF was largely prompted by the intersection of several political, economic, and social conditions, the festival also had to negotiate between the central and the local governments. As illustrated above, throughout the 1990s, a rapid social transformation was affecting every part of South Korea. Residual authoritarian and emergent democratic interests and ideologies converged in the establishment of film festivals.[37] In this context, the organizing processes illustrate the complex ways in which groups with local power and decision-making powers negotiate and struggle with one another.

As discussed, the 1990s saw a shift away from the authoritarian military dictatorship towards a democratic, civilian government. Despite the latter's ambitious decentralization policy, local governments and civil society were still extremely weak in comparison to the strong central government, on which local governments continued to be significantly dependent.[38] As all festivals face economic pressures, both local and national subsidies were crucial to the PIFF's survival, but due to the enactment of the local self-government system, the central government only provided around USD300,000, less than 20 percent of the annual budget for the first festival.[39] However, instead of falling apart as a result of this meager funding, the PIFF maintained a certain autonomy and was put under less pressure from the Seoul-based political bureaucracy than might previously have been the case.

On top of relations with the central government and other problems such as administrative management and a lack of media savvy, the PIFF had to resolve a series of issues in relation to local concerns. For instance, the fact that only a few members of the founding group were originally from Pusan while the majority was from Seoul could have given rise to some resistance from the local community. How were the founders able to negotiate the tensions between local and national interests?

The official launch of the PIFF Committee was announced in February 1996, just seven months before the opening in Pusan. The organizing body was divided into two parts: the Organizing Committee and the Executive Committee. Whilst the Executive Committee consisted of film intellectuals, professors, and local media executives, the Organizing Committee was mainly composed of local government officials, representatives of local business, theater owners, and hotel owners in Pusan. This division was intended to facilitate arbitration between the various local interests. While the Executive Committee was in charge of envisioning the festival identity, programming, and recruiting staff, the Organizing Committee was responsible for financial affairs. In this structure, the central decision-making power was with the Executive Committee. The relatively smooth process of negotiation was partly attributable to the well-organized distribution and balance of roles played by the local and non-local founding members. For example, Kim Dong-Ho, the festival director and member of the Executive Committee, who had specialized in cultural policy for many years in the government in Seoul, played a crucial role in mediating conflict and tension between central and local interests. At the same time, natives from Pusan concentrated on resolving local issues, such as negotiating resistance from local business people and encouraging "local spirit." This clear division of roles has been maintained throughout the life of the festival and enabled the PIFF to prevent any extreme conflict in spite of differences in perception between different parties about the festival's functions and aims. This reciprocal relationship between film industry insiders and local government officials differentiated PIFF from other festivals in Korea, as many other festivals, including Puchon and Jeonju, failed to build co-operative relationships with their respective local governments.[40]

However, different components of the power structure perceived PIFF in different ways. One example of this is worth commenting on in more specific detail in order to expose the complicated relationships the festival developed with many of those in power. It is a little known fact that the city government had initially planned PIFF as a temporary event. Inspired by the huge success of the 1988

Olympic Games in Seoul, the *Segyehwa* drive, and the inauguration of the local government, the newly-formed Pusan city government sought to host international events. After a successful bid in May 1995 to host the 2002 Asian Games as the first international sporting event held in the city, the Pusan government wished to generate a new, non-industrial image for the city, and sought to realize this aim in part through organizing an event to precede the Games. Significantly, the government's desire to promote a new East Asian identity for Pusan was reflected in the festival committee's Northeast Asia-focused programming.

However, while the founding PIFF members had been preparing for the event since mid-1995 and awaiting a firm confirmation from the local government regarding its status as an annual event since that time, there was no definite answer until the end of that year. Before the official announcement on February 13, 1996, one major local newspaper reported, "Pusan city has suddenly abandoned its long neglect of PIFF and decided to support it, so it can open the event this year to promote the 2002 Asian Games."[41] It is therefore not surprising to learn that the first PIFF was accompanied by an event called "Asian Week," which acted as a promotional event for the Asian Games and the successful *Segyehwa* process in Pusan. These twinned events opened and closed on the same day.[42] Originally, the PIFF was supposed to be fundamentally restructured or even terminated after the Asian Games in 2002 by the local government.[43] While this initial plan was dropped soon after the huge success of the first PIFF, the fact that it had even existed clearly demonstrates that the local government perceived it as supporting the sports event rather than standing alone as an important cultural practice. In fact, this kind of thinking, motivated by the economically oriented *Segyehwa*, was pervasive in local governments in South Korea at the time. This case highlights how heterogeneous forces surrounding one cultural organization worked in different directions.

Key Founding Members

Film intellectuals and industry insiders involved in the festival organization constituted one of the newly emerging social groups which flourished in Korean society in the 1990s. According to Kim Soyoung's classification of South Korean film festivals—those derived from a coalition of the state, local government, corporations, and intellectuals equipped with film expertise; those which are primarily corporate-sponsored; and those which are organized by new and more established activist groups[44]—the PIFF fits the first category as it is closely related to the state and the local government.[45] Kim further observes that the politics of the status quo influenced the whole process of festival organization in Korea in the late 1990s. Among many other different groups, there were "collectives and identities engaged in film festival politics, some are not only recognized but also heavily supported by the authorities whereas others are refused recognition or they themselves resist recognition by the authorities."[46] She suggests:

> [F]inding themselves in the ever shifting space between the residual authoritarian government of military dictatorship and hegemonic quasi-democratic government, the non-majority groups tend to employ the discourse of radical differences less than the idea of universal humanism. The appeal to human rights reverberates through the array of feminist and gay/lesbian movements.[47]

Examined within this framework, PIFF belongs to a privileged group who were recognized and supported by the authorities in contrast to the Queer Film and Video Festival or the Human Rights Film Festival which have both been severely interrupted and censored by the central government. Kim focuses on the establishment of cultural events by "non-majority groups"—using her term—in the 1990s in Korea. In a similar fashion, special attention is paid in this work to how other "non-majority groups" strived to negotiate and engage with the authorities to create a film festival under the shifting, transitional circumstances in the same period.

Amongst the founding members of PIFF were young filmmakers and film critics.[48] These were largely divided into two groups, depending on their links to the local community. Most of the local intellectuals were engaged with local film communities via film education activities such as those at Gyeongsung University. Their enthusiasm for cinema was evident as far back as the 1980s when the same generation organized a small film society named "Cineclub," showing classic Hollywood and European art films.

Regarding the cinematic legacy of Pusan, in September 1950, during the Korean War, the Korean Film Critics Association was established in Pusan, the first such body established in Korea. While its establishment in Pusan was due to the city's temporary status as the capital, the formation of the Association encouraged local film intellectuals to establish their own film society named the "Pusan Film Critics Association" as well as the "Buil Film Award" in 1958.[49] Although local film production in Pusan deteriorated over the following three decades, local film intellectuals sought to draw on and promote Pusan's legacy in film culture through this tradition so as to support and justify the establishment of the PIFF.

In a similar vein, the organizing process was marked by the involvement of a wide range of organizations. While most of the founders hailed from Pusan's film community, the Executive Committee quickly expanded to include a broad range of social groups, including an opposition party and non-party politicians, various religious groups, and women's organizations in Pusan. This network also grew to include foreign film festival consultants such as Tony Rayns, Simon Field, Paul Yi, and Wong Ainling.[50] As noted, the Executive Committee, rather than the central or the local government, assumed a leading role in organizing and developing the festival. The committee used this wide network to enlist the efforts of two key figures: festival director Kim Dong-Ho and deputy director Park Kwang-su, the quintessential Korean New Wave director.

Park Kwang-su, who played a central role in the PIFF founding group, is significant in Korean film history. When President Roh Tae-woo enacted a new constitution which allowed for a gradual easing of censorship laws in 1988, the first film to take advantage of this was *Chilsu and Mansu* (1988) by first-time director Park Kwang-su. This film marked the rebirth of political expression in Korean films. Park showed a consistent interest in social reality, going on to direct acclaimed films such as *Black Republic* (1990), *To the Starry Island* (1993), *A Single Spark* (1995), and *Uprising* (1999).

Furthermore, Park was the first film director and producer to receive funding from the West. From the 1980s, the arrival of new directorial talent brought about a revival in the South Korean film industry; every sector of the film industry was dramatically transformed. Multiplex theaters were built and the old distribution monopolies broken down. Filmmakers at all levels, from young independents working on 16 mm to well-known names like Park Kwang-su, sought and found new sources of finance. Park directed and produced *To the Starry Island* in 1993, the first Korean film to benefit from co-financing from the West, in association with Samsung Nices in Korea and Channel 4 in Britain. At the time of production, he founded and ran his own independent production company in order to open up new funding options for his films outside the mainstream *Chungmuro* industry.[51] Park thus adopted an intriguing pioneering position within the Korean film industry.[52]

As well as bringing a symbolic association with the image of the New Wave in the Korean film industry to his relationship with the PIFF, it is important to note that Park had a firm connection with Pusan. Though born in Sokcho, in the Gangwon province, he lived mostly in Pusan until he joined the film group *Yallasung* in Seoul in his twenties. This link bolstered his effectiveness as an advocate for the establishment of a film festival in Pusan, as did his personal ties to global film critics through his experience at various Western film festivals as a film director. Park Kwang-su's positioning sheds light on the PIFF's identity and boundaries. Most importantly, it provided legitimacy in the organization of this event in Pusan as a successor to the 1980s political movement. In other words, his presence and active engagement with the festival enabled the Executive Committee to position this cultural event as "an important extension of Korea's cultural movement." It also meant a symbolic break away from "authoritarianism and the first dynamic step towards a more open society."[53]

While Park Kwang-su played a pivotal role in bringing together local and global resources to assist the establishment of the festival, Kim Dong-Ho, the

festival director, had a more pragmatic role as he was responsible for eliciting corporate funding and mediating tensions with the central government. As he was a
former Vice Minister of Culture and Tourism, and specialized in cultural policy
with long administrative experience in this field since 1961 (including his position as chairman of the Korea Public Performance Ethics Committee from 1988
to 1992), he made the most of a broad and diverse personal network. As discussed
earlier, political networks in Korea are often largely economic in character. The first
PIFF was financed largely through a KRW300 million donation from the Daewoo
Group, a top ranking *jaebol* (*chaebol*) in the region.[54] While Kim played a decisive
role in making this happen by using his networks, the availability of such funding
was also largely attributed to the rapid transformation of the Korean film industry
at the time.

Just prior to the establishment of the PIFF, a shift in production capital had
occurred in the film industry. The traditional chain of distribution rooted in
Chungmuro capital prevailing during the 1980s shifted as key *jaebol* groups such as
Samsung and Daewoo began to invest in film production from the mid-1990s on.
The inflow of new capital and film industry marketing strategies rapidly restructured the pattern of film production. In addition, the government's globalization
drive, *Segyehwa*, had propelled the film business by offering tax incentives, making
it a highly profitable investment option. These conditions encouraged corporations
to fund cultural institutions, a situation of which the PIFF took full advantage.
Kim Dong-Ho personally played a distinctive role which contributed to the relatively smooth development of relationships with both the central government and
the conglomerate Daewoo Group. Because of this, although he was not a native
of Pusan, he successfully positioned himself in PIFF and gained a positive appeal
amongst the local community.[55] Overall, these particular characteristics of the
founding members played a crucial role in generating a balance between the local
and the central governments, which was necessary for the successful establishment
of the festival.

Local Economy and PIFF

No matter how carefully the structure of the organizing committee was set up,
local commercial interests were an unavoidable issue for PIFF. The local economy
of cities is closely related to the rise of international film festivals as such globally
scaled cultural events can attract revenue to the local industry.[56] Festivals in cities
can stimulate low-season tourism which helps to justify the local subsidy on which
most festivals depend. In this sense, culture has become more and more significant
to the meaning and function of cities as they are converted from places of production to places of consumption and as they are forced to compete for finance
capital in an increasingly competitive global economy.[57] The PIFF's establishment

in Pusan and the city's specific urban economy reflect the changing function of culture, which became an increasingly important commodity for entrepreneurs. For example, a local newspaper editorial emphasized that "through this festival, the city of Pusan can attract tourists each year and ultimately enhance its reputation as a cultural center" by concentrating on the merits of the PIFF to attract more attention to the local community.[58] This rhetoric underlines the fact that, initially, economic motives trumped cinematic ones in the establishment of the film festival as it was seen primarily as a tourism-related enterprise to boost the local economy.

Although Pusan was primarily regarded as an industrial port city, it also maintained its reputation as a southern tourist center. It has been estimated that during the summer season, over eight million people visit the local beaches, making it one of the most popular vacation places in Korea with a huge tourist entertainment industry. However, since the 1990s, the local infrastructure began to change. In particular, cinema chains run by local syndicates began to be transformed in the wake of the multiplex construction boom in Seoul. Consumer spending patterns in Pusan also changed dramatically: the Gwangbok-dong and Nampo-dong area in the city center, for example, became one of the south's most prosperous zones in the 1990s. Both areas played important roles in the festival, either hosting screenings or parties.

Just before the PIFF was launched in 1996, local authorities and the Executive Committee sought to persuade local businesspeople and other interest groups, mainly in the tourism and entertainment sectors, to contribute financially to its founding. However, local businesses were skeptical about the immediate outcomes of the PIFF and therefore some failed to follow through on their promises. For example, one of the major local hotel chains promised to be the festival's anchoring sponsor but reneged on its commitment at the last minute.[59] Moreover, when the festival and the city government planned to build a prestigious space devoted solely to the PIFF, intending to symbolize Pusan as a "film festival city," local businesspeople who ran stalls in the open-air markets objected fiercely and protested against the redevelopment of the Market Square.[60] Traditionally, the Market Square, surrounded by four cinema venues and open-air stalls, symbolized the city center. In order to construct a new PIFF cinema square, existing open-air markets would have been forced to move.[61] In the first year of the festival a compromise was reached: a temporary PIFF Square was constructed, and businesspeople agreed to relocate the market during the festival period. In subsequent years, a permanent structure was completed.

In addition, individual venues to screen films constitute a crucial part of the infrastructure for film festivals. In this respect, the participating festival cinemas in Pusan were clustered in the center of the city, creating a focal point which resulted in ideal opportunities for socializing among the festival guests and audiences. This spatial configuration, with four cinemas placed around a central square, worked well during the festival even though there were no modern multiplexes in 1996. However, local cinema syndicates in Pusan did not welcome the PIFF initially. To screen festival films, it needed access to their venues, yet owners could see no reason to make them available, as they were making good money screening Hollywood blockbusters. The Pusan city council and the PIFF committee had to persuade them to rent out their venues during *Chuseok*, the Korean Thanksgiving festival, the most lucrative time of the entire year. Through the influential mediation of the Pusan city council, the PIFF was able to use these venues to screen festival films by paying expensive rental fees.

As it became clear that the first PIFF could attract enormous attention from local and global audiences and media, public opinion rallied behind the festival and local enterprises quickly fell in line with the shift in attitude. Thus, the initial situation was reversed in a few years. In the wake of the success of PIFF and the rapid redevelopment plan in place for Pusan, from the year 2000, many new multiplexes were built in both the city center and suburban areas of Pusan, for example, in Hauendae. These cinemas aggressively promoted themselves to attract young consumers, offering their venues to the PIFF on favorable terms.

These tussles lay bare how the PIFF was perceived by the local community in its initial stages. While culture was generally considered a profitable product to rejuvenate the local economy, businesspeople, who had never experienced a global cultural event in their own city, were reluctant to support the demands of the festival. Overall, these processes reveal the conflicts, resistances, and compromises among the newly inaugurated local government, the commercial power structure, and the founding members of the festival committee.

Censorship and the PIFF

Censorship was one crucial factor in the transformation of the Korean film industry. Specifically, the pre-release review system had long been a serious obstacle to the development of Korean cinema. However, ironically, it affected the PIFF's success in a different way. According to the law, the PIFF was not allowed to screen films without advance permission from the government. Amongst the regulations that affected the festival in this way was the Enforcement Ordinance of the Film Promotion Act. In effect since 1996 this act stipulated that "unless an international film festival has more than three participating countries and more than three years of history, all invited entries shall be subject to review by the Korea Public Performance Ethics Committee."[62] While the founding members of the PIFF strove to construct an image for the festival that was free from the reach of authoritarianism, they had to avoid any extreme confrontation with the central government to inaugurate the festival on schedule. Being aware of the difficulty in dealing with this political issue, the PIFF coped with the situation at several different levels.

As this was the first time an international film festival had been held in Korea, there were concerns about the ability of the Ethics Committee members to review more than one hundred films in a limited time. In an attempt to resolve this issue, festival director Kim Dong-Ho, who had once headed the Ethics Committee, mobilized his personal network: he met the review board members in order to "appeal for leniency."[63] In addition, around this time there had been serious legal discussions about the validity of the act as it was contradictory to the spirit of the dominant *Segyehwa* campaign.[64] Thanks to these efforts and circumstances, from the first year the PIFF committee enjoyed a dispensation allowing it to show all films uncut.[65] Thus, the PIFF was able to exist as a censorship-free zone, and the majority of films, which would have been prevented from being shown in full had there been a pre-release review, were shown uncut at the PIFF. While this fact was in itself of historical significance to Korean cinema, at the same time it also helped attract a huge audience to the festival.

Furthermore, the screening of particular films, such as Japanese films, aroused much interest because these had not previously been available to the Korean public. Japanese cultural products—including films, songs, and TV programs—had been prohibited following the founding of the Republic of Korea in 1948.[66] The first PIFF in 1996 featured fifteen Japanese films, including the animation feature *Ghost in the Shell* (1995) by Oshii Mamoru and *Sleeping Man* (1996) by Oguri Kohei, the first such public screenings in Korean film history. Viewers in their teens, twenties, and thirties, too young to remember the occupation and attracted by Japanese pop culture, responded with particular enthusiasm.[67] Furthermore, Mainland Chinese films, such as *Behind the Forbidden City* (1996, also known as *East Palace, West Palace*) by Zhang Yuan, banned by the Chinese government for their homosexual and/or political content, were given their world premieres at the PIFF. These films soon aroused controversy and attracted attention from the press and foreign film critics as well as local audiences; ticket sales hit the roof.[68]

However, the PIFF still had to grapple with the thorny issue of North Korean cinema. It is worth noting that since its inception, the PIFF had consistently attempted to screen films from North Korea. Despite difficulties due to the National Security Law,[69] the PIFF aggressively tried to announce that the festival would show North Korean films to the public in Pusan. Under the particular political conditions of Korea as a divided nation, such rhetoric tended to attract huge media and public attention to the festival, whether the films were ever actually screened or not. Given that the Human Rights Film Festival was severely censored by the central government around the same period, the PIFF's deliberate manipulation of the political situation is noteworthy. As well as taking advantage of loosened government regulations during a transitional political period, the festival also actively exploited those negative national conditions to garner attention for itself at local, national, and global levels.[70]

Part 2: "Making a Hub of Asian Cinema": Regionalization Strategies

In the previous section, I highlighted a number of inter-related factors which influenced the inauguration of the PIFF, casting light on how this complex process reflects the multilayered aspects of Korean society and the Korean film industry in the 1990s. The successful establishment of the PIFF was certainly the result of negotiation among a number of different and conflicting interests and forces. Globally, East Asian cinema—including Korean cinema—was emerging in Western international film festivals at this time. Concurrently, the HKIFF, which had long been a key showcase of Asian cinema for the West, was gradually becoming less important as a platform. The PIFF took the opportunity created by this short-lived vacuum, during which the HKIFF was in decline due to the city's handover to China in the late 1990s, to claim for itself the status of being the new hub for Asian cinema.[71]

The PIFF's regional approach was tied to a range of other developments, including an urban regeneration project aimed at transforming the industrial port of Pusan into a cultural center. It was also incorporated into a global networking strategy that exploited the changes and differences in local and regional attitudes towards the global film market. The PIFF forged substantial ties between Asia and Europe in two major ways: by appealing to pan-Asianism and anti-Hollywood sentiment towards Asia, and by using a strong market-oriented approach towards Europe. By focusing on two interlinked themes, urban regeneration and networks, I will explore how this strategy has interacted with local and global forces.

Becoming a Global City of Cinema: Urban Regeneration

The shaping of urban spaces by cinema as a cultural, material, and social practice is one of the distinctive features of globalization. As Mark Shiel notes, cinema as an industry provides cities with a sub-national driving force in developing civic identities and a renewed function to cope effectively with the changing global economy. He outlines:

> Industrially, cinema has long played an important role in the cultural economies of cities all over the world in the production, distribution and exhibition of motion pictures, and in the cultural geographies of certain cities particularly marked by cinema (from Los Angeles to Paris to Bombay) whose built environment and civic identity are both significantly constituted by film industry and films.[72]

This description corroborates the view held by large numbers of commentators today, for example, Saskia Sassen, that the city—more so than the nation-state—is the fundamental unit of the new global system which has emerged and of which the mobility of capital and information is the most distinctive feature.

As argued, film festivals today tend to interact with other political, social, and economic factors so as to build up a sense of distinctive festival identity and to survive both local shifts and the increasingly competitive global economy. In this context, Julian Stringer notes, the development of global cities has been bound up with the prominence of international film festivals since the 1990s. Stringer suggests that many festivals actually now market and project a city's own festival image within the global space economy especially in relation to other cities and other festivals.[73] Hence, global-scaled festivals self-consciously tend to expand their events to compete with rival festivals, actively benchmarking existing big festivals, often claiming to be a regional hub and operating according to dual goals: to be globally accessible and locally distinctive within the global space economy.[74] As Stringer states:

> In order to compete within the terms of this global space economy, such events must operate in two directions at once. As local differences are being erased through globalisation, festivals need to be similar to one another, but as novelty is also at a premium, the local and particular also becomes very valuable. Film festivals market both conceptual similarity and cultural difference.[75]

The more festivals desire to be fixed in a global festival map, the more they need to differentiate themselves from others by reconstructing the host city into a more attractive place. In this regard, the PIFF's regionalization strategy is aligned with the local development project so as to compete for global financing. In order to make its regional identity a marketable trademark, the urban regeneration of Pusan was significant. Urban planning, including building up an efficient and comprehensive infrastructure, aimed to suit the image that the PIFF wished to construct. The links the festival forged "between local councils, businesses, governments, and communities, as well as some discussion of how all of these relate to global networks of power and influence" also require consideration.[76] Hence, the processes of urban regeneration depend to a large extent upon multiple levels of networks.

With regard to the PIFF's choice of a regional identification, there are two ways to explain why it has focused on Asian identity from the start. First, as mentioned in the previous chapter, the PIFF was initially created as one of the special events of Asian Week, which Pusan organized to promote the 2002 Asian Games in the city. Therefore, the PIFF committee had to enhance the spirit of Asian community in line with the main goal that Pusan city had already established.

Second, as a newcomer competing against world-renowned and well-established film festivals, the PIFF had to find a niche and differentiate itself from them. As the PIFF committee stated, "it would have been impossible for an unfamiliar country like Korea and an even more unfamiliar city like Busan to invite the 'world premiere' that other more famous international festivals had their eyes on."[77] Moreover, the PIFF committee was aware of the potential for a niche market in Asian films, which had been apparent in the warm reception given to Iranian productions at Western festivals such as Cannes, Venice, and Berlin.[78] Although Hong Kong had established an official platform for Asian cinema over the past two decades, it had been deteriorating since the mid-1990s. The PIFF hoped to take its position. The widespread use of rhetoric elevating "Asianness" to promote the festival was evident in a number of cases. The most distinctive examples were the focus on Asian cinema in the main programs and the project market known as the Pusan Promotion Plan (PPP). In addition, the establishment of new awards such as Asian Filmmaker of the Year reinforced the message of Asian identity.[79]

Despite its negative civic image as an industrial port city and lack of cinematic heritage image, Pusan managed to host the first international film festival in Korea. The success of Pusan's first cultural event influenced a new civic identity and boosted self-confidence in Korea's second largest city, and a gateway to the outside world with growing geopolitical importance. It also stimulated local attempts to develop valuable cultural and economic activities, encouraging promoters such as sponsors, the local government, and other related tourist industry groups to make it a regular event.

In spite of the time gap, the PIFF seems to share a similar experience with many European film festivals such as those in Berlin and Rotterdam in terms of urban development. Both European cities were bombed during World War II, while Pusan suffered extensive damage in the Korean War. Moreover, the three cities carried out prestigious cultural projects to enhance their credentials as future economic and cultural capitals of Europe and East Asia. Like many cities that have endeavored to become global economic hubs, this urban trio strove to revive the local economy through cultural events. In this respect, Rotterdam has a few extra points of comparison with Pusan.

First, the urban regeneration in Rotterdam was driven by the city council's initiative for the invention of a "new Rotterdam," while in Pusan the success of the festival preceded the development of Pusan, and subsequently, the festival's initiative was combined with support from the local government.[80] As shown in the introduction, the local government was initially doubtful about the feasibility of PIFF and was not actively engaged with its establishment. Yet, the PIFF's success stimulated local government plans for urban regeneration.

Second, although both cities are non-capital port cities, their specific approaches for urban regeneration were different. In Rotterdam, art and design was adopted by the city council to change the urban city image. Pusan, relatively lacking cultural heritage, had to create its legacy of culture—cinema—to support its city image. Under such circumstances, the PIFF adopted the concept of being a hub of film industries in East Asia, an impulse rapidly propelled by the establishment of the project market—PPP. The PPP has certainly provided the PIFF with a major justification to grasp the new role of the film festival in the process of urban regeneration in Pusan.

Also, there were a variety of factors that prompted the PIFF's successful establishment; one crucial circumstance was the newly inaugurated local government in Pusan. Responding to the shift in the political environment in Korea and the demand from the local community, the PIFF's establishment is understood as a local rather than nationally orchestrated initiative. In this respect, the PIFF's moves to link its festival identity and brand image with a strong Asian identity is closely incorporated with the desire of Pusan's local community, which also tried to gain a distinctive civic image to remain competitive in the global economy. Both the city and the festival had to position themselves beyond the divided nation-state and place themselves into a global arena.

Importantly, local economic development strategies in any individual city must increase revenue stability and decrease vulnerability to external forces. They must also provide good jobs for local citizens, and increase the overall satisfaction of city residents.[81] For instance, there was intense debate about the economic benefits from hosting an international film festival. These included the rapid increase in PIFF-related tour packages, including transportation, accommodation, and tickets to films during the festival. Typical advertising lines included "Movie Lovers Get a Chance to Tour Pusan and Attend the Film Festival,"[82] and "Five-Star Hotels in Pusan are Fully Booked Due to the Special Procurements of PIFF."[83] Kim Joo-young, a journalist for a national mainstream financial newspaper, calculated the economic impact of the PIFF on Pusan and reported, "With a budget of just 25 billion won, the PIFF secured revenues of 250 billion and significantly contributed to the local economy of Pusan."[84] In short, the local community paid special attention to the extent that this cultural event could contribute to the economic development of Pusan.

The PIFF's continued success and growth have accelerated the transformation of Pusan from a manufacturing port city to a culturally driven modern city. Multiplexes, an aquarium and mega-sized shopping malls were constructed in the suburban area of Pusan including Haeundae, where the PIFF's headquarters are located. The cityscape has been changed and this has begun to have an impact on the festival image and vice versa. Indeed, the PIFF has proved that the cultural industry could revitalize the local economy. The role of culture in urban regeneration in Pusan seems to be dominated by a combination of economic and marketing considerations in this regard. The success of the PIFF has enhanced the entrepreneurial function of culture within the local economy. In the national context, it has also prompted the proliferation of local film festivals in Puchon, Jeonju, and Seoul.

As well as boosting the local film industry, the PIFF redefined the identity of Pusan as a cinematic city. After the PIFF and the PPP, Cinematheque Busan, the Busan Film Commission,[85] the Busan Cinema Studio at the Yachting Centre Haeundae, the Asia Film Industry Centre, and the Asian Film Commissions Network (AFCNet)[86] were subsequently established. Most importantly, it was decided by the government that the Korean Film Council (KOFIC) would relocate its base from Seoul to Pusan by 2012 according to the state's decentralization policy.[87]

However, it was not until the first PPP proved to be successful that the PIFF started to have full self-confidence and a decisive initiative in its Asian-oriented direction. While the PIFF tended to carefully stress the locality of Pusan at the start, it began to be more aggressive in evoking its Asian identity when the PPP was launched in 1998. In order to differentiate itself from the Hong Kong and Tokyo film festivals, the PIFF created new channels of finance and co-production for Asian films to access the global distribution circuit right after launching the festival. Propelled by the prominent development of regional film industries, the PPP has carved out a major network within Asia's rapidly rebounding film (co)-production sector. In the wake of PPP's success, the Hong Kong and Tokyo film festivals competitively established their own programs: the Hong Kong-Asia Film Financing Forum (HAF) and the Tokyo Film Creators' Forum.

Overall, the PIFF has attempted to develop links between the urban image of Pusan and its festival identity as a hub of Asian cinema. To achieve this aim, the festival and the local community have established an efficient infrastructure to become an industrial base of Asian cinema. Furthermore, the PIFF has strategically established a pre-market PPP to attract transnational capital to invest in Asian cinema and to share information for participating in the production, distribution, and exhibition in the early stage of production. This effort reflects the pervasive trend of globalization, as Manuel Castells has described: the flow of transnational capital, or the flow of information in a highly technological society into a global space, namely global cities.[88] In this regard, the PIFF's urban regeneration project is interlinked with its global networks strategy which was simultaneously carried out. Obviously, the particular process of regional approach shown at the PIFF and Pusan corroborates the argument that globalization is a complex, dynamic coexistence of overlapping and contradictory modes at local, national, and regional levels.

Global Networks

The PIFF's effort to build global networks is observed at different levels. It focused on forging strong regional ties with Asia by joining specialist networks such as the Network for the Promotion of Asian Cinema (NETPAC).[89] At the time of its establishment in 1996, the PIFF tended to focus on Northeast Asian cinemas including those of Japan, China, Taiwan, and Hong Kong. After its successful launch, however, in order to meet the key concept of an Asian hub, the festival had to include other parts of Asia such as India, the Philippines, Malaysia, Indonesia, as well as Iran. To this end, the PIFF actively participated in and became a significant member of NETPAC, which was initially based in the Philippines and India. In November 2002, the NETPAC general conference was held in Pusan during the seventh PIFF. Members agreed to relocate its headquarters from Manila to Pusan for the following five years.[90]

Moreover, in rebuilding and creating these networks, the PIFF seems to have become imitative of the networking style of politico-economic relationships practiced within the boundaries of many Asian states in the past such as with ASEAN. For instance, as ASEAN's primary aim is "to accelerate economic growth, social progress and cultural development in the region," the AFCNet—a group of organizations in Asia that provides shooting support services—received its official launch at the ninth PIFF.[91] The network's major goals are to collaborate in marketing Asia as an attractive shooting location and to encourage the professional development of its members through educational activities.

It is worth pointing out that the PIFF has appealed to pan-Asianism and anti-Hollywood sentiments to generate regional solidarity in Asia. As mentioned in the previous chapter, key members of the PIFF committee such as Park Kwang-su and Lee Young-kwan were associated with the National Cinema Movement (*Minjok Younghwa Woondong*) which attempted to "construct the possibility of meaningful political and social change."[92] The executive members tried to establish the PIFF "without turning the festival into an exhibition fair or showcase for predominantly Hollywood films" and regarded this Asian film festival as "an important extension of Korea's cultural movement."[93] Therefore, even before its inauguration, the PIFF invoked anti-Hollywood sentiments to protect the local film industry from its dominance. At an international seminar on June 5, 1996 for the successful launch of PIFF, festival consultants and participants pointed out that the South Korean film industry had been dominated by Hollywood commercial films and that PIFF needed to show a new spectrum of world cinema by focusing on Asian cinema.[94] *Variety* reported in 1997 that "[s]trategies for combating Hollywood's grip on foreign audiences dominated the discussion at the second Pusan Int'l. Film Festival, which ran Oct.10–18 in South Korea's second largest city."[95] PIFF's anti-Hollywood sentiments were most visible in its active participation in the screen quota movement, a strong defense campaign against US pressure for the abolition of the system which required Korean theaters to screen local films for between 106 and 146 days a year.[96]

However, at a regional level, the PIFF's anti-Hollywood attitude was incorporated with pan-Asianism to protect the Asian film industry from Hollywood. During the first PPP in 1998, the PIFF and the PPP announced the first co-production project, "Y2K," embracing Japan, Taiwan, and Hong Kong. At the official press conference, renowned Hong Kong director Stanley Kwan stated, "We looked at the increasing dominance of Hollywood and decided we had to change, to do something different. [...] We hope this sets new standards and provides a model for the future."[97] In addition, the festival kept generating this discourse to invigorate the Asian film industry network by arranging a conference on "The Impact of the WTO on the Asian Film Industry" during the 2002 PPP.[98]

The other strand of the PIFF's global networks is its market-oriented approach to Europe. The PIFF used a market-oriented approach to build a network with Europe as South Korea attracted huge amounts of capital from the West when it gained the status of "tiger economy" in the late 1980s. In particular, PPP's solidarity with CineMart at the International Film Festival Rotterdam (IFFR) and its close ties with the European Film Promotion (EFP) are clear examples of this approach. As the PIFF became popular in East Asia as a platform for Asian cinema, the EFP, the Hamburg-based umbrella network of all European national promotion and export organizations, wanted to promote European cinema in Asia through PIFF. Since the 1990s, the EFP had been looking for a base from which to promote European films on and to the Asian market. Following the decline of the Hong Kong and Tokyo Festivals, the PIFF emerged as a representative market. European cinema's eastward thrust thus encountered Pusan's ambitions to become a nodal point within the Asian market. In the process, the PIFF's European bias also helped.[99] As a result, every year the PIFF has invited rising European stars to introduce the films produced in Europe, helping to promote them to the local cinema chain and Asian film distributors.

This market-driven networking style was most obvious with the establishment of the PPP. Spurred on by its initial success, the PPP carved out a major network within Asia's rapidly growing film production sector. It is worth noting that PPP's initial success was enormously attributed to the partnership with CineMart, the IFFR's co-financing and co-production market. For instance, every year the Asian projects at CineMart were considered by the PPP and, in turn, PPP projects were considered by CineMart, providing a strong collaboration for supporting new Asian films. Furthermore, the PIFF and KOFIC launched the Asian Film Industry Network (AFIN), closely modeled on the EFP, and kicked off the expanded launch of a film market—the Asian Film Market (AFM)—in 2006.

Overall, the PIFF forged substantial ties between Asia and Europe in different ways by appealing to an anti-Hollywood sentiment and a feeling of Asianism, and by emphasizing the mutual interests in the region. The PIFF's wide-scale adoption of this strategy indicates that it is a conscious and reflexive player aware of changing cultural and political circumstances. It has adapted to the growing commercialism of the film industry, analyzed its economic implications, and adapted its capacity to cope with changes in the regional and global context.

Two distinctive features of PIFF's regionalization approach merit special attention: the festival's unique ability to position itself in the region by a specific regionalization strategy, and its close link with the national film industry, to be discussed in detail in the next chapter. These two aspects are, in turn, intertwined with each other. The PPP's transnational co-operation and its outcomes for investment, production, and distribution are inter-related to the transformation of the South Korean film industry in terms of shifts in funding sources and the rapid development of the infrastructure for film production. Forging of global networks and the city regeneration project were carried out at the same time. For instance, the festival schedule had to be negotiated with the tourist industry in the local economy of Pusan and within the festival circuit at the global level. Significantly, spatial and temporal aspects of the film festival economy are inter-related.

Festival Economy in the Festival Calendar

Festivals are cultural events where complex economic, cultural, social, and political threads come together for a limited time. Various factors influence attendance at festivals and the reputation of each festival. These include the quality of the program (the line-up of "names"), accessibility (accommodation, transportation, ease of purchasing tickets), and the ease of movement through a festival and its various events, as well as additional attractions in the surrounding city. Among them, as many commentators point out, much as festivals create a powerful sense of place, the temporal aspect of film festivals is significant in order to survive amongst many rival film festivals.

Clearly, there has been inequality between established film festivals and newcomers within the structure of the international film festival circuit. For example, it is widely believed that the respected, oldest Western film festivals such as those in Venice, Berlin, and Cannes have long dominated the annual festival calendar. Hence, scheduling is a key factor since it determines the activities of cities in relation to one another. In addition, it is notable that within the mutual relationships forged with the local tourism and leisure industries, there exist particular high-peak festival seasons—especially between September and November, when film festivals such as those in Venice, Locarno, Pusan, Tokyo, and Toronto take place. Within this competitive global map, conflict, negotiation, and cooperation are all evident.

Furthermore, as more film festivals compete to be prestigious showcases, as mentioned earlier, the film festival economy has changed. Since the 1990s, many international film festivals have begun trying to insert themselves into this fixed calendar, creating new opportunities for being an established film festival. To avoid clashing and overlapping with other festivals, co-operation becomes as important as competition. To find a place in a calendar dominated by established Western film festivals, it is necessary to negotiate and link with rival cities and inter-regional counterparts at a variety of levels.

As the PIFF has to rent venues for the festival period, it is usually scheduled to open three weeks after the Korean Thanksgiving holidays (which change every year according to the lunar calendar). In the PIFF's case, the annual event begins between late September and early October, although the range of dates may shift slightly.[100] For instance, the sixth PIFF opened one month later than the previous year. By opening the festival during this season, the PIFF aimed to find a niche market between the Hong Kong Film Festival in April and the dates of the major Western festivals. Obviously, this seems to be the outcome of having considered the major festival circuit to avoid competition with Cannes in May, Venice in September, and Berlin in February. Since the PIFF has focused on Asian films, it has become important for it to obtain high-impact new titles produced in Asia for a quality line-up.

However, the Venice Film Festival in September—one month earlier than the PIFF—potentially poses a threat to PIFF's selection because high-quality Asian films made during the year may be chosen for Venice rather than Pusan in the same autumn period. To avoid this overlapping, PIFF has been set up as a non-competitive festival, as I discuss further in the following chapter. To better understand the political process in which festivals negotiate and compete with one another, it is worth noting that this temporal aspect of film festivals is closely related to the premiere system.

More attractive world premieres provide a clear reason for the media to go to the event and consequently increase the presence of film distributors and sales agents. The premiere at festivals often accrues the value of the film, in the name of "international premiere," "world premiere," or even "national premiere." Pointing out the significance of the temporal aspect of film festivals and its relation to the premiere system, Janet Harbord further emphasizes that the notion of the premiere forges a hierarchical relationship among different festivals. She states:

> Films screened in or out of competition at other international festivals will automatically be excluded from selection. Such a stipulation automatically places the festivals in competition with each other at sites of cultural significance, and confirms their status in the register of importance [...] but in addition to intra-festival premieres, the notion of the premiere constructs a hierarchy of viewing through a temporal axis, securing the originality of the moment of festival viewing as a first.[101]

In this context, in order for a film to be nominated in the official competition of major film festivals, such as those in Cannes or Venice, the commitment to a sole film festival is necessary.

On top of this, the rules of competition limit the film's ability to move or flow around many film festivals at the same time. It is worth briefly mentioning the regulations of the International Federation of Film Producers Associations (FIAPF) here.[102] According to its rules, once festivals are classified as competitive, they are not supposed to accept or exhibit films which have previously been in competition at other festivals. For example, films screened at Cannes are automatically excluded from selection for Venice. Such a stipulation helps determine the hierarchical positions between festivals, as Harbord notes above.[103] Put simply, FIAPF has played a role in distributing territories to film festivals around the world.[104]

In this climate, it is very difficult for the PIFF, as a newcomer in a non-western nation, to obtain new Asian titles. To overcome this disadvantage, the PIFF has pursued a special tie with the IFFR. Both festivals co-operate in programming Asian films through various channels, even by sharing the pre-production stage of Asian films such as the Hubert Bals Fund (HBF) in the PPP.[105] In other words, the IFFR, held at the beginning of the year following the PIFF's October, takes the initiative to show the most recent Asian films prior to Berlin and Cannes. Since the IFFR has aimed to discover and introduce some alternative and experimental films and to offer a different focus on Asian films from its two counterparts, it does not necessarily block Asian cinema's subsequent route to Berlin in February and Cannes in May in the same year. By avoiding competition with other well-established film festivals, the PIFF has actively co-operated with a European film festival, the IFFR. This mutual relationship has enabled PIFF to obtain new titles from Asia and a firm position in the festival calendar as a platform for Asian cinema.

In sum, the PIFF's strategy to differentiate (and conceptualize) itself through the process of negotiating the festival period and the non-competitive system indicates the complicated cultural politics operating on the festival circuit. By building a vital co-operative relation with other European festivals, PIFF has tried to be the leading platform for Asian films. As shown, interdependency and inequality in the film festival economy necessitate a link to other film festivals. It is for this reason that the PIFF has strengthened ties with the outside world: the rest of Asia and Europe.

Conclusion

The general argument presented is that the PIFF, as it is currently constituted, is the result of an ongoing process of negotiation and renegotiation of its position and identity between the local and the national. Hence, the establishment of the PIFF should be understood within the context of the multitude of factors which have contributed to the event itself and the transformation of the Korean film industry as a whole. As the above discussion has demonstrated, the complicated process through which the PIFF was established reflects the multilayered aspects of Korean society and the Korean film industry in the 1990s. I have highlighted a number of inter-related factors which influenced the inauguration of the PIFF, casting light on how this process reflects the specificities of Korean society and relates to the Korean film industry. In addition, I explored how the PIFF navigated the regional and global landscape with aplomb, building networks and helping renew the city of Pusan.

As the global film festival circuit is growing fast, it becomes increasingly difficult to map out the complex set of festival connections, currently comprising around 2,000 networked events.[106] Of particular concern for this chapter is the fact that spatial and temporal aspects of the film festival economy are closely inter-related. Whereas I have focused on spatial developments through which urban regeneration and global networks were operated, I have tried to elucidate the significance of the temporal aspect of film festivals through the PIFF's non-competitive policy and through the particular circumstances that determine the festival schedule.

Indeed, the PIFF's focus on regionalization shows that there is a significant change in the way festivals are now entering the global market. At the same time, it also shows that today's regionalization interacts aggressively and multi-dimensionally with local and global forces. In this context, the PIFF is of particular importance since its distinctive approach to cultural politics in East Asia demonstrates the ways in which festivals have begun to negotiate and renew their roles and identities within the national, regional, and global economies.

2

Negotiating a Place between Korean Cinema and Asian Cinema: Programming Politics

This chapter seeks to reveal some of the institutional dynamics of film festivals by focusing on the programming sections of the PIFF between 1996 and 2005. It specifically aims to illustrate how the festival's programming of its national/regional sections is closely tied to its political, economic, and social interests. While the PIFF has served as a showcase for Asian films by evoking a strong Asian identity to differentiate it from its regional counterparts, it has equally striven to promote the national film industry by acting as a gateway to the global market for Korean films featured in its prime sections. By examining the tensions between the national and the regional in the PIFF's programming, I explore how the festival is attempting to stake out its own unique position within an ever-changing global landscape.

The international recognition of Korean cinema has mainly been achieved through an increased presence on the festival circuit in the West and a concurrent growth in the national film industry since the 1990s. In conjunction with this global visibility of Korean cinema, the PIFF has, in a relatively short period since its inception in 1996, established a firm position in East Asia as a showcase for Asian cinema. Recent scholarship on Korean cinema tends to agree on the key role that the PIFF has played in promoting Korean cinema and its globalization.[1] Consequently, the festival's evolution is very much inter-related with the boom in the Korean film industry and its increasing visibility worldwide. However, despite the importance of the close links between the PIFF and the Korean film industry, existing scholarship in this area largely elides any sustained empirical research on the relationship itself. That is, it has largely been taken for granted that the PIFF's success rides on that of Korean cinema's or, conversely, that Korean cinema's global success is a result of significant support from the PIFF. Nevertheless, in spite of the keen connection between the two, neither assumption can fully explain the distinctive relations between Korean cinema and the PIFF without further empirically verifiable research.

As Julian Stringer observes, just because a festival is internationally established and successful, it does not necessarily imply that the national film industry will follow suit.[2] In this regard, European film festivals and the PIFF differ significantly in their relations with their respective local film industries. For example, Derek Elley, senior critic of *Variety*, states that the PIFF was "exceptionally lucky" as Korean cinema has been growing remarkably since the 1990s compared to its counterparts in other nations. Elley further claims that although the International Film Festival Rotterdam (IFFR) tried to promote Dutch cinema on the international film market through its own festival site, it failed to reverse the decline in the Dutch film industry.[3]

In this context, the particular relationship between the PIFF and Korean cinema requires serious consideration and raises important questions. How do the PIFF and the Korean film industry inter-relate? If the former has played a role in promoting Korean cinema, how specifically and to what extent has the festival functioned in this respect over the decade? How did it correspond to individual Korean filmmakers' self-positioning strategies aimed at breaking into the global film market? And finally, how does it relate to the Asian identity that the PIFF has established as its festival identity?

To answer these questions, a close examination of the PIFF's key sections will act as a useful baseline to understand the complex negotiations of the contemporary Korean film industry within a local/global context. First, the chapter looks at Korean films in two key sections: "Opening" and "Korean Panorama."[4] Between 1996 and 2005, three Korean films were shown in the Opening section: *Peppermint Candy* (2000), *The Last Witness* (2001), and *The Coast Guard* (2002). *Peppermint Candy* is of particular interest for this chapter as the film offers a discursive site to demonstrate the substantial transformation of the Korean film industry. This shall be followed by a consideration of "Korean Panorama", examining how the PIFF reacts to developments within the local film industry. Lastly, pan-Asian programs such as "New Currents" and "A Window on Asian Cinema" will be examined to discuss the ways in which the PIFF has used a regionalization strategy to respond to changing industrial circumstances.

Opening the Festival with a Korean Film

Despite the significance of the roles that festivals have played in global film culture, there has been little research on programming itself. In her essay, "Film Festivals, Programming, and the Building of a National Cinema," Liz Czach discusses how the festival programming process at the Toronto Film Festival is related to the Canadian film industry and Canadian cinema. Developing the concept of "critical capital" from Pierre Bourdieu's "cultural capital," Czach argues that a film's critical capital is accrued and often determined through the film's placement within the festival structure as well as from being screened at prestigious festivals such as Cannes.[5] She asserts that a focus on national programs is common in every film festival because it promotes the national film culture to the global market. Furthermore, the slot where a film is placed often determines its hierarchical position and indicates the way in which it may be circulated and interpreted in the global market.

In light of this consideration, opening films are significant since they are the first encounter with festival audiences, especially with film professionals and journalists. Opening films can attract more attention to the festival in terms of promoting it to the media and general audience, and through establishing its own festival image.[6] Therefore, the "Opening" section often becomes the most prominent slot especially in non-competitive film festivals. Whilst it is the closing night with the winning results that generally gains the most attention in competitive festivals, the opening night in non-competitive festivals attracts the media spotlight, drawing strong interest from foreign critics and the public. At the same time, and exactly for the same reason, the reverse is also true. If the opening film fails to gain critical, public, and industrial attention at the festival site, it may severely damage the reputation of the festival. Due to this risk, the decision-making process about this key section necessitates great consideration. Under these conditions, featuring a new local title as the opening film reflects a strong nationalistic concern to place an emphasis on the local film industry, and it contains a number of political dimensions and consequences.[7]

The PIFF's overall program consists of nine sections: "Opening"/"Closing," "A Window on Asian Cinema," "New Currents," "Korean Panorama," "World Cinema," "Wide Angle," "Special Program in Focus," "Korean Retrospective," and "Open Cinema."[8] As shown in the chart below, films in the "Opening" section largely compromise some combination of Asian directors and films. It is noticeable, however, that the first opening film was *Secrets and Lies* (Mike Leigh, 1996), a British production that does not reflect the festival's identity as "the platform of Asian cinema." Park Kwang-su, deeply engaged in the selection process as deputy festival director of the first PIFF, said the programmers were desperately looking for a "big, quality film" that could represent the event in that year.[9] Since the debut festival was launched in haste, as discussed in Chapter 1, the emphasis was on a safe choice rather than on taking a risk with a less acclaimed film. For example, *Secrets and Lies* had just won the Palme d'Or in competition at Cannes a few months earlier and had already gained a Korean distributor.[10] However, apart from this case, the section has tended to show new titles of prominent Asian directors such as Wayne Wang, Mohsen Makhmalbaf and Hou Hsiao-hsien.

As we can see, it was not until the fourth PIFF that the festival committee chose to open the event with a Korean film. *Peppermint Candy*, Lee Chang-dong's second feature film, engages with issues of trauma and recovery from the Korean historical experience, such as the Gwangju Uprising, the International Monetary

Table 1

Opening Films at PIFF 1996–2005

	Year	Title	Director	Country
1	1996	*Secrets and Lies*	Mike Leigh	UK
2	1997	*Chinese Box*	Wayne Wang	France/UK/USA
3	1998	*The Silence*	Mohsen Makhmalbaf	Iran/France
4	1999	*Peppermint Candy*	Lee Chang-dong	South Korea
5	2000	*The Wrestler*	Buddadeb Dasgupta	India
6	2001	*The Last Witness*	Bae Chang-ho	South Korea
7	2002	*The Coast Guard*	Kim Ki-duk	South Korea
8	2003	*Doppelganger*	Kurosawa Kiyoshi	Japan
9	2004	*2046*	Wong Kar-wai	Hong Kong
10	2005	*Three Times*	Hou Hsiao-hsien	Taiwan

Source: PIFF program booklets from 1996 to 2005

Fund (IMF) crisis, and the military dictatorship since the 1980s. On opening the fourth PIFF with this film, the programming committee ambitiously asserted:

> This year's festival celebrates Asian cinema with the Korean entry of *Peppermint Candy* as its curtain raiser. Lee Chang-Dong, whose acclaimed *Green Fish* (1996) exposed the essence of Korean society, captures the process of recovering lost time with a new cinematic form. [...] Simply put, this film is a personal history of Young-Ho. Through his character, however, we experience twenty years of Korean history. The changes in Young-Ho echo the turmoil in our society.[11]

Drawing most plaudits from foreign guests and local audiences, this film was highly acclaimed during the festival. At a press conference after the world premiere screening, director Lee said, "I am honored that this film was selected as the opening film. Without PIFF, it would be impossible to screen Korean films including my film to many film professionals from the entire world."[12] Spurred on by the success at the PIFF, it won multiple awards at the Karlovy Vary International Film Festival including the Don Quixote Award, the Special Prize of the Jury, the Network for the Promotion of Asian Cinema (NETPAC) Award, as well as the Grand Bell Award for best film of 2000 in Korea. In addition, the film was invited to the Cannes Film Festival's Directors' Fortnight. On top of the critical applause, the film was successful at the national box-office.[13] After being shown at PIFF and accompanied by significant support from the media, it was released to the general audience on January 1, 2000.

Alongside this critical success at several international film festivals,[14] the local media paid enormous attention to *Peppermint Candy*, as the film suddenly became a phenomenon in Korean society and altered the broader cinema-going culture. Its realistic approach to a series of traumatic events in the 1980s began to attract a large number of viewers who were between thirty and fifty years old. As the main audience of Korean films has been generally considered to be females in their twenties, the film was celebrated for attracting attention from middle-aged viewers who rarely attended the cinema. Titled "Peppermint Syndrome Changed Cinema Culture," one major newspaper article reported that "this film was highly spotlighted as it hugely contributed to digging up a niche market in the Korean film industry."[15] Among those audiences who had experienced the historical circumstances depicted in the film, famous opinion leaders within the cultural arena such as Park Wan-seo (the renowned novelist) and Hwang Ji-woo (the poet) praised this film publicly. Park acclaimed, "I found a deep consolation when I saw this film. Ah, a film can be made in this way! This film is truly a good example of Realism cinema."[16] In addition, as a consequence of this phenomenon, a fan community called "People who Love *Peppermint Candy*" was established.[17] Although this was part of a media-orchestrated public relations campaign, the group continues to be popular with its annual New Year special screening of the film that attracts large audiences.

The success of *Peppermint Candy* was a turning point in the PIFF's programming and subsequent direction.[18] Indeed, it gave the festival and the wider Korean film industry some confidence that Korean films were able to appeal globally. Two years later in 2001, the PIFF selected another Korean film, *The Last Witness*, for the "Opening" section. Director Bae Chang-ho was one of the most prominent directors of the 1980s. After his directorial debut, *Slum People* (1982), he shot a number of box-office hits including *Flower on the Equator* (1983), *Whale Hunting* (1984), and *Deep Blue Night* (1985). Based on a true story and a legendary Korean novel, *The Last Witness* is a film about people who suffered during the Korean War and the ideological conflicts between democracy and communism during the fifty years that followed.

A similarity between *Peppermint Candy* and *The Last Witness* is worth noting. Although the former uses a unique reversed narrative time scheme, both films engage with the history of South Korea in the latter decades of the twentieth century. This common element was confirmed as a trend when *The Coast Guard* was chosen the following year. *The Coast Guard* is a story about a soldier in an observation point whose greatest goal in life is to arrest North Korean spies attempting to infiltrate the coastal area. After he mistakenly shoots a young villager who is having sexual intercourse with a village girl, the girl goes insane and becomes the observation point sex toy, while the guilt-ridden coast guard also suffers from mental problems. Hur Moon-yung, the programmer of the Korean section, introduced this film as "a shocking report on the oppressiveness that permeates Korean society."[19]

These three films commonly demonstrate how national narratives are constructed cinematically and how individual identity is brutalized by institutional repression.[20] In *Peppermint Candy*, lead character Young-Ho's innocence is destroyed by police and military brutality during the 1980s and 1990s, while Private Kang in *The Coast Guard* becomes crazy as a result of the hair-trigger atmosphere of guarding the volatile North-South Korean border. The tragedy in *The Last Witness* comes from the political situation in the divided nation and the prisoners of the Korean War. In this respect, despite the specific textual differences among the three films, they all display an exploration of national history that is pertinent to an understanding of the way in which the PIFF presents and promotes national films to the global market.

Alongside the thematic similarity in their engagement with Korea's national history as a divided nation, it is interesting that there was an attempt towards blockbuster filmmaking in both *The Last Witness* and *The Coast Guard*. It could be argued that by mixing national history with popular genres, these two opening films reflect the same trend prevalent in contemporary Korean films since the late 1990s, as exemplified by *Shiri* (Kang Je-kyu, 1999) and *Joint Security Area* (Park Chan-wook, 2000). As Chris Berry points out, whilst using recognizable Western aesthetics such as the blockbuster model to appeal to global audiences, recent Korean films since the late 1990s have drawn on an interest in local political issues. He argues:

> [B]oth of the most successful Korean blockbusters to date (*Shiri* and *Joint Security Area*) provide a space for examining and exorcizing the anxieties associated with the division of the Korean peninsula.[21]

For veteran director Bae, once a leading director of the 1980s, *The Last Witness* was his ambitious comeback to commercial filmmaking by casting top stars Ahn Sung-ki, Lee Jung-jae, and Lee Mi-youn. In a rare instance of local government funding, the film received financing from Koje city in Korea and Miyazaki prefecture in Japan, which amounted to around twenty percent of the film's total budget.[22] Yet this film attracted praise neither at the opening screening nor on subsequent general release in Korea. Indeed, there was a significant amount of negative media coverage regarding its choice as opening film. Film critic Yang Yoon-mo complained to a major local newspaper:

> Firstly, PIFF made a critical mistake in selecting *The Last Witness* as an opening film, since the film was full of cliché.
>
> The film discouraged local audiences from being enthusiastic about the festival and Korean films alike. The festival committee, in particular,

must not tie the current human relationship to the Korean film industry or certain reputation of a filmmaker.[23]

Journalist Park Eun-eu was equally critical:

> It is doubtful that such a high-budgeted blockbuster like *The Last
> Witness*, whose production cost amounted to a staggering 4 billion
> Korean won, could incorporate the festival's spirit about Asian cinema.
> The committee needs to be aware that it is not obligated to screen a
> Korean film as the opening selection of the festival.[24]

The quotations above indicate that a discrepancy exists between how the PIFF
prioritizes a local film by placing it into a prominent section and how it is then
received at both global and local levels. Despite the PIFF's endeavor to highlight
Korean films as opening titles, the choices were not always successful in satisfying
the demand of the local film industry and audiences.

In *The Coast Guard*, director Kim Ki-duk also attempted a blockbuster that
was very different from his previous films by casting a big star, Jang Dong-kun, and
invoking a strong political message but, ultimately, it was proved that "his films are
hardly commercial blockbusters in Korea despite the considerable weight of the
opening slot at Pusan."[25] Several extremely provocative scenes, including brutal
rapes and a miscarriage, seemed to be unbearable to the audience.[26] In fact, those
have always been typical characteristics of Kim, with British film critic Tony Rayns
describing his films as "sexual terrorism."[27] Ironically, however, and partly due to
this aspect, his films were praised and awarded at major Western film festivals
such as Venice and Berlin, whereas they were turned away by the local audience.[28]
Furthermore, in contrast to this critical praise from the West, it is noticeable that
the PIFF never paid attention to Kim's films until he started to gain an international reputation. In this context, the PIFF's choice of this film as an opening title
gave rise to controversy as it symbolized a sort of official ratification of his films
which had been "ostracized" by the local film industry.[29]

Such a contrast in the reception of Kim Ki-duk's films illustrates how taste
regimes operate in the process of festival programming: some films are included
and others excluded according to what the film festival particularly likes. Indeed,
festival programming and the notion of taste are closely related. Despite his rather
journalistic approach, Kenneth Turan usefully describes the nature of the selection
process at festivals:

> If there is one thing that is generally agreed about the official competi-
> tion, it's that the selection process is baffling at best [...] The uncom-
> fortable truth is that for a film festival that is the cynosure of all eyes,
> Cannes' taste, at least as far as the competition goes, is surprisingly
> narrow.[30]

The festival programming process of decision-making can never be neutral. It depends highly on the current political, economic, and social interests of the institution. However, programming national sections tends to be treated as an exceptional occasion as it is bound up with a different agenda, what Czach describes as a "national interest." She explains that "[p]ersonal taste and value judgements might be downplayed more often in national spotlight programmes than in other programming decisions as these decisions are in the national interest—so to speak."[31] If this is true, then how can one clearly explain the choice of Kim Ki-duk's film as operating within this taste regime?

A possible answer may become clear when Kim Ki-duk is compared with Lee Chang-dong. The two directors show different pathways to reach global access, particularly in relation to the PIFF's programming. Whilst all of Lee's films to date—*Green Fish*, *Peppermint Candy*, and *Oasis*—were shown at the prestigious and more important sections, none of Kim's nine films from 1997 to 2002 were ever invited to them. For example, in the same program catalog in 1997, Lee's first feature film *Green Fish* was shown at "New Currents" and accompanied with critical praise such as "characters share similarities that represent the distortions of Korean society,"[32] whereas Kim's debut film *Crocodile* was allocated to "Korean Panorama" and described as "*Crocodile* is reminiscent of a painting, yet that doesn't compensate for the lack of good storytelling."[33]

Considering this situation, it is apparent that the world premiere screening of *The Coast Guard* as an opening title was an exceptional occasion, and a decision that seems to have been prompted more by the global recognition of the director rather than by the PIFF's self-motivated determination. In short, this process illustrates the complex negotiations of the festival's taste regimes, particularly around notions of "national agendas," and the complex, uneven, and political process of programming.

Furthermore, the discussion above reveals the dilemma which the PIFF faces when programming local films and the conflicting relationship with the local film industry. While the festival committee has tended to rely on established or globally recognized directors for the "Opening" section, the Korean film industry has begun to evolve and grow rapidly both in terms of industry infrastructure and creativity.[34] For example, in 2001 when *The Last Witness* was shown at the PIFF, Korean audiences experienced huge box-office hits such as *Friend* (2001), *My Sassy Girl* (2001), *Kick the Moon* (2001), and *My Wife is a Gangster!* (2001). Hyangjin Lee speaks of a new trend emerging in Korean cinema:

> The hybridism of commercialism and artistic experimentalism is a significant factor in contemporary Korean cinema as it has successfully created its new identity politics in Asia. The creative adaptation of Hollywood dramatic conventions flavoured by the locality is essential to capture the audience.[35]

In other words, as Berry points out, it is not only the type of film that has been driving Korean cinema's international success that is different from the "new waves" of art cinema that made Taiwanese and Mainland Chinese films well-known overseas in the mid- to late 1980s.[36] Moreover, as we saw with *The Last Witness* and *The Coast Guard*, the fact that a film is chosen and shown as an opening film does not necessarily imply that commercial gain or enhanced reputation will follow. Czach admits that although the programming process can be a crucial way to understand the important relation between film festivals and the formation of a national cinema, programming itself is only one of the multiple factors implicated in these processes and its operation is often uneven at many levels.[37]

As illustrated above, an examination of Korean films at the PIFF enables us to consider the particular conditions, considerations, and criteria around decision-making processes. It also provides one of the indicators that may reflect the way in which the PIFF attempted to promote Korean cinema to the global film market. However, to fully account for the key factors surrounding the PIFF and the Korean film industry, it is important to trace the transformation of the contemporary Korean film industry since the 1990s. To demonstrate this, I will look at the example of *Peppermint Candy* again. The film can provide a contested discursive site to observe the transformation of the Korean film industry during this crucial period. Apart from consideration on a textual level, it also invites a number of wider questions; for instance, why was this film chosen from among the many new local titles, such as *Lies* (Jang Sun-woo, 1999), *Chunhyang* (Im Kwon-taek, 2000), *Barking Dogs Never Bite* (Bong Joon-ho, 2000), *The Isle* (Kim Ki-duk, 2000), *The Virgin Stripped Bare by Her Bachelors* (Hong Sang-so, 2000), and *Die Bad* (Ryoo Seong-wan, 2000), and why in this particular year, between 1999 and 2000?

To address these questions, it is necessary to pay attention to the period from the late 1990s to the early 2000s. For the Korean film industry, 1999 was the year when the first Korean blockbuster, *Shiri*, was released.[38] Its commercial success and the subsequent large amounts of capital available for filmmaking quickly transformed the structure of the local film market. The emergence of the PIFF thus became an important part of a local film industry looking for a route to the global film market. As it marks the beginning of a crucial period of substantial transformation for the Korean film industry, the positioning of *Peppermint Candy* within this situation is significant.

Firstly, the film was financed by UniKorea, a new investment firm founded in 1999.[39] The importance of UniKorea lies in its founding members and target films for financing since it was created by actors and filmmakers in order to support diverse films outside the mainstream.[40] *Peppermint Candy* was the first film that UniKorea financed.[41] As this shows, the founding of UniKorea indicates a space for niche products such as *Peppermint Candy* to exist in, alongside the resurgent blockbuster and other popular genres in the Korean industry.

The legacy of UniKorea becomes most obvious in the presence of its cofounder, actor Moon Sung-keun.[42] Moon starred in various works of New Korean Cinema, such as *Black Republic* (Park Kwang-su, 1992) and *A Single Spark* (Park Kwang-su, 1995), and also served as vice-chairman of the newly launched Korean Film Council (KOFIC) in 1999.[43] Alongside the transformation in structures of capital in the film industry, there has been considerable struggle between the so-called old and new generations in the local film industry in terms of governmental film policies. When the former Korean Motion Picture Promotion Corporation (KMPPC) was replaced with a body named KOFIC, the new leadership—presided by members including Moon Sung-keun—was challenged by older film professionals such as former KMPPC president Yoon Il-bong and Kim Ji-mi, head of the Korean Motion Picture Artists Association. Although Moon had to resign due to resistance from the old generation, KOFIC had successfully taken the initiative and played a key role in establishing a new governmental cultural policy during this period.[44] The unique position of UniKorea and the dramatic transformation in terms of cultural policy at governmental level at that time are intertwined with *Peppermint Candy*'s position in the local film industry.

Meanwhile, it is also crucial to look at the position and status of director Lee Chang-dong in the local film industry. Following the screening of *Green Fish* in the "New Currents" section in 1996 and *Peppermint Candy* as an opening title in 1999, Lee finished his third film *Oasis* (2002) with the financial support of the Pusan Promotion Plan (PPP), a project market or a forum through which selected filmmakers pitch new projects to potential producers.[45] This film was subsequently nominated for a Golden Lion at the Venice Film Festival and received the Special Director's Award in 2002. In this way, Lee has been closely involved with the PIFF and used this to establish himself within the Korean film industry. The fact that Lee worked as Minister for Culture and Tourism between 2003 and 2004 further indicates the exalted position he has gained in Korean society. As we can see, this case illustrates the ways in which the festival engages with particular filmmakers, offering a perfect marriage of interests between filmmakers and institutions.

Another significant point is that *Peppermint Candy* is the first co-produced film between Japan and Korea to be followed by a theatrical release in both countries. Considering that there were still some restrictions in cultural exchanges and collaborations at that time, a new finance initiative from NHK (Nihon hōsō kyōkai, Japanese National Broadcasting Corporation) determined the film's distinctive position in the local industry. Despite geographical contiguity, there was little cultural exchange among East Asian countries before the 1990s due to the colonial history, especially with Japan. For example, Japanese cultural products, including films, songs, and television programs, were prohibited following the founding of the Republic of Korea in 1948, as illustrated in Chapter 1. The position and success of *Peppermint Candy* should be considered within this political and historical context since there has been growing attention from the public on this sensitive issue. *Hollywood Reporter* stressed this fact by reporting that:

> Confirming its groundbreaking role in Asian cinema, the Pusan International Film Festival will open on Oct.14 with the first Japanese-Korean co-production to be released in South Korea, organizers said Thursday. *Peppermint Candy*, directed by Korea's Lee Chang-dong and financed by Japan NHK, will premiere at the huge 5,000-seat outdoor theatre as the first of more than 200 films to be shown at the 10-day festival. It will be the first co-production to be screened in South Korea since the country's President Kim Dae-Jung announced a gradual lifting of the ban on Japanese cultural products last year, according to NHK.[46]

In addition, at the opening ceremony of 1999, a special message on the importance of "cultural exchange" between Japan and Korea from President Kim was delivered on the big screen. After the PIFF, *Peppermint Candy* was also screened in the opening section at the third NHK Asian Film Festival in December 1999 in Japan amid a huge media spotlight. All these rhetorical and political circumstances around this film precisely mirror the transformation in the local film industry and show how these factors were activated and contributed to the PIFF's aim to promote Korean films and highlight the event.

The final point regarding PIFF and *Peppermint Candy* concerns the screen quota, a system which required Korean theaters to show domestic films for between 106 and 146 days a year,[47] claiming that, without it, Hollywood products would completely dominate the local market. When the United States demanded the removal of this system, it provoked an enormous defensive campaign from Korean filmmakers. Following a huge dramatic demonstration in Seoul, the fourth PIFF in 1999 provided a climatic moment for this nationalistic campaign by spotlighting the screening of *Shoot the Sun*, directed by Cho Jae-hong, a documentary film dealing with this very issue. By occupying PIFF Square in Nampo-dong street in Pusan during the festival, local filmmakers fervently supported the quota system. Indeed, newly emerging members of the local film industry—such as Lee Chang-dong, Myung Kae-nam, and Moon Sung-keun, who were also key producers of the film—were always at the head of the parade. As the nature of a screen quota arguably indicates a strong nationalistic agenda, this was, ironically, the same place where Japanese films that could now be shown, were enthusiastically received by the young audience. Consequently, the space where PIFF is located reveals a complex and contradictory interplay between the local and the global. Indeed, the screening of *Peppermint Candy* at the PIFF in 1999 should be read within these new complexities caused by such transformations in Korean society.

Putting Korean Panorama into a Global/Local Context

Whilst Korean films screened at the "Opening" section over the past decade have mirrored some of the ways in which institutional dynamics interact with the local film industry, "Korean Panorama" is the key to understanding how individual filmmakers have responded to these institutional dynamics. The emergence of the PIFF in the late 1990s has become an important part of local cinema. For instance, there has been recognition that films shown and spotlighted at the PIFF frequently achieve global distribution. However, as will be argued, this position has gradually shifted since many new local titles have begun to find a direct route to the global market without the mediation of local institutions such as the PIFF or KOFIC.

Within the overall festival program structure, apart from the "Opening" and "Closing" sections, locally or regionally defined programs generally receive less media attention and are even perceived as "ghettos."[48] Furthermore, although a film may benefit from the critical, public, and industrial attention that the festival brings to a national section, this success at the festival site does not necessarily lead to a consequent success at the local box office. For example, Czach succinctly analyzes the way in which Canadian films at the Toronto International Film Festival are enthusiastically received and sold during the festival by creating "otherness," while they do not attract local audiences throughout the rest of the year.[49] In contrast, however, the PIFF's "Korean Panorama"—which aims to showcase the latest spectrum of Korean films by featuring around twelve to fifteen films each year— has been widely spotlighted by both foreign guests and local audiences since its inception. As a number of international film festivals have similarly used their own national cinema sections to achieve overseas visibility, the PIFF has attempted to manipulate this section so as to "break through" to the global film market. It is worth looking at the initial goal of the PIFF, as shared by festival director Kim Dong-Ho at the first event:

> Finally, the first and foremost objective of PIFF is to present and promote Korean cinema. For the most part, exposure of Korean cinema has been limited to single film screenings at individual festivals or week-long retrospectives at various cinematheques around the world. From now on, however, we will showcase the strength and complexity of Korean films through our own self-determined and uncompromised film festival. This, I believe, is also the most effective way of advancing Korean films distribution into foreign markets.[50]

Such phrases as "exposure of Korean cinema" and "through our own self-determined and uncompromised film festival" suggest the ways in which the PIFF perceived the status and problem of Korean cinema at the time of launching the festival. Kim further emphasized that the "Korean Panorama reflects the most definite aim of the PIFF, featuring outstanding Korean films made in the past year with the utmost artistic, commercial and critical merit."[51] Unlike "New Currents," which strictly limits its selections to only art-house cinema from Asia, "Korean Panorama" operates with a broader remit to showcase a range of local productions.[52] Thus, this section served to introduce a variety of Korean films to programmers and distributors from the major Western film festivals. As a growing number of Korean films at the PIFF participated in these, "Korean Panorama" became something of a gateway to the West, its powerful position attributed to the relatively strong possibility for global distribution. Consequently, it has led the local film industry to believe that the PIFF can guarantee the exhibition and distribution of its products. Furthermore, because many more local titles are being produced, it has become increasingly competitive to be selected as the opening or closing Korean films. In this context, "Korean Panorama" has often been the only available section for the Korean film industry to exhibit films to the global market before theatrical release.

However, as many new titles have begun to be premiered at other prestigious international film festivals such as Cannes, Venice, and Berlin, the PIFF has started to lose its special position as a showcase for Korean movies, and since 2003, has failed to stage the world premiere of any major local titles. At this point, it may prove useful to consider some examples. The majority of the films selected in the "Korean Panorama" in 1999 had already been shown abroad earlier. In September of that year, *Lies* (Jang Sun-woo) had been in competition at the Venice Film Festival. In July, E Jae-yong's *An Affair* had won the main prize at the Fukuoka Asian Film Festival, while Song Il-gon's *The Picnic* had garnered top prize at the 1999 Melbourne Film Festival. Also, Park Kwang-su's *The Uprising* had been screened in competition at Locarno. As British film journalist Stephen Cremin notes, overseas guests no longer seem to visit Pusan to watch—let alone discover—Korean cinema. Indeed, in May 2006, in addition to the world premiere of Bong Joon-ho's *The Host*, Cannes attendees could catch over twenty different Korean films in the market.[53]

Meanwhile, there has been much criticism of the "Korean Panorama" focused on the small number of titles and the lack of diversity in the section. For instance, in 1999 it featured eleven local films made over the previous year. Derek Elley commented that this section failed to encompass "the full breadth" of current Korean production.[54] Tony Rayns also complained that "there are many people who mainly come here to see Korean films, so they want to have a good panorama. Panorama should mean panorama, it should mean wider view."[55]

As seen in the examples cited above, the "Korean Panorama" was unable to offer the first showing of Korean films since several filmmakers constantly sought to establish an international reputation for their artistic achievements though securing a premiere abroad. Another clear example is the case of Park Chan-wook, whose films have recently gained a strong reputation in the global film market. Although almost all films from *The Trio* (1997) to *Sympathy for Mr. Vengeance* (2002), and from *Old Boy* (2004) to *Sympathy for Lady Vengeance* (2005) were shown at the "Korean Panorama," not one of Park's films was ever world premiered in Pusan. As this example illustrates, individual filmmakers and distribution companies have begun to present many local titles directly to the global market, more specifically to the competition sections of global festivals such as Cannes, Berlin, and Venice, without the institutional support of the PIFF. Being aware of this difficulty in premiering local films in the "Korean Panorama" section, the festival has begun to find a way to adapt to a more competitive film festival environment by strengthening its Asian identity and remapping Asian films through its programming strategies.

Building up an Asian Identity through Asian Programs

The world of film festivals is always in "a state of flux."[56] Some older festivals vanish while new ones flourish. The Hong Kong International Film Festival (HKIFF), once one of the top festivals in East Asia, has been upstaged by its young and dynamic counterpart, Pusan, since the late 1990s. More recently, the position of the Tokyo International Film Festival has been threatened by its domestic counterpart in Tokyo, FILMex, initiated in 2000.[57] Considering these circumstances, the PIFF's self-reflexive regional identification to differentiate it from competing festivals is notable. As argued in the Introduction and Chapter 1, the PIFF's strategy to survive the highly competitive global film industry is not only to link its festival identity to its city identity, but also to develop this identity so as to integrate the region of (East) Asia through industrial links. The PIFF's reclaiming of Asian identity and Pan-Asianism could be said to reflect an attempt to build up the idea of "region" as a unified entity as a strategy to compensate for the lack of internationally renowned directors in Korea, unlike Japan, which has Ozu Yasujiro and Kitano Takeshi, or China which has Zhang Yimou. Thus, the concept has evolved from the vulnerable "in-betweenness" and "indistinguishableness" of Korea as a cultural entity.

From this context, it is notable that while the PIFF has responded to local imperatives through local programs, it has always equally stressed its position as an East Asian hub. In order to be a platform for Asian cinema, the PIFF has established two key Asian sections: "New Currents" and "A Window on Asian Cinema." Featuring between ten and twelve films, "New Currents" aims to discover talented Asian directors and to present a cash award of USD30,000. "A Window on Asian Cinema," covering between thirty and forty films, serves as a showcase for brand new and representative films by talented Asian filmmakers with "their diverse points of view and style."[58] Although both sections focus on Asian films, each has a slightly different goal. Whereas "New Currents," the only featured competition at the PIFF, includes an award by using an ambivalent tactic of a non-competition and competition system, as shall be discussed later, "A Window on Asian Cinema" aims to be a portal of East Asian cinema by extensively selecting Asian films ranging from North to South Asia. As the program catalog states:

> PIFF includes the New Currents Award to promote and encourage emerging film talents from Asia by selecting the best new film by an Asian director. First or second time directors of a feature film are eligible. An international jury, made up of eminent film professionals, judges films for the competition with the award guaranteeing a USD 30,000 cash prize to a winning director.[59]

Considering that the PIFF has been classified as non-competitive according to the International Federation of Film Producers Associations (FIAPF),[60] the dual operation of competition and non-competition draws attention. Under the regulation of FIAPF, once festivals are classified as competitive, they are not supposed to accept or exhibit films which have previously been in competition at other festivals. Due to this regulation, and in order to avoid disadvantages in supplying and screening films within this system, some smaller or newly opened international festivals tend to operate with less strict selection criteria in order to be categorized as non-competitive festivals such as the IFFR and Edinburgh Film Festival. In the same vein, as a recently launched festival in a non-Western region, PIFF had to self-consciously position itself as non-competitive to survive in the competitive global festival world of uneven power and hierarchical relationships.

In fact, the PIFF's dual approach to this particular section seems to closely model the Asian programs of the IFFR and Vancouver Film Festival. The IFFR is classified as non-competitive but includes the VPRO Tiger Awards, a competition for first or second features as a platform for discovering new talent.[61] At each festival, an international jury grants three VPRO Tiger Awards consisting of EUR10,000 each as well as guaranteed television airing in the Netherlands. Interestingly, the majority of the recent winners have been from East Asia including China, Japan, and South Korea. For example, winning films include *Postman* (He Jianjun, 1995), *Suzhou River* (Lou Ye, 2002), and *Walking on the Wild Side* (Han Jie, 2006) from Mainland China; *Like Grains of Sand* (Hasiguchi Ryosuke, 1996) from Japan; *Last Holiday* (Amir Karakulov, 1997) from Kazakhastan; *The Day a Pig Fell into the Well* (Hong Sang-soo, 2000) from South Korea; and *The Missing* (Lee Kang-sheng, 2004) from Taiwan. Another similar case is the "Dragons and Tigers: The Cinemas of East Asia" section at the Vancouver International Film Festival. As the largest annual exhibition of East Asian films outside Asia, the festival has, since 1988, offered the Dragon and Tigers Award for Young Cinema to "the most creative and innovative feature by a new director from the Asia-Pacific region."[62]

As Thomas Elsaesser observes, while the IFFR has pursued a platform of Asian cinema *outside* Asia and has played a role in "building bridges between Asian cinema and European audiences" as a specialty for two decades,[63] the PIFF's goal has been to act as a platform for Asian cinema *within* Asia. That is to say, instead of dispatching films and people to achieve recognition from the West, the PIFF has set up its own festival platform to attract Western film professionals with a "self-determined point of view" toward its own cultural products.[64] Although the HKIFF had played a key role in introducing Asian films inside Asia for about two decades, this role has been severely weakened since the late 1990s.[65]

Given these examples, the PIFF has striven to establish its image as non-competitive so as to remain competitive in the festival world. At the same time, however, the festival has also deliberately extended its desire to create and brand its own new product, "Made in Pusan," by dually operating a competition system in the "New Currents" section.[66] Equally, in "A Window on Asian Cinema," the festival has also highlighted its wide scope as a showcase of Asian films ranging from Northeast Asia to the rest of Asia. When the PIFF was launched, it differentiated itself from its counterparts in Japan and Hong Kong by focusing on Northeast Asian cinema. As PIFF organizers announced in 1996:

> PIFF emphasizes films from Asia, especially Northeast Asia. In recent years, films from China, Taiwan and Hong Kong have been acclaimed at international film festivals. Likewise, filmmakers from Southeast Asia and Middle East countries such as Iran, India, and Vietnam are also enjoying world-wide attention, proving that films out of Asia have improved with each passing year. PIFF strives to further this exciting movement and to discover and support promising filmmakers and their stunning cultural productions.[67]

Yet this boundary has changed and rapidly expanded. Since 1997, the festival has started systematically to showcase Asian films through the section, "Special Program in Focus." In 1997, PIFF showed twenty-two films from Korea, Japan, Mainland China, Indonesia, and India at "Early Asian Cinema: Close Encounters with Asia's Past." In 1999, thirteen films entitled "Celebrating 20th-Century Asian Cinema: 20th-Century Asian Masterpieces" were introduced. In 2000 the festival ambitiously established a special series of screenings of Central Asian cinema, "Cinema over the Tien Shan Mountain: Special on Central Asian Cinema," which covered the little-seen cinemas of Kazakhstan, Turkmenistan, Uzbekistan, Tajikistan, and Kyrgyzstan. In the same year, it also focused on Iranian cinema in "Salaam Cinema!, Films of the Makhmalbaf Family." In such instances, and as the cinema of Central Asia had generally been elided since the collapse of the Soviet Union,[68] the PIFF attempted to cover this territory by actively including such films and integrating them within an Asian-themed special section.

This expansionist tendency in programming can be understood, as Stringer notes, as one of the crucial components of the survival strategies used to differentiate a festival from other rivals in the same region.[69] Consequently, the expansionism of the PIFF, as a regionalization strategy, uses a wide range of tactics centered on programming. For instance, the tenth PIFF can be considered a significant moment in terms of its overall structure, identity, and position within a local, regional, and global context.[70] This event was accompanied by a promotional crusade involving a massive 31 screens, 307 films including 122 Asian films from 73 countries, the launch of the Asian Film Academy, and the announcement of the launch of the new Asian Film Market in 2006.[71] By aggressively programming Asian films in the name of "Remapping Asian *Auteur* Cinema: Asian Pantheon," the festival has claimed its position as a critical hub in Asia, upstaging the Hong Kong and Tokyo festivals to become the portal for a first contact with "the other new Asian cinemas."[72]

By contrast, the HKIFF attempted to redefine its festival identity in a different way. Celebrating its twenty-fifth anniversary in 2001, the festival organized a special program integrating ethnic Chinese cinemas including those from Mainland China, Taiwan, and Hong Kong.[73] In its subsequent year, the HKIFF deleted the key section named "Asian Vision" which showcased between fourteen and sixteen contemporary Asian films. Instead, films produced in Asia were now allocated to the "Global Vision" section as well as a new Asian digital competition section named "Age of Independence: New Asian Film and Video." These examples indicate a struggle over the festival's status and identity through self-consciously differentiating itself from its regional counterpart.

This regionalization strategy in programming Asian sections is closely aligned with local (and regional) film industries, such as in the interplay between the PIFF and the Korean film industry. On the industrial side, the PIFF's regionalization approach was achieved by the PPP, a project market, which is one of the most distinctive marketing strategies allowing the festival to survive the dramatic transformations of the local/global film market. Since its establishment in 1998, the PPP has positioned itself as a gateway to Asian film projects by demonstrating that a number of previous projects have been completed, prizes awarded at other prestigious festivals, and films distributed to a global audience. These are issues that I will explore further in Chapter 4.

In summary, to actively respond to the transformation of the local film industry and to survive the competitive environment of the global film market, the PIFF negotiated its own position between the local and the regional film industry, and attempted to reconstruct an Asian identity through its particular programming strategies.

Conclusion

The recent momentum towards establishing the PIFF as representative of East Asia reflects a change in the festival's relationship with the global film market. Furthermore, the recent trend for co-productions on a transnational, regional level has challenged the idea of narrowly defined national values in East Asia. This chapter has tried to suggest how the PIFF has negotiated its own position within these changing global/local dynamics by examining the festival's ambivalent and complex programming politics.

By showcasing Korean titles such as *Peppermint Candy* (2000), *The Last Witness* (2001), and *The Coast Guard* (2002) as its opening films, the PIFF attempted to use programming as a way of promoting national films to the global market. Among the three films, the chapter focused on *Peppermint Candy*, as it usefully demonstrates some of the substantial transformations in the Korean film industry. The "Korean Panorama" section has also reflected these changes, as many of the films exhibited in this section had been previously premiered at Western film festivals. Alongside the programming politics in national sections, Asian-focused programs such as "New Currents" and "A Window on Asian Cinema" have reflected the way in which the PIFF has used a regionalization strategy to respond to these changing industrial circumstances. To negotiate the new complexities emerging in the local film industry, the PIFF has reconstructed and reinforced a pan-Asian identity as a way to appeal to the regional and the global film industry.

However, the ambivalences of the politics of simultaneous regional/national identity precipitated by globalization are intrinsically intertwined. These are frequently at odds with changing political, historical, and economic contexts such as the screen quota movement and the lifting of the ban on Japanese cultural products. From this perspective, new complexities have spawned a drive for the festival to establish a new approach by expanding its strong sense of regionalization in tandem with a transnational and globalization framework. Furthermore, the PIFF's transformation in cultural politics seems to prompt shifts in East Asia, such as in the case of the Hong Kong and Tokyo Film Festivals' attempts to reconstruct their status and identities. Indeed, the cultural politics of cultural industries in East Asia seem to be moving from the national to the regional in order to participate more fully in globalization. Overall, the PIFF's programming politics over a decade demonstrate how the festival has attempted to negotiate a place between the national and the regional within rapidly changing national, regional, and global circumstances.

3

Re-imagining the Past: Programming Retrospectives

"In the past 10 years, Korean cinema has spread rapidly in France, where it is much loved by local audiences. Considering the fact that Korean cinema history boasts no great master such as Kurosawa Akira in Japan, isn't this global spotlight amazing?"

"Have you ever wondered why classic Korean films have long been unknown in Europe? The absence of information about old Korean films may be attributed to Korea's history. I don't think the quality of Korean cinema at that period was inferior to other countries in East Asia. When Kurosawa made films in Japan, there were quite a few film *auteurs* in Korea whose work was just as excellent. Yu Hyun-Mok, who made *An Aimless Bullet* (1961), is representative of those masters."

When one French audience asked a question to Bong Joon-ho in a Q&A session after the screening of *The Host* (2006) in France, director Bong jumped up from his chair to answer.[1]

Following the discussion of contemporary Korean cinema and the PIFF in the preceding chapter, this chapter explores the relationship between *older* Korean films and the PIFF. The chapter specifically looks at a series of retrospectives organized by the PIFF between 1996 and 2005.[2] By recirculating classic Korean films in this particular section, the PIFF has sought to redefine the concept of Korean cinema and play a key role in sanctioning old films made in Korea as a legitimate agent of memory within South Korea.[3] At the same time, the PIFF has highlighted old Asian films in these retrospectives in an attempt to justify the festival's identity as a platform for Asian cinema. I will demonstrate how the PIFF strategically exploited this section to promote the festival and highlight the mediation and negotiation that appeared in the process of remapping old Korean and Asian cinema.

It is an often-overlooked fact that film festivals have provided a significant location for screening "old" films. Research on the global phenomenon of international film festivals tends to focus on the discovery of "newness." As discussed earlier, these festivals have continued to select many innovative, "cutting-edge" contemporary films for world premieres in order to attract more global attention and to secure a high profile within an increasingly competitive film festival economy. Dudley Andrew calculates that approximately 3,000 films are produced annually around the world and make up a "sea of films" at festivals in every corner of the globe.[4] A series of processes for identifying and categorizing these thousands of films has been developed for differentiating between them. Among these new films, some are identified as "New Wave," breaking through existing trends in cinema, and then categorized by a group of film professionals—for example, festival programmers of and critics—while others disappear from public view.[5]

Furthermore, this obsession with "newness" at festivals has enabled festivals to become a key location for the buying and selling of projects and ideas at the pre-production stage: these are films which are not yet produced but will be completed in the near future. More and more film festivals have created their own project film markets alongside the main event. For example, the Pusan Promotion Plan (PPP) at the PIFF and CineMart at the International Film Festival Rotterdam (IFFR) have played a key role in producing "new" films and branding them as their own distinctive products, a phenomenon which will be discussed in detail in the following chapter.

Conversely, Julian Stringer claims that festivals today play a crucial role in the recirculation of old films:[6]

> As with the process of labelling that happens at museums and art galleries, any movie shown at a film festival needs to be positioned for public display, and this is achieved through acts of classification and identification. At its moment of reception by a festival audience, a title will be made sense of, in part, through the weight of the interpretative frames provided at and around such events.[7]

By analyzing the relationship between Hollywood "classics" and the London Film Festival between 1981 and 2001, Stringer attempts to reveal the role that festivals play in the re-circulation of old films. Focusing on the materialization of film memory through a particular logic of re-release sequencing of classic Hollywood titles at film festivals, he points out a hidden logic in the commercial agenda around festival viewing.[8] In other words, he explores a series of specific memory narratives that the London Film Festival drew on to collect, categorize, and present old films, such as technological developments and "firsts," special modes of public presentation, traditional concepts of authorship, and opportunities for recommodification.[9] Importantly, Stringer suggests that the growth of the international film festival circuit makes it possible to open up "a more decentred and de-territorialised view of Hollywood's reception history." That is, the same "old" films may be viewed differently in different contexts and with different preservationist concerns.[10]

From this perspective, exhibiting old films at the PIFF can provide an opportunity to understand one such different context and raises several important questions: Are the retrospectives at Pusan different from ones in the West? If so, how have different institutional interests become intertwined within this particular section over the past decade? And how does the decision to screen old Korean and Asian films at the PIFF support the formation of the festival's identity and its strategy to enter the global market? To address these questions, this chapter considers how such strategic activities around retrospectives are closely related to the particular political, social, and cultural circumstances of South Korean cinema.

Exhibiting old films produced in host countries is one of the most important programming features of film festivals around the globe. Despite considerable national variation, retrospective sections serve to justify and legitimate the current status of each national cinema, often coalescing with the festivals' interest in promoting their own events. In this respect, by connecting the past to the present through its Korean retrospective program, the PIFF has attempted to both establish and maintain a sense of "continuity" in Korean cinema as well as to solidify the position of the festival in the local and the global market. Similarly, as one of the PIFF's key aims and sources of identity is to be a hub of Asian cinema in both a critical and an industrial sense, the festival also highlights old Asian films through retrospective programs alongside its contemporary Asian programming.

Taking this into account, this chapter considers one pan-Asian and three key Korean retrospective programs from 1996 to 2005: "Korean New Wave" (First PIFF, 1996); "Kim Ki-Young, Cinema of Diabolical Desire and Death" (Second PIFF, 1997); "Shin Sang-Ok, Prince of Korean Cinema, Leading the Desire of the Masses" (Sixth PIFF, 2001); and "Rediscovering Asian Cinema Network: The Decades of Co-Production between Korea and Hong Kong" (Ninth PIFF, 2004).

These programs have been chosen for two reasons. First, they clearly illustrate significant processes of negotiation and mediation in refiguring the past of Korean and Asian cinema and in constructing the PIFF's festival identity. Second, they were the most controversial and widely discussed programs over the decade. They can therefore provide an opportunity to grasp the multifaceted roles and complex motivations involved in marketing retrospectives to the local and global markets. In short, they can help us to understand the ways in which these old films were received within the political, social, and cultural context of South Korea.

Retrospectives at the PIFF, as a key means of constructing the festival identity, will be examined at two levels. On the one hand, I discuss how this section played a crucial role in connecting Korean cinema's past with its present. Korean retrospectives established "continuity" in Korean cinema history and legitimized old Korean films at the festival site. This becomes most apparent when looking at the establishment of the first retrospective, "Korean New Wave," in 1996. Significantly, such an effort to continue the legacy of South Korean cinema was inter-linked with the desire of the Korean film industry to "break through" into the global film market. Furthermore, this interdependency between the PIFF and the Korean film industry can also be observed in the case of retrospectives focusing on the works of Kim Ki-young and Shin Sang-Ok.

On the other hand, the strategic exhibition of old Asian films in this section is one way in which the PIFF has tried to build up the festival's brand image as an official platform for Asian cinema. Although this effort operates within various programs to remap Asian cinema's history over the decade, "Rediscovering Asian Cinema Network: The Decades of Co-Production between Korea and Hong Kong" at the ninth PIFF in 2004 provides the most interesting case. This particular retrospective clearly pinpoints the very moment at which a critical review of the past was linked with the ongoing transformation of the Asian film industry.

Before examining these programs in more detail, it is worth noting that there are significant differences between the re-circulation of old Korean films at the PIFF and how classic Hollywood film is viewed in the West (both in Europe and North America).

Firstly, the way in which Korean cinema is remembered should be understood within its particular historical context. Unlike old Hollywood films, which tend to be extolled as an "emblem of the good old days" and as helping viewers remember a "glorious" or "better past," the past in Korean cinema has often been depicted as traumatic and painful due to colonization, the Korean War, and the subsequent dictatorship and compressed modernization processes.[11] Cinematic imagery of the nation in Korean cinema, therefore tends, to be interpreted pessimistically as a response to the historically, politically, and socially traumatic consequences of modernization put in place by the authoritarian government. In this sense, the ways in which Korean cinema are remembered should be understood within its particular historical contexts. For example, one Western journalist described Korean cinema after the first PIFF as follows:

> All these films, however, do retain the sad ending; in a nation that has been colonized for centuries, suffering is a necessary element of its drama. The New Wavers do it with style, though, making the art film's art film. For a country historically known as the "Hermit Kingdom," the emergence of these New Wavers signals a move toward worldwide recognition. There is, no doubt, more to come.[12]

Secondly, it should not be forgotten that there are relatively fewer old films left in Korea, since the vast majority of Korea's early film footage was destroyed in the 1950s during the Korean War, and not a single feature film produced before 1945 survives in complete form today. It is therefore difficult to find materials and resources for public exhibition. For these reasons, when the PIFF launched in the mid-1990s, academic research on Korean films made before the 1950s had yet to be systematically undertaken.

Due to these conditions, archival activities to preserve historical materials have been less developed in Korea than in the West. As retrospective programs are usually conducted in co-operation with major film archives across the country, the program's relation to one archival institution in particular—the Korean Film Archive (KOFA), the national archival body—requires attention. Although many previous Korean retrospectives had been made possible through the co-operation and support of KOFA, due to the short history of archival activities and the particular historical situation of Korea, the PIFF did not historically have a great range of old films to choose from, especially in its early stages. Therefore, decisions concerning which retrospectives to show depended heavily upon the condition and availability of films.

For example, before the first event was launched in 1996, the PIFF made a special effort to look for a way to find a lost film entitled *Arirang* (Na Woon-kyu, 1926), which was made during the colonial period, to highlight the launch of the inaugural event. However, even though the festival committee desperately tried to contact the Japanese owner of a rare print, negotiations failed and in the end PIFF could not display this historically crucial film.[13] Films made during the colonial period were not restored and made available to the public until very recently. A systematic and strategic cooperative effort with the archive for the preservation of films made during the colonial period was finally realized at the eleventh PIFF in 2006, when the PIFF was able to organize a retrospective of colonial films entitled "The Time of Change and Choice: Discovery of Films from the Japanese Colonial Period."

Furthermore, the lack of market value placed on old films in Korea is the most influential factor in understanding differences in the context of the recirculation of old Korean films. Before the first PIFF, no Korean film institution could claim sustained success in exhibiting films as objects of lasting cultural, aesthetic, or historical value. For instance, the Korean Film Archive was only founded in 1974 and did not receive government funding for the preservation of moving image materials until 1994.[14]

To compare this situation with circumstances in the West, in the 1930s film libraries in Berlin, London, and Paris had already started to function as powerful articulations of nation, film, and educated citizenship.[15] Additionally, when the Museum of Modern Art (MoMA) in New York launched its screening of Hollywood classics at the Film Library in 1935, Korea was still suffering from colonial suppression by Japan. These examples suggest that different national contexts should be considered when understanding the ways in which national film culture is formed in relation to the perception of the value of heritage.

For this reason, the systematic reissue of films in ancillary venues in Korea is not as fully developed as that of Hollywood classics both in Korea and internationally. The DVD/VHS market in Korea has been particularly unstable since the late 1990s due to the increasingly frequent occurrences of illegal downloading prevalent in East Asia.[16] Unlike the presence of Hollywood commemorative activities, the revival of old films in retrospectives at the PIFF is not therefore aligned with the commercial power of the DVD market.

Lastly, the critical status of films exhibited at the PIFF is totally different from that of old Hollywood films screened at festivals in the West. While Hollywood classics exhibited at the latter are "all safe, stellar attractions from the global film canon which have in effect already been voted as worthy of preservation by international film culture," old Korean films shown at the PIFF tend to be films that have been largely ignored both in the West and in Korea.[17] The meaning and aim of recirculation should thus be discussed in a different way. The PIFF cultivated the re-evaluating of old Korean films so as to challenge the previous perception of these films which were less frequently viewed and were previously considered to be less important than contemporary movies.

It is widely believed that Korean films made before the 1990s have been largely unknown in the West. This ignorance can be attributed to the fact that South Korean cinema has only very recently and rapidly emerged onto the global stage.[18] As discussed in the previous chapter, since the West's recent encounter with Korean cinema has been heavily dependent upon its appearance at film festivals in the West, global recognition of Korean cinema as a national cinema has focused primarily on contemporary Korean films. This is partly due to the absence of a distinctive brand image associated with Korean cinema. Korean films made before the 1990s have therefore been less acknowledged than old Japanese and Chinese films on the global art-house circuit.

In Britain, for instance, particular films made by contemporary filmmakers largely construct the available image of Korean cinema. An article in the *Guardian* attempted to identify the particular timing of Korean cinema's emergence on to the world stage. Whilst Japanese cinema was described as being associated with the Japanese "golden era of Kurosawa and Ozu in the 1950s," the article placed the golden age of Korean cinema in the "present" (early 2000s) rather than the "past."[19] In this special section on World Cinema, Hannah McGill, director of the Edinburgh International Film Festival, wrote: "[e]nter South Korea, with daring, convention-busting auteurs such as Park Chan-wook and Kim Ki-duk."[20] She adds:

> South Korea: 2002–2005. Far East cinema got a new injection of venom from a batch of hyper-violent, hyper-stylish films, among which Park Chan-wook's *Old Boy* (2003) has arguably had the most significant impact. Balance is provided by more serene offerings from art

film director Kim Ki-duk and Im Kwon-taek. Key film: *Old Boy* (Park Chan-wook, 2003).[21]

From this, it is possible to conclude that although global (in particular, Western) audiences were intermittently exposed to several old Korean films through festival exhibition before the 1990s, these films failed to create an international currency constituting a distinctive image of South Korean cinema in the West.

It is important to examine the relationship between old Korean films and the PIFF in this context. Although there have recently been significant improvements in the understanding of old Korean films in academia—especially Korean films of the colonial era—there has been to date no sustained empirical research on how old Korean films *per se* have been displayed and relabeled by international film festivals. This includes how they have been presented at the PIFF, the leading film festival associated with Korean film culture itself. Nancy Abelmann and Kathleen MacHugh have recently discussed old South Korean films—specifically South Korean Golden Age Melodrama—and their work contributes to the research on old Korean films by providing a rare opportunity to enhance understanding of them. However, their studies were largely conducted on a textual level, and institutional perspectives toward old Korean films have not been seriously considered.

This chapter focuses upon the context and backdrops of the particular PIFF retrospectives rather than undertaking a full textual analysis of each program. It considers the role that retrospectives at the PIFF play in the strategic re-imagining of the past. It examines how the PIFF's arrangements reveal an institutional endeavor to restore continuity between older and newer films in an effort to renew confidence in the past of Korean and Asian cinema, as well as in contemporary movies.

Redefining Korean Cinema in "Our Own" Critical Perspective: Korean New Wave Retrospective from 1980 to 1995

"Korea's New Wave: Retrospectives from 1980 to 1995"[22] was organized in 1996 as the first retrospective in the PIFF's history. It is worth paying particular attention to the fact that PIFF decided to show relatively recent rather than older films in its debut retrospective. Highlighting seventeen Korean films from the fifteen years prior to 1996—including *Mandala* (Im Kwon-taek, 1981), *Why Has BOHDI-Dalma Left for the East?* (Bae Yong-kyun 1988), *Black Republic* (Park Kwang-su, 1990), *Sopyonje* (Im Kwon-taek, 1993), and *301, 301* (Park Chul-soo, 1995)—this event is significant because it shows how the PIFF perceived its role as a key mediator between the global and the local in the promotion of Korean cinema at this time.

It is significant that the time around the mid-1990s when the first PIFF launched was just prior to when Korean cinema was on the verge of "breaking through" into the global market.[23] In this respect, the PIFF's choice of "Korean New Wave" as the first Korean retrospective suggests that the festival self-consciously sought to position these recent Korean films within a legacy of Korean cinematic history in order to forge a sense of "continuity" between the past and the present. The PIFF attempted to identify Korean films produced during this period as a starting point to display old films in subsequent events. That is to say, by exhibiting recent Korean films which were relatively well known and already circulating to the Western film festivals, the PIFF was attempting to reconfigure the legacy of Korean cinema as a legitimate agent to sanction national products.[24]

In examining the backdrop to the establishment of this first retrospective, it is helpful to look at the particular historical situation of South Korea in the mid-1990s. At that time, no material infrastructure had been successfully built to secure lasting studious attention to films. Furthermore, as mentioned above, the unavailability of films which were made before the 1980s affected the PIFF's initial decision to screen more recent films rather than older Korean films.

Just as new exhibitions at museums are often influenced by research taking place in academic circles, the retrospective program at festivals often relies on the work of scholars who are specialists in related fields.[25] In this sense, it is noticeable that the choice of these films at the first PIFF was influenced by work going on *outside* Korea. A number of diverse retrospectives focusing upon Korean cinema had earlier been organized in the West earlier, such as Im Kwon-taek's retrospective in 1990 at the Munich Film Festival and at the Centre du Pompidou in 1993. Moreover, a retrospective with the exact same title was held at the Institute of Contemporary Arts, London, in 1994. South Korean cinema was poised to appear on the global stage just at that time and the retrospective at the PIFF was precipitated by the rise of attention paid to Korean cinema in the West. For this reason, the majority of films included in the New Wave retrospective at the PIFF had been previously exhibited at other film festivals outside of Korea. A report in a local Pusan newspaper reinforced this perspective, introducing the first retrospective to the local audience as "a collection of Korean films from the 1980s and 1990s which proudly demonstrate the power of Korean cinema in international film festivals."[26]

Regarding the labeling of these films with the categorization "New Wave," it should be mentioned that the PIFF tried to redefine this term through its first retrospective. Before then, the term "Korean New Wave" had already been circulating in the West to describe a distinctive trend in Korean cinema. In introducing Korean films to the UK audience, for example, Tony Rayns paralleled the Korean New Wave with other new wave trends such as the French, German, Japanese, and Chinese new cinemas.[27] Dudley Andrew describes the term "new wave" as arbitrary and suggests that "[c]ritics and festival programmers continue to invoke the term because the original New Wave inundated world cinema so decisively in the '60s that a total renewal of the art seemed imminent." He further states:

> As European art cinema was moribund, desperate festivals began looking elsewhere for signs of life. And life was found in what I call the Second Set of New Waves. By the early '80s, as if sucked into a vacuum, came films from places never before thought of as cinematically interesting or viable: Mainland China, Senegal, Mali, Ireland, Taiwan, and Iran. This second set of waves is distinct from those of the 1960s not only in their provenance but in the way they functioned in a greatly changed international system.[28]

In fact, many scholars attempted to periodically identify a new movement in Korean cinema around the course of the early to mid-1980s and across the 1990s.[29] However, as Julian Stringer admits, defining a particular group of directors and films in this era of Korean cinema can be problematic. While differentiating "New Korean Cinema" from "Korean New Wave" both in terms of period and focus, Stringer points out difficulties in the placement of boundaries since Korean cinema is still in the process of formation as a new national cinema.[30] Considering this situation, it is noteworthy that the PIFF attempted to redefine the Korean New Wave according to its own criteria—from 1980 to 1995, just *before* the first PIFF. For both the PIFF and Korean cinema, it was imperative to build up a certain distinctive image as a national cinema to support the entering of the global market. In this sense, reinventing the term "New Wave" and re-identifying this trend at the first retrospective helped construct clear identities for both, in order to securely position themselves in the global film market.

In this process of renegotiation and reconfiguration, however, there was a sense of hesitation when the PIFF used the term. In an official publication, local critic Yi Hyo-in attempted to clarify the definition of the term:

> It may not be completely justifiable to label the group of directors that joined the Korean film scène in the mid 1980s the "new wave," as the term usually indicates filmmakers with a subversive ideology contrary to the existing film values. And in any event, to warrant the appellation they should at least share common characteristics that can tie them into a single category. Of course, another convenient way to organize the "new wave" would be to look for common elements related to specific film ideologies and methodologies, or a tendency to lead film movements. One cannot say for certain that the new directors who started their career in Korea in the mid '80s share such qualities. In a broad sense, however, it is a fact that such directors do keep a distance from the conventional filmic practices in terms of ideology and techniques that had been prevalent to that point in time, and they were seen as

actually implementing their own beliefs regarding film. Therefore, they will be termed the Korean New Wave in this sense.[31]

To justify connecting the films made in the 1980s to ones made in previous years, Yi also carefully states that "mainstream movies in the 1980s inherited the conventions of Korean films of the 1960s and 70s."[32] As the term "New Wave" was not created by the PIFF or the Korean film industry, there was a necessary self-consciousness surrounding the festival's attempts to reclaim the meaning of the term, reflecting the series of struggles to determine and invent its own identity in order to retain continuity both with Korean cinema and itself. As festival director Kim Dong-Ho asserts:

> The reason that we are holding a Korean Retrospective section in the first PIFF is to convey a clear image to the audience from Korea and abroad who are interested in understanding the Korean cinema. We do not expect to accomplish everything through this initial attempt, yet we expect that we will open a new venue for international cultural exchanges and discussions, which should include not only appraisals but also sharp criticism of Korean cinema.[33]

In this regard, the exhibition of Korean New Wave cinema at the first PIFF was crucial to the PIFF and the Korean film industry because it addressed the rupture and discontinuity in the legacy of Korean film history and began to constitute a clear identity for Korean cinema and the PIFF for the future.

It is notable that responses to this first event show clear discrepancies between global and local audiences. Although foreign viewers at the first PIFF paid special attention to the Korean cinema sections, including the retrospective, this section largely failed to evoke interest from the local audience.[34] For instance, statistics published in a local Pusan newspaper show the lowest attendance among local viewers in the retrospective section that year, demonstrating how local media and audiences perceived its lowly importance. The World Cinema section was the most popular program, quickly selling out and recording 26.5 percent of tickets sold in advance. However, the Korean New Wave retrospective only had 2.4 percent of seats sold in advance and no film in this program ever sold out during the festival.[35] An editorial in one of the mainstream national newspapers pointed out the unwelcoming reception experienced by this event by noting that "[a]lthough the Korean Panorama and New Wave retrospective contributed to promoting Korean cinema to overseas audiences at PIFF, these sections seriously asked us to reflect on the current problems in Korean cinema."[36]

Furthermore, the PIFF opened an exhibition at the Yachting Centre in Haeundae, entitled "From Na Woon-kyu to Namyangju Seoul Studio," as a side event to promote the retrospective. This exhibition displayed historical materials related to old Korean films which had seldom before been displayed to the public. It was also organized to celebrate the KOFIC's studio in Namyangju, which was due to be constructed soon after the PIFF ended that same year. Despite the PIFF's endeavor to highlight the value of its cinematic heritage through this event, however, the event completely failed to attract attention from the local audience.[37] This suggests that there was a discrepancy between the public audience and the PIFF in terms of perceptions about the value of old cultural products, despite the PIFF's attempts to bridge this gap. However, overall, the first retrospective allowed the PIFF to begin to constitute a legacy for Korean cinema and it played an important role in revealing the different perspectives on Korean cinema present at this time.

Kim Ki-young: Rediscovering a Director from the Past

Kim Ki-young's retrospective, entitled "Kim Ki-Young, Cinema of Diabolical Desire and Death," was the first on an individual Korean director to be held at the PIFF. With the co-operation of the Korean Film Archive, new prints were made for this program. For the PIFF, this retrospective of eight films—from *The House Maid* (1960) to *Carnivore* (1989)—was a challenge, since films made by Kim Ki-young had never before been the subject of critical study nor been systematically exhibited to the public in Korea.[38] Due to the particularly "excessive" nature of his films, director Kim was considered a maverick figure and his films were classified as cult movies in Korean cinematic history.[39] For these reasons, the PIFF was not sure whether this retrospective could appeal to local or global audiences and doubts continued "as late as two months before the festival."[40]

This can help explain why the results of this program were often described using terms such as "discovered," "unexpected," "sudden success" or "surprising appeal."[41] Although he made thirty-one films over three decades, including his debut *The Box of Death* (1955), he had previously received scant attention from critics at home and abroad, and had not been seen as an important filmmaker in Korean film history. Through exhibition at the PIFF, however, he became the first director to receive international recognition. In particular, Western viewers enthusiastically responded to his work by highlighting his films when covering the PIFF. As *Moving Pictures* commented with the title "A Star Is Born—Aged 78":

> The new discovery at this year's 2nd Pusan International Film Festival was not to be found in the New Currents section, a competitive event for new Asian directors. Instead, it was the name of 78-year-old director Kim Ki-Young [...] Critics from around the world delighted in films like *Killer Butterfly* and *Insect Woman*, movies which quickly established Kim as a fully-fledged auteur in the Russ Meyer/Roger Corman scheme of things.[42]

Another critic from the US also described Kim's work as a "never-too-late rediscovery" and enthused that "his films may well be poised to enter the ranks of the world's most sought-after cult flicks."[43] After this exhibition, festival programmers and critics subsequently invited his films to numerous international events such as the 1998 Berlin Film Festival in the following year. Through the PIFF, Kim had clearly been "discovered by the international film world."[44]

Significantly, the success of this section reveals the PIFF's insufficient awareness of the unconscious assumptions that lay behind its own exhibition decisions. For the PIFF—or more specifically, for programmer Lee Yong-kwan who chose Kim Ki-young for the second retrospective—this enthusiastic response from Western viewers was surprising since the organizers had somehow underestimated the value of Kim's films.

Despite such doubts, there were two factors that may have propelled the decision to hold this retrospective. First, as Kim Soyoung argues, an increasingly cinephile culture in Korea in the 1990s encouraged this retrospective program devoted to Kim Ki-young.[45] In addition, just one year before (in 1996), the twentieth Hong Kong International Film Festival (HKIFF) had organized a special program entitled "The Rediscovering Korean Classics' Retrospective, " which brought in twelve South Korean films made between the 1960s and the 1980s. Amongst them, Kim Ki-young's *The House Maid* received special attention from Western participants due to its unique style.[46]

However, this successful event reveals several problems, including the absence of diverse perspectives and local voices in constructing discourses on Korean films at the festival site. According to Kim Soyoung, despite overseas guests' enthusiastic reaction to contemporary Korean cinema, little opportunity to examine it across discursive positions between local critics and foreign participants was provided during and after the festival. Overseas viewers such as festival programmers and critics who had been invited by the festival therefore shared major comments and criticism about Korean cinema shown in Pusan mainly amongst themselves.[47] This apparent inability to include local Korean voices in the discussion created an imbalance in constructing discourses about the current status of Korean cinema, as the discussion about Kim Ki-young's films was shaped mainly by Western participants and failed to connect with the local reception and interpretation of these same films.

As a clear example of this, whilst the majority of the Western press praised Kim Ki-young, the local media did not pay much attention to this retrospective and many did not even realize the program's success.[48] National and local newspapers went so far as to criticize the apparent failure of the retrospective for the poor attendance at its screenings. Even after they recognized the positive response from Western journalists, they still did not know how to understand it. This confusion in interpreting the Western reception of Kim Ki-young, who had long been neglected by local audiences, is most apparent in an article written by well-known local critic Lee Dong-jin. In a major newspaper, Lee lamented how "the popularity of Kim's films to the western film professionals conversely reflects that we don't have any representative Korean *auteur* available at the moment to show to the global film market."[49] The confusion and lack of consensus in looking at Kim's films demonstrate that both the PIFF and the Korean film industry were struggling to find (or invent) a way to accommodate the perspectives about Korean cinema then constituted by the West. Moreover, importantly, this illustrates the PIFF had failed in establishing its own aesthetic norms and tended to lean on such international aesthetics already sanctioned by Western film festivals.

At the time of the retrospective, Korean cinema had, to repeat, not yet established an image for itself in the international art-house circuit. Although numerous Korean films had been screened at international festivals, few or none were to generate much of an impact until the late 1990s. The "blank" image of Korean cinema was considered one of the main obstacles preventing it from achieving international success. Few spectators differentiated Korean films from those of Japan or Mainland China. In this respect, as Chris Berry suggests, Korean cinema had to establish its own distinctive image as a national cinema which could thus be easily distinguished from other East Asian countries on the "globalized art-house circuit."[50] It is thus essential for a film or group of films to establish a distinctive and appealing image as a new product, defined in national and *auteur* terms.[51] Berry further explains the reason for the failure of many Korean realist films to receive global attention, pointing out the necessity for a unique product image. Comparing Kim's films to other Korean realist films, he emphasizes:

> Although many Korean realist films might be considered very fine, they do not have this type of distinctiveness among realist films [...] In some ways, it is reminiscent of other recent Asian films that have revisited the traumas of the fifties.[52]

In this respect, Kim's films seemed to get around this obstacle as their "analytic excess" set them apart from the mainstream.[53] This also explains why subsequent PIFF retrospectives did not receive as much critical attention as Kim's. When Yu Hyun-mok's retrospective, "The Pathfinder of Korean Realism Yu Hyun-Mok" followed Kim's, there was considerable expectation of success since Yu holds a firm position in Korean cinematic history and his films realistically depict the traumas of the Korean War. However, this program failed to receive much attention both from the local and the global audience.

In other words, although Korean filmmakers had previously targeted the film festival circuit, before the emergence of the PIFF and its strategically orchestrated exhibition of old films, international film festivals paid scant attention to such Korean films. For example, few critics showed interest in Kim Ki-young's *Fire*

Woman (1982) when it was screened at the Pesaro Film Festival in 1983, clearly showing that the conditions of exhibition are crucial to a film's life—or afterlife.[54] The presence of Kim Ki-young at the PIFF enabled the rest of the world to reconsider the legacy of Korean cinema. For example, David E. James told a national newspaper when he visited Pusan in 1997, "I always thought that Korean cinema began from Im Kwon-taek until I knew Kim Ki-young. I didn't know there was another master before Im. It's Kim Ki-young."[55]

The success of the first solo retrospective, focusing on Kim Ki-young, gave the PIFF confidence to approach the global film market with old Korean films as well as contemporary ones.[56] Since then, it has tried to sustain the "heat" that Kim's retrospective generated and has striven to develop further discourse around his films. When Director Kim suddenly died the following year, the PIFF presented the world premiere of his posthumously discovered film, *A Moment to Die For* (1988), as a tribute to him. Furthermore, the PIFF re-exhibited Kim's films at Busan Cinematheque and tried to generate critical attention from the local film community.[57] It is worth pointing out that a large-scale retrospective featuring eighteen of Kim's films was held in December 2006 at the Cinémathèque Française in Paris to celebrate a century of diplomatic relationships with Korea. Indeed, the PIFF's continuing effort to rediscover old Korean masters has been prompted by the huge success of Kim Ki-young's Retrospective.

Shin Sang-Ok: The Politics of Memory and the Articulation of History

The PIFF featured the films of Shin Sang-Ok in a solo retrospective at the sixth festival in 2001. This retrospective is distinctive as it demonstrates how the PIFF promoted this particular exhibition by emphasizing political issues. Benefiting from a promotional campaign focusing on Shin's career in North Korea, the retrospective obtained huge media attention from the local and global media, and was also the first PIFF retrospective sponsored by a private corporation. Moreover, it illustrates a rare case of the recirculation of old Korean films in other local film festivals and the process of shaping different discourses.

After his debut feature in 1952, Shin directed over seventy films until he died in 2006. The cinematic world of Shin Sang-Ok illustrates diverse aspects of Korean cinema: he founded his own film studio, Shin Film (with two hundred full-time workers in the mid-1960s, a recording room, its own generator, and even an engineering department to maintain machinery to make films); he was the producer of about three hundred films; and the director of two movies per year on average during the 1960s and the 1970s.[58]

He was often called a "legend" who led the boom of the 1960s Golden Age. However, what made him more famous in the West was his political involvement with North Korea. In 1978, Shin was kidnapped and taken to North Korea, where he was held captive until his escape in 1986. Since his dramatic escape, which was an unprecedented event, it has been impossible to consider Shin Sang-Ok without reference to North Korea. For example, John Gorenfeld wrote an article on him in the *Guardian* entitled "Producer From Hell" and begins his detailed account mainly by focusing on his relationship with Kim Jong-il:

> The North Korean dictator Kim Jong-il has a passion for cinema. But he could never find a director to realise his vision. So he kidnapped one from the South, jailed him and fed him grass, then forced him to shoot a socialist Godzilla. Now, for the first time, Shin Sang-ok tells the full story of his bizarre dealings with—and eventual flight from—the world's most dangerous dictator.[59]

Shin's image as it is tied to this particular story has been increasingly reinforced since his death in 2006. Much of the Western as well as local press repeated this story in obituaries and articles which appeared after his death, highlighting his personal history with North Korea. In these writings about Shin it is often difficult to determine whether it is a story about Shin or Kim Jong-il in North Korea.[60] In other words, both local and global audiences paid more attention to Shin's filmmaking career in North Korea and his subsequent experience of escape rather than his films. In this context, the image of Shin Sang-Ok has played an intriguing position within the Korean film industry, the director and his work remaining undiscovered and rather ambiguous until the retrospective was held at the PIFF in 2001. This may be attributed to the fact that he was never completely able to separate his film career from politics, especially in relation to North Korea. Although the local film industry and public were aware of his contribution to the Korean film industry, Shin's films were not actively talked about since his name was always associated with the North Korean issue which was prohibited from public dialog in South Korea.

In fact, even before 1978 when he was kidnapped and taken to North Korea, Shin was regarded by the Korean public more as a political figure than a filmmaker. In the 1960s he maintained good relations with the government and benefited from them, but by the mid1970s he suffered from financial problems resulting from the regime's strict regulations. After his escape from North Korea in 1986, he produced *Mayumi* (1990), *Vanished* (1994) in South Korea and *Three Ninjas* (1995) and its sequels in Hollywood. During this period, Shin Sang-Ok had become a political figure in both Koreas.

Considering this situation, the PIFF retrospective was significant because it was the first exhibition to cover the whole period of his filmmaking by screening ten films, from *A Flower in Hell* (1958) to *Vanished* (1994), including two films which were made in North Korea, *Runaway* (1984) and *Salt* (1985). The PIFF insisted on screening and putting the two films in the official catalog although the organizing committee was aware of the risk.[61] Consequently, this decision caused a public outcry. Just one day before the scheduled screening of *Runaway*, the public prosecutor of Seoul halted the showing by invoking the National Security Law, which forbids any action that could benefit the North. Banned from public screening by the government, this film was exclusively presented only to festival guests, including professionals from Western film festivals such as Berlin and Cannes.[62]

Furthermore, it is worth noting that the films in this retrospective were selected after consultation with director Shin and Western festival consultants. Programmer Han Sang-jun expresses the PIFF's "deepest gratitude to ex-programmer Lee Yong-Kwan and Mr. Pierre Rissient from France for all the help they have provided,"[63] suggesting that the PIFF had carefully orchestrated the selection process by including the views of a Western consultant—specifically one involved with the Cannes Film Festival—in an attempt to appeal to global participants more than local audiences. After this retrospective, Shin's film *The Evergreen Tree* (1961) was invited to the special programs section at Cannes in 2003.

Because one of his films produced in North Korea had been banned, the major Western media dealt with such a restriction as a hot issue which no doubt met the PIFF's goal to attract attention from the global media. *Variety*'s report is typical:

> Drawing more attention was the fest's other sidebar, a long-delayed retrospective of the legendary Shin Sang-Ok (aka Simon Sheen), the only Korean director to have made movies in both South and North Korea. Now a sprightly 75, and still talking about further projects, Shin remains a political hot potato in the divided country—one North Korean movie in the retro "Runaway" was withdrawn at the last moment—but the sensuality and invention of some of his pics from the '50s and '60s delighted foreign attendees.[64]

While the Western media mainly highlighted the fact that his films were banned by the government because they had been made in North Korea, local papers blamed the PIFF's relaxed attitude toward the screening. On the one hand, they harshly reprimanded the PIFF for its ignorance about this serious political issue, although it was clearly expected that the government would take strong action before the screening. On the other hand, the PIFF was also criticized for "easily" canceling the screening due to governmental pressure.[65] It is unclear whether the PIFF responded to these pressures by negotiating with the government authorities at the last moment. However, although the PIFF had apparently previously negotiated an alliance with the state authority, it is true that the retrospective's success hugely benefited from political elements of exhibition which were carefully orchestrated by the festival.

The lesson that is possible to take away from an examination of this situation is that Shin's political engagements and subsequent narrowly defined image have long acted as deterrents to the development of a fuller understanding of his work. In this way, his case echoes that of Zhang Yimou. Yingjin Zhang suggests that apart from the international applause for Zhang's films, his reputation in the Western world can be attributed largely to the fact that most of his films were banned by the Chinese government.[66] Though political issues are not the sole reason for Shin's global appeal, they can help market his films at global festivals.

Furthermore, and importantly, this retrospective was the first to attract a corporate sponsor in Hermes Korea. Local newspapers highlighted Shin's retrospective during the festival due to the marketing activities of this famous international cosmetics corporation. For example, large pictures covering a special event organized by Hermes Korea and a complimentary "Director's Chair" specially manufactured in France were spotlighted in major newspapers and broadcast news. A party dedicated to Shin and his actress wife, Choi Eun-hee, was also widely advertised through national newspapers.[67] Such media exposure was not accorded to previous retrospectives. Rather, glamorous parties or sidebar events were devoted to particular programs, such as Korean Panorama or to the opening night film, which provided promotional opportunities for private companies. Naturally, following information about the event in the press, a short introduction to Hermes was added: "Hermes Korea has been supporting various arts and cultural events in the form of *Mecenat* (business art association) activities in Korea and operates an arts award program worth 20 million won every year."[68] Moreover, this company announced that it had agreed to sponsor the retrospective for the following four years up to 2005.

Thus, although the Korean retrospective program was less popular than other sections featuring contemporary movies, it demonstrated that it could attract commercial interests and link up with commercial agendas. It also suggests that there was a shift in perceptions about the role of old films as cinematic heritage in Korea. In short, Shin's retrospective provided both the PIFF and the Korean film industry with an effective starting point from which an awareness of the economic value of old national films at the festival could become visible in new ways.

Lastly, this retrospective presents a rare case of the recirculation of Korean classic films at the local level. Five years after the first Shin retrospective at the PIFF in 2001, another film festival in Korea, the tenth Puchon Fantastic Film Festival (PiFan), organized a similar program entitled "Fantastic Shin Sang-Ok: A Legend in Korean Film in the '60s and '70s." Although it was organized mainly because Shin had died in that year, this event, comprising six films, demonstrates a different point of view on Shin's work and position in Korean film history:

> Although he made big hits in the '60s, starting with *A Romance Papa*, Shin's debut film, the quality of his work over-all was uneven. This was because of his complicated desire to be an outstanding movie technician and producer as well as a director. Unlike other rival directors such as Kim Ki-Young, Kim Soo-Yong, Lee Man-Hee and Yu Hyun-Mok, he made it clear that commercial success is as important as critics' success. [...] Although there are some exceptions, including movies made during his stay in North Korea, through his movies we can see a complicated Korean film history which cannot be defined in one frame. He did not pursue a revolutionary style but he nonetheless created innovations in realms such as shooting, editing, use of colours, music, studio set, and many others.[69]

In this second festival retrospective which placed an emphasis on his innovative technical contribution to the Korean film industry, Shin was regarded as "an outstanding movie technician and producer" rather than a director.[70] While the programmers at the sixth PIFF produced a nebulous definition of Shin's position, questioning whether he was an *auteur* or a commercial master, the tenth PiFan clearly illustrated his industrial engagement with Korean cinema:

> Like Howard Hawks in Hollywood, director Shin had a huge influence in Korean film history. His filmography included various genres such as *Guest and Mother*, a prototype of melodrama; *The Red Muffler*, a popular war action movie; *A Romantic Papa*, a home sitcom; *Prince Yeonsan*, a historical drama; *The Sino-Japanese War and Queen Min the Heroine* and *Female Bandits*, action films; and *Evergreen Tree* and *Rice*, campaign movies. He also tried hard to modernise Korean film techniques but establishing economies of scale in the industry was not easy.[71]

Shin has a remarkable record: he was the first filmmaker to make a color cinemascope film, *Sung Choon-Hyang* (1961), using a 13-mm telephoto lens and a 250-mm zoom lens for *Rice* (1963). Furthermore, he was the first Korean director to attempt synchronized sound in *King's Father* (1968) during the 1960s. In short, he was a pioneer of new film technology as well as industrial and artistic development in Korean cinema of that era.[72] In this way, Shin and his films were redefined through the particular recirculation process organized by film festivals. The discrepancy in how his work was presented and discussed between these two festivals points out some significant procedures in the refiguring of the past of Korean cinema. It also demonstrates how different institutional interests had an impact on the various displays of old national films.

Overall, these three PIFF Korean retrospectives played a key role in allowing the festival to sanction the legitimacy of old Korean films, creating and establishing a sense of continuity within Korean cinema history. While the first retrospective on Korea's New Wave in 1996 provided a useful starting point to establish the legacy of Korean cinema, the retrospective on Kim Ki-young in 1997 contributed to increasing the self-confidence of the Korean film industry and the PIFF in approaching the global film market. Furthermore, by initiating a retrospective on Shin Sang-Ok and highlighting the controversial issue of North Korea in its attendant promotional campaign, the PIFF attempted to maximize local and global media attention. In short, the development and presentation of Korean retrospectives at the PIFF illustrate the close links between the interests of the Korean film industry and the PIFF, whose mutual aim is to break through into the global market. Overall, an examination of these three programs over the past decade provides an opportunity to grapple with the multifaceted and complex roles played by retrospective exhibitions at film festivals.

Remembering the Regional Cinematic Past: Asian Retrospectives at PIFF

While the PIFF has presented a number of old Korean films in retrospectives over the decade of its existence in order to establish a sense of continuity with the legacy of Korean cinema, the festival has equally attempted to highlight old films produced in Asian more generally. This corresponds with the aim of the festival to promote itself as a platform for Asian cinema. I will argue in the remainder of this chapter that Asian retrospectives at the PIFF illustrate a growing self-awareness of the importance of the preservation of a regional cinematic heritage to justify and enhance a sense of Asian identity.

I examine the PIFF's efforts to achieve this aim along two lines of inquiry. First, rather than devoting itself to one national filmmaker, the PIFF established a transnational framework to examine the past of Asian cinema. Second, its focus on old Asian films served the festival's regional drive to reinforce industrial networks in Asia, such as the Asian Film Commissions Network (AFCNet) and the Asian Film Industry Network (AFIN), as discussed in Chapter 1. For example, the festival's drive to support archival networks in Asia is in tune with its industry-oriented approach in the region. In addition, it is possible to discern the festival's desire to present a pan-Asian perspective and contribute to the development of an integrated approach to Asian cinema in the programming decisions related to the PIFF's retrospective sections. By strategically displaying old Asian films from a diverse array of countries, the PIFF has pursued the construction of a reputation as the gateway to the Asian film industry in the global market.

From the early stages of the festival, the PIFF included films from Hong Kong, Taiwan, the People's Republic of China (PRC), and other parts of Asia in its retrospectives. For instance, alongside the Korean Retrospective of Kim Ki-young, the PIFF organized a special exhibition of two Asian retrospectives—"Hong Kong

Cinema" and "Early Asian Cinema"—in 1997. Whereas the special retrospective on Hong Kong cinema was organized in commemoration of the city's handover to the PRC, "Early Asian Cinema" aimed to review, in a more general fashion, early films from the region including those from the PRC, India, Indonesia, Japan, and Korea. In addition, this program was accompanied by a seminar, "The Beginnings and Development of Early Asian Film," to shape discourses around the heritage of Asian cinema. It is important that the PIFF acknowledged the display of old Asian films as a crucial means of promoting the festival's pan-Asian identity as well as that of contemporary Asian cinema from the start. The PIFF self-consciously outlines the aim of this section in its 1997 program brochure:

> The focus and mainstay of the Pusan International Film Festival are the regional cinemas of Asia. In this year's Retrospective section, we offer three special programs salient to the world of Asian cinema. This year PIFF is proud to present a very strong retrospective, with the discovery of rare films and the programming of significant works. Reaching back into Asian history is a crucial step in looking forward to Asian futures as this area becomes more of a regional community in today's age of transnational flows.[73]

Since being a platform for Asian cinema formed an important plank of the PIFF's self-defined festival identity, it was necessary for the festival to showcase the diverse spectrum of Asian cinema. In this sense, there were a number of special retrospectives focusing on Asian cinema, including independent films produced in Asia, and one particular period of one national cinema. For example, in the subsequent year, two special programs were introduced: "Another Korean Cinema: Works by Overseas Koreans" and "The Double Wall: Becoming a Woman Director in Asia."

In 1999, the PIFF attempted to refigure classic Asian cinema by displaying thirteen films under the title, "Celebrating 20th Century Asian Cinema: 20th Century Masterpieces" to "coalesce and point towards a bright new future."[74] In 2002, it presented "The 20th Anniversary of New Taiwanese Cinema 'From New Wave to Independent': Taiwanese Cinema 1982–2002" and "Seen from the Perspective of Nagisa Oshima" alongside the Korean retrospective of Kim Soo-yong. However, the PIFF's efforts to connect with the past of Asian cinema reached its peak during the tenth event in 2005. That year produced the festival's most ambitious, in terms of scale and diversity, and highly promoted Asian retrospectives such as "Remapping of Asian Auteur Cinema 1" and "10th PIFF's Asian Pantheon" held to celebrate the festival's tenth anniversary. For the latter, the festival aggressively selected and screened an extensive selection of thirty films from seventeen Asian countries in an attempt to claim its place as a critical hub in Asia.

It is significant that the PIFF's strong focus on Asian cinema was maximized both by displaying old films from Asia and by launching a massive Asian network on an industry-wide level. For its anniversary, the PIFF established the AFIN with the Korean Film Council and announced the inauguration of the Asian Film Market to advocate the concept of the pan-Asian film network. In short, a critical remapping of Asian cinema in these retrospectives was closely aligned with the PIFF's drive to consolidate important industrial networks.

On the one hand, while the PIFF's diverse Asian retrospective programs served to reconceptualize a distinct festival identity, the PIFF actively participated in archival activities at the regional level in conjunction with the national film archive, KOFA. Sharing mutual interests in restoring and preserving moving image materials as a form of cultural heritage, both these institutions were fully aware of the importance of "(re)discovering" old Korean and Asian films. It is apparent how the PIFF considered the preservation project at the regional as well as national level when the International Federation of Film Archives (FIAF)'s annual conference was held in Seoul for the first time in 2002.[75] There, PIFF director, Kim Dong-Ho spoke on the current perception of Asian cinema's past and the PIFF's role:

> I believe the main cause for Asian films remaining relatively unknown, lies upon the lack of active cultural exchange for film culture between East and West, as well between the Asian countries. [...] Fortunately, thanks to various international film festivals taking place in Asia in recent year, active film exchanges between the Asian countries are taking place, along with increased numbers in co-productions between them. Pusan International Film Festival has been contributing greatly in shedding the lights on Asian cinema that was relatively unknown previously and introducing it to the Western society.[76]

Thus, to enhance cultural exchange in the region Kim emphasizes the significance of "collaboration" rather than individual effort within each country. He further suggests that the most efficient plan to achieve this is to establish a system of close collaboration among each nation's film archives and cinematheques. Kim further states:

> Unfortunately, Asian countries went through numerous wars and lost so many precious audio-visual materials in the process, even losing the desire to preserve what is left. Because of this, it is quite difficult to discuss the history of cinema in Asian countries. It is very fortunate to see that, in recent times, many countries have acknowledged the importance of the film archive and its role, after experiencing such heavy losses of many valuable audio-visual treasures.[77]

As Korea has a relatively short archival history compared with others in the region, such as the Hong Kong Film Archive and the Singapore-based Asian Film Archive, the PIFF and KOFA self-consciously joined regional archival organizations such as the Association of Asian Film Archives (AAFA) and FIAF. This active engagement shows how film festivals are co-operating with relevant film institutions to strengthen regional identity within the cultural heritage industry.

On the other hand, the presentation of Asian retrospectives at the PIFF over the past decade illustrates how the role and function of retrospectives can be expanded and systematically organized within the institutions' interests alongside shifts in the regional industry. The relatively recent Asian retrospective program is distinctive in that it clearly demonstrates the potential to expand the boundaries of this section, thus differentiating it from others. The ninth retrospective in 2004 is a good example of this. Titled "Rediscovering Asian Cinema Network: The Decades of Co-Production between Korea and Hong Kong," it features nine such film collaborations. As the PIFF asserts:

> Entering into the new millennium, the flourishing Korean cinema now expands its range to the rest of Asia. Having shared its markets and resources, the Asian film industry enters into the age of full-scale co-production, and Korean cinema is expected to play a central role in this movement more than ever. However, Korean cinema has always tried to make Korean-Asian co-production alliances, ever since the early 20th century, under Japanese rule, and later in the 1950s [...] Throughout the co-production years with Shaw Brothers in its 1960s golden years, and then with Golden Harvest in the 1970s, the Korean film industry could exert its distinctive voice by encountering "Chinese martial art films" (*Muhyupyounghwa*) and "Fist Fight Films" (*Kwongkyukyounghwa*).[78]

Despite these manifestations of an existing legacy of co-productions in Asia, it has often been pointed out that a lack of experience and understanding of co-production among East Asian countries could be an obstacle to future transnational collaborations. Programmer Huh Moon-yung notes:

> Most people think that Asian countries, especially Northeast Asian countries, have only recently started co-producing films. But in fact, Korea, Hong Kong and Japan have experimented with co-production since the mid '50s, driven by one need or another. *The Last Woman of Shang* (1963) is one accomplishment borne of such efforts. Looking back on Korea-Hong Kong co-productions now is an attempt to both recognize the significance of the achievements of Asian film collaboration, and provide meaningful guidelines for the current revival of co-production and the Asian Cinema Network that has captured the attention of Korean filmmakers today.[79]

This consciousness is further strengthened by the recent increase in the number of co-production bodies across East Asia such as the PPP and the AFIN. Within such a context, this particular retrospective reflects the PIFF's efforts to surmount a vulnerability—a perceived lack of co-production experience—by rediscovering the hidden, unknown history of co-production in East Asia. In this sense, the retrospective served a diverse set of interests contained within the current film industry and played a key role in justifying the festival's pan-Asian identity.

Furthermore, the recent Asian retrospective programs at PIFF demonstrate that there has been significant progress in expanding the range of films in this section and in increasing awareness of the importance of preserving old films within the public and academic arenas. However, and significantly, it should be mentioned that this progress could not have been made without considerable and increasing financial support directed towards the Asian retrospective section from the PIFF's resources. Although the budget for this program has typically been far smaller than for others, the budget allocated for the display of old Asian films, in particular, rapidly increased over the past decade. To be more specific, no separate budget allocation for Asian retrospectives existed before the sixth festival in 2001. However, from the seventh the PIFF in 2002, the festival began to earmark KRW9 million (approximately USD9,800) for Asian retrospectives, separate from Korean films. The budgetary allocation for Asian retrospectives then gradually increased to KRW15 million (approximately USD16,300) for the ninth festival in 2004.[80]

Conclusion

This chapter has looked at retrospectives over the decade of the PIFF's existence and tried to demonstrate how displaying old films at the festival provides a potentially contested place for reconstructing cinema's past in the Asia region. On the one hand, by recirculating old Korean films, PIFF sought to re-examine the legacy of Korean cinema and so establish for itself a role as a legitimizing agent for Korean cinema. Similarly, the PIFF attempted to reconfigure the history of old Asian films to justify the festival's identity as a platform for Asian cinema. I have elucidated how the PIFF strategically used this section to promote the festival and examined the mediation and negotiation processes employed.

While the first retrospective, "Korean New Wave," shows how the PIFF tried to re-identify Korean cinema to continue a historical legacy, the Kim Ki-young event illustrates how PIFF perceived its own old national films as a form of cultural heritage and how different discourses were shaped between the local and the global through the exhibition of his films at the PIFF. Furthermore, a retrospective on Shin Sang-Ok demonstrates how the festival deliberately orchestrated this special exhibition to maximize the marketing potential of the retrospective section by highlighting Shin's role in the ongoing political conflict with North Korea. The re-exhibition of old Korean films at PIFF provides an opportunity to grasp the complex roles of retrospectives at film festivals and understand its interlinks with the promotion of the contemporary national film industry. These retrospectives, however, also illustrate the festival has failed in creating aesthetic norms at the international level and rather attempted to accommodate international aesthetics already sanctioned by Western perspectives.

As the PIFF has aimed to construct for itself a new position in East Asia as an official showcase for Asian cinema, the festival has gradually begun to pay more attention to displaying old films from a broader cross-section of East Asian countries. Co-productions between Korea and Hong Kong, spotlighted at the ninth event, suggest how the PIFF has sought to create a strong link between the screening of old regional films in the retrospective section and a recent development in the regional film industry—transnational film production. In this respect, retrospectives at the PIFF reflect a complex transformation of the festival's approach to the global market: the focus of the festival has begun to move away from the national and towards the regional.

It is still too early to accurately or systematically measure the impact of the recirculation of old films in retrospectives at the PIFF. Nevertheless, as observed above, the retrospectives of the past decade have enhanced the credibility and reputation of the PIFF and Korean cinema both locally and in a global context. These retrospectives also prove that there is still much room for the PIFF to explore the "past" in Korean and Asian cinema, and that doing so may improve the PIFF's overall appeal to the global market as a showcase for both old and contemporary cinema in the region.

4

A Global Film Producer: The Pusan Promotion Plan

This chapter aims to show how the PIFF's regionalization strategy has been furthered by the Pusan Promotion Plan (PPP), a market in which new Asian feature film projects can seek co-financing and co-production partners from all over the world.[1] By looking at the PPP, the purpose of this chapter is to demonstrate that festivals have become a key location to sell and buy projects and ideas in the pre-production stage. The key argument of this chapter is that film festivals are beginning to play a new role in the global film industry, that of being a new kind of *producer*, by actively engaging with the production, as well as exhibition and distribution process. Through the effective operation of the PPP, the PIFF has expanded the boundaries of its festival functions and intensified the hype surrounding this event. By doing so it has also made a name for itself as "a prime regional mover."[2]

As argued in earlier chapters, for the past few decades international film festivals have played a key role in introducing world cinema to the West. Among the film industries' three conventional modes—production, exhibition, and distribution—film festivals have established themselves as important centers of exhibition and distribution. As Julian Stringer states, it is festival exhibition that determines the distribution of certain films in particular cultural arenas. As such, festivals have enabled Western scholars to encounter non-Western films.[3]

Yet, despite the close link between festivals and the film industry, there has been little academic discussion of the new role of festivals in film production. Their involvement in film production is increasingly visible as the global film market becomes more competitive. The new relationship between film festivals and industry is best explained by Yingjin Zhang. Although Zhang focuses on big-budget Chinese films of the late 1990s, his research encompasses the whole process of production, exhibition, and distribution. A study of all of these elements is necessary to understand the content and impact of any given film. Zhang asserts:

> [A]part from some basic facts and film texts themselves, very few research publications to date can tell us what went on behind the scenes in the processes of planning, financing, scripting, shooting, editing,

marketing, distributing and receiving big-budget films such as *Red Cherry* (Hong Yingtao, 1995) and *The Emperor's Shadow* (Qinsong, 1996).[4]

Considering that transnational co-financing and co-production have become dominant trends in the global market, the modes of production, exhibition, and distribution are increasingly interlinked and simultaneously determined by a variety of structural and situational factors. In this regard, the production-oriented role of festivals in the global film market has been overly downplayed and should be redefined as one of their crucial functions. In this context, a critical focus on a project market in Asia, such as the PPP, can provide a useful base from which to understand the ways in which festivals are involved in the planning, financing, and production of films in the region. The PPP serves an exemplary example of how festivals position themselves within the global film economy.[5]

Focusing on the years 1998 to 2005, I will first explore how and why the PIFF established the PPP by investigating the background, aims, and achievements of this project market.[6] Second, the chapter will discuss how the PPP has attempted to brand its products in the name of Asian cinema and has forged a link between exhibition at the PIFF and projects at the PPP. Third, I will show that the PPP has achieved its industrial objectives by building networks with other film institutions at the local, regional, and global levels. Finally, the chapter will consider the necessary compromises made between the PPP's regional approach and its goal of promoting local products in South Korea.

Overall, by examining tensions between national and regional forces through the PPP, the chapter will seek to reveal how the festival deliberately played up to and manipulated Western expectations as a means of reaching the global market. It also attempts to show that the PPP's development and success were linked with strong commercial imperatives prevalent in the national and regional film industries as a result of globalization.

The Pusan Promotion Plan (PPP)

The PPP is a co-financing and co-production market for Asian films established in 1998 as a side event of the third PIFF. Each year the festival showcases a select number of Asian film projects in the development or production stages, giving out cash awards and providing an opportunity for filmmakers to meet prospective financiers. More specifically, as it is a project market, the PPP candidates are film projects that are in the pre-production stage, including scriptwriting, casting, and budgeting. By arranging one-to-one meetings between investors and filmmakers, the key aim of the PPP is to provide Asian filmmakers with an opportunity to get funds in order to complete their films, and in return, to encourage the investors to acquire rights for distribution as one of the important conditions of the contract. The PPP selection committee, consisting of the festival programmers and specialists in the local film industry, chooses projects which are submitted from Asia. Over three days during the festival, PPP guests and a limited number of festival guests participate in panels, roundtable discussions, and pitch presentation events. This project market ultimately aims to encourage and educate buyers and investors to support and finance new film projects from Asia.

The PPP runs a number of awards that offer production financing to Asian filmmakers. Year on year, the number of awarding bodies has increased. The main awards were the Busan Award (Pusan, USD20,000), the Hubert Bals Fund (HBF) Award, the CineMart Award [International Film Festival Rotterdam (IFFR), USD10,000],[7] the Kodak Award (Eastman Kodak, negative film worth USD20,000), the Busan Film Commission (BFC) Award (USD10,000), and the New Directors in Focus (NDIF) Awards (various funding bodies, KRW10 million).[8] As shall be discussed, the biggest indication of the PPP's effectiveness is the success of the market's past selections.[9] By completing each project, the PPP has become more closely involved in all three stages of filmmaking—pre-production, production, and post-production—in the global market.[10]

It is important to consider how and why the PIFF established the PPP from the earliest stages of the festival. In 1997, the PIFF staged a forum to lay the foundations for the launch of the project market the following year. It gathered the key producers, distributors, sales agents, and investors of Asian films in the international market and tried to find new models of co-financing and co-production for Asian films. The following comment from festival director Kim Dong-Ho is helpful in understanding how the festival self-consciously perceived its role in the global film market when launching the PPP:

> The critical element in filmmaking is often not the script, the producer, nor the actor: it is *money*. To further the goal of supporting Asian cinema, the festival will launch in 1998 the Pusan Promotion Plan (PPP), a co-financing and co-production market for Asian films. PPP will invite Asian producers and directors with projects at the development, pre-production or production stage to meet invited financiers, distributors, television buyers, sales agents and other funding sources. PPP is unique in being the only pre-market in Asia for Asian films. The potential influence and impact of PPP on Asian cinema is thus rather high, especially when considering the emerging strength of the festival itself.[11] (italics added)

This demonstrates PIFF's pro-market stance when establishing its own market within the festival. As I argued in chapter 1, the economic role of culture and cultural industries in East Asia has become closely incorporated within the logic of market functionalism or corporatism. Within this context, it also indicates how the PIFF focused on boosting the Asian film industry. For example, although the forum in 1997 was divided into three areas (Asia, North America, and Europe), the focus was on the Asian films in overseas markets, funding issues, joint investments, and co-productions. In the Asia session, participants discussed several issues specific to Asia such as "How have Asian films fared in their own backyard?" and "Who is emerging as key players in Asia-wide distribution?" The Europe session dealt with questions such as "What influence do festivals have in presenting Asian films to the wider European public?" and "In which European countries have Asian films been most successful and why?" By contrast, in the North America session, the main topic was why it was difficult to sell Asian films in North America.[12]

In recent years, Asian films have been enthusiastically received by international audiences. Indeed, this has become something of a global phenomenon. However, this warm reception depends heavily on the availability of films, especially those with English subtitles. In this respect, it becomes apparent that film festivals have played a key role in circulating Asian cinema to the West. For example, as Stringer notes, contemporary Korean cinema is most obviously associated with two specific forms of modern-day film consumption: high-profile international film festivals and home viewing on commercial video, VCD, and DVD.[13] In this way, many Asian films have been discovered by Westerners through the festival circuit. Consequently, films produced in certain regions of the world are often underacknowledged until they have been recognized by Western film festivals. Stringer states, "scholars tend to approach them through the nostalgic invocation of those moments when non-western industries were 'discovered'—that is 'discovered' by westerners—at international competitions."[14] Being aware of the limited funding opportunities in the global film market, the PIFF has actively worked with the Asian film industry to create new channels of financing and co-production. Rather than relying on being discovered by the West in their film festivals, the PIFF has attempted to create indigenous regional products and to brand films produced, discovered, or financed in Pusan through the PPP.

As I explained, in the late 1990s, many East Asian film industries, including Korea, were facing hard times in the wake of the International Monetary Fund crisis. Film production had fallen sharply in most countries in this region. Moreover, the structures for trans-regional co-operation which the PPP attempted to consolidate were less familiar than the ones in Europe. Despite these obstacles, the PPP has achieved considerable success. The first event attracted record attendance and much positive feedback from delegates.[15] Seventeen Asian projects, including five from Korea, won USD10,000-prizes, awarded by the HBF and the Korean investment company Ilshin. Ishi Sogo won the PPP Award for his science-fiction Samurai story, *Gojo-Reisenki*, and Chinese filmmaker Jia Zhangke took the

HBF Award for *Platform*. The success of the PPP that year was, as *The Hollywood Reporter* stated, a case of "triumph amid adversity."[16]

Throughout its eight-year history until 2005, the PPP positioned itself as the gateway for Asian film projects by proving it could recognize and promote success. Many projects submitted during the early years went on to become award-winning films that reached a global audience. As evidence of its effectiveness, the organizers released data relating to the number of completed projects. For example, the following films were among the completed projects funded by the PPP: *Platform* (Jia Zhangke, 1998), *THE CIRCLE* (Jafar Panahi, 2000), *Beijing Bicycle* (Wang Xiaoshuai, 2001), *Address Unknown* (Kim Ki-duk, 2001), *Oasis* (Lee Chang-dong, 2002), *Woman Is the Future of Man* (Hong Sang-soo, 2004), and *The Bow* (Kim Ki-duk, 2005).

However, why did PIFF have to organize a pre-market rather than a market to buy and sell completed films, such as the Cannes Film Market and the American Film Market (AFM) or the International Multimedia and Film Market in Milan (MIFED)? Furthermore, why did the PIFF devote itself to a more production-oriented strategy rather than other types of investment or distribution arrangements?

There are several factors which determined the PIFF's choice of a project market. First of all, it was aware that the recent international spotlight on Asian cinema could not guarantee the long-term stability of supply and demand in the global market. In spite of the growing interest in Asian cinema and the prolific film production in the region at the time, there was a sense in the Korean film industry that Asian cinema had been restricted by limited releases as well as other unexpected factors in the global film market.[17] For this reason, the creation of a new brand—through incubating, developing, and marketing products—was a significant step into the global distribution system. Moreover, as other major film festivals in the West had already established their own film markets, the PIFF had to find a niche to avoid competition and differentiate itself from others in the global film industry. Lastly, it was CineMart, an established project market of the IFFR in Europe, which specifically influenced the establishment of the PPP. In launching the PPP, the PIFF closely examined and modeled it after CineMart and has continued building a partnership with it over the past decade.

The PIFF's choice of a project market mirrors a trend for festivals to be more involved with their local and regional film industries. Recently, more international film festivals have become aware of the significance of the project market and begun to establish their own. For example, during the 2004 Berlin Film Festival, a co-production market was launched in tandem with the festival. Although there was already a European Film Market (EFM) affiliated with the festival which dealt with completed films, the need for a project and co-production market prompted the Berlin Film Festival to launch this initiative separately. Additionally, the Locarno International Film Festival began to widen the scope of its "Industry Office" by focusing on the functions of a project market such as co-financing and co-production. Despite the existence of film markets within renowned festivals, the growing visibility of project markets indicates their increasing importance in the global film industry. Indeed, it is a response to the shared needs of film industries and festivals, both of which are looking for more opportunities in a competitive global market.

Asian Identity Meets Asian Products

Since its inception in 1996, the PIFF has stressed its Asian identity as a vehicle to reach beyond national boundaries to the global market. This strategic regional approach has been aligned with the festival's link to the regional film industry in the fields of production, exhibition, and distribution. The PIFF forged strong links with the PPP by consolidating the relationship between projects completed through the PPP and programming at the PIFF.

The festival specifically engaged with film projects that had not been completed by arranging financing or financiers and attempting to brand these products as "PIFF films." It tried to implant some credit signs of its efforts into the film in order to maintain a legitimate identity as "made in Pusan," insisting that this product was chosen and created by Pusan. To achieve this aim, the festival has used the PPP as a means of identifying those titles that "belong" to Pusan. This is linked with the PIFF's efforts to integrate its image as a hub of Asian cinema with attempts to establish a reputation as a market-oriented festival.

In this context, it is significant that many PPP projects have been specifically linked with the PIFF's main program. For instance, the choice of *Chinese Box* (Wayne Wang, 1997) as the opening film at the second PIFF was made in consideration of the key agenda of the PPP: the co-finance and co-production of Asian films. *Chinese Box* was a suitable model for the PPP as it had been co-financed with capital from France, Japan, the UK, the USA, and Hong Kong through CineMart. To learn about the specific process of co-production, the PPP established a roundtable by inviting director Wayne Wang and the key producer and distributor.[18]

Furthermore, the PPP has enabled the PIFF programming committee to have access to much greater variety and availability of films for selection and exhibition in the various festival sections focusing on Asian cinema. As the PPP was able to prove it can provide funding opportunities for Asian projects and help to complete films, increasingly large numbers of Asian directors began to attend PIFF and the PPP. Since the second PPP, the organizers have been able to boast that many projects taken on previously through the PPP were completed, invited to renowned film festivals elsewhere, and also shown at the PIFF itself. For example, at the fourth PPP, they announced:

As of September 2001, already 19 projects have been completed of the 55 projects (56 films) introduced at PPP in the last three years. These films have been awarded, completed or were invited to many historic and prestigious film festivals including the Cannes, Berlin, Venice and Rotterdam Film Festivals. Of these completed films, 5 will be screened at this year's 6th Pusan International Film Festival (PIFF).[19]

The films which were selected and completed through the PPP in previous years were screened at the PIFF in 2001. These films include *The Monkey* (Aktan Abdykalykov, Kyrgyzstan), *Address Unknown* (Kim Ki-duk, Korea), *The Road* (Darejan Omirbaev, Kazakhstan), *All About Lily Chou-Chou* (Iwai Shunji, Japan), and *Weekend Plot* (Zhang Ming, People's Republic of China). In this way, the PPP provided the PIFF with potential opportunities to obtain more products for its programs. This vital link between exhibition at PIFF and projects at the PPP demonstrates a collusion of the conventional modes of production, exhibition, and distribution.

However, while PIFF pursued the creation of its own brand through the PPP, the results did not always match its aim, suggesting a complex and negotiated relationship between Asian filmmakers and the PIFF, which cannot be simply defined as an exchange and barter system. Rather, the relationship between the awarding bodies and winning filmmakers points to a complex and negotiated process through which specific films tie in with particular festivals and funding bodies. In particular, in its early stages—that is, before the PPP established a reputation—the PPP's role was to provide a meeting place rather than to directly offer funding to projects.[20] As a case in point, the official 2001 PPP Report, released to guests prior to the opening of the festival, proudly announced, "*Weekend Plot*, which won the HBF Award at the previous year's PPP, was co-produced by Les Films De L'Observatorie and this film will be making its world premiere at this year's PIFF."[21] Notwithstanding PIFF's expectations, however, *Weekend Plot* was screened at the Toronto International Film Festival in September 2001 at the last minute, and was shown again at PIFF two months later, when it could be billed only as the Korean premiere.[22] Considering that Zhang Ming's *In Expectation* (1996) was the winner of the New Currents at the first PIFF, this meant that if his new PPP-funded film *Weekend Plot* had been world premiered at PIFF, it would have provided PIFF with a successful example of its achievement by combining the interests of PPP (a funded project) with PIFF (a world premiere screening).

In view of this situation, and in order to activate and maximize the impact of the PPP from its initial stages, PIFF had to create its own so-called Asian star who was "discovered" or "made" in Pusan from the first event. Jia Zhangke from the PRC was the most likely candidate with films in the most high-profile sections of the festival, New Currents, and the PPP. At the festival, Jia received the New

Currents Award in the competition section for his film *Xiao Wu* (1997); he was financed by the HBF Award for his project *Platform* at the PPP. The PIFF committee declared the birth of an Asian star as follows:

> A new master in Asian cinema was discovered during the 3rd PIFF. Chinese filmmaker Jia Zhangke, who presented a superb self-examination on the lives of Chinese youths in *Xiao Wu*, stormed the festival by receiving the New Currents Award and the Hubert Bals Award for his new project presented at PPP, *Platform*, and thus arose an up and coming talent in Asian Cinema.[23]

Some international media reports concurred with the PIFF's focus on this director. *The Hollywood Reporter* comments:

> The brightest star to emerge was Chinese director Jia Zhangke, who won PIFF's main prize—the New Currents Award—for his film *Xiao Wu*, a tale of a pickpocket in provincial China. The award, which is given to the best new film by an Asian director, guarantees distribution in South Korea or USD 10,000. It was Jia's second success of the week. Earlier, he was given the USD 10,000 Hubert Bals award for *Platform*, which was deemed one of the most promising of the 17 scripts presented at the promotion project. The New Currents jury hailed Jia as 'an auteur in the making.' One of them, Gohei Oguri from Japan, said Jia's success at Pusan marks the birth of a rare filmmaking talent which appears only once every few years.[24]

Jia received huge amounts of media attention during the third PIFF and the first PPP in 1998 and became a regular guest at Pusan thereafter. Although *Xiao Wu* had already been shown and had received the NETPAC Award at the Berlin Film Festival earlier in February, the PIFF insisted that it had discovered Jia and never mentioned his previous award at Berlin when releasing press material during the festival. Spurred by the media and financial support, his new project *Platform* was subsequently completed in 2000 through co-financing from Hong Kong, France, and Japan. This film was nominated at the competition section, world premiered, and won the NETPAC Award at the Venice Film Festival in 2000. In addition, it won multiple awards such as the best film at the Buenos Aires International Festival of Independent Cinema and the Don Quixote Award at the Fribourg International Film Festival in 2001.

By helping film projects receive production financing, PIFF sought to consolidate the exhibition role of the festival with the production role of the PPP. If film projects funded through the PPP are completed and exhibited at PIFF, the festival is able to secure some world premieres of Asian films in return for its initial investment in sponsoring and organizing the PPP. However, the response of Asian filmmakers who benefited from the PPP was different from what PIFF had hoped for.

It is significant that although *Platform* was significantly supported by the PIFF and IFFR, Jia Zhangke chose to be world premiered in Venice, a more influential film festival than Pusan or Rotterdam. It was also shown at the Toronto Film Festival in September of that year. After being shown at two major Western film festivals, it was screened in October at "A Window on Asian Cinema," a non-competition section of PIFF.

There are a number of similar cases. In 2000, examples of such films include Jafar Pahani's *The Circle* (Iran)—which won the Golden Lion, the top competition prize at the Venice Film Festival—and Fruit Chan's *Little Cheung* (Hong Kong), which won a Silver Leopard at the Locarno International Film Festival in 2000. Korean projects are no exception: *Address Unknown* (Kim Ki-duk, 2001) was selected as the official project by the second PPP, funded by the Korean Film Council, and screened in Venice after being nominated for the Golden Lion and invited to Toronto before the PIFF in 2001. In 2002, Hong Sang-soo's project *Woman is the Future of Man* received the Busan Award, a top award funded through the PPP, but this film went to the competition section of the Cannes Film Festival before the PIFF.

These Asian filmmakers' choice of major Western film festivals rather than Pusan to premiere their films reveals a complicated hierarchical relationship both among global film festivals and between festivals and filmmakers. An unequivocal barter arrangement between the PPP and the filmmakers who have benefited from participation at the market is not always guaranteed to occur as part of this relationship. This also reveals how Asian film directors cope with the complex relationship between the different interests of international film festivals and their own desires to get easier access to the global market.

Global Networks and the PPP

Globally-scaled film festivals are emerging as a new type of producer through their powerful involvement with the creative production process via project markets such as the PPP and CineMart. Project markets are connected in "complex webs of alliance, partnership and joint venture," competing and co-operating with each other.[25] The PIFF and the PPP have developed an important relationship with the IFFR and CineMart, which allows us to understand a set of significant characteristics of film markets and festivals. It illustrates how this kind of alliance is created among different film festivals and how this relationship affects all the parties involved. Furthermore, it specifically shows how cultural intermediaries act through both markets and festivals.

CineMart has been the prime partner of the PPP since 1998. Every year the Asian projects presented at CineMart are considered for the PPP official project selection and, in turn, the PPP projects are considered by CineMart, providing a strong collaboration in supporting new Asian films. In addition, CineMart sponsored the HBF Award in the amount of USD10,000 every year between 1998 and 2003.

Initially, when CineMart was launched in 1983, it was a regular film market. However, the IFFR shifted it to a pre-market for film projects which were looking for additional financing. By differentiating itself from major film festivals such as Cannes, Venice, and Berlin, the IFFR has positioned itself as one of the distinctive international film festivals in Europe specializing in the presentation of innovative and independent films. In the same vein, the IFFR established CineMart and enhanced its function of arranging co-financing and co-production to differentiate it from the other film markets of major festivals in Europe. Across its twenty-three-year history, approximately 315 films have been realized at CineMart. The organizers boast that around twenty former CineMart titles were premiered at leading global festivals, including Cannes, Venice, Locarno, Toronto, and Berlin, as well as its home festival in Rotterdam. Indeed, the establishment of CineMart as a pre-market to support talented young filmmakers has been successful and has successfully matched the aim and identity of the festival as it pursued the selection of worldwide independent, innovative and experimental cinema and visual arts.[26]

The prime benefit to the PPP of modeling itself on CineMart was the know-how of running a project market. From the formula of introducing projects to potential co-producers, sales agents, TV buyers, distributors, and financiers, to the setting up of one-to-one meetings, all the important knowledge was shared with the PPP organizers, who did not have any experience in this field. In the meantime, as a new international body in a non-Western region, there was a need for the PPP to gain international authority by associating itself with a more renowned counterpart.

In turn, CineMart, geographically located outside of Asia, received materials and resources of Asian filmmakers from the PPP. The IFFR had been paying special attention to East Asian cinema for the previous decade. As discussed in Chapter 3, many of the winners of the VPRO Tiger Awards have been from East Asia, including the PRC, Japan, and South Korea. In the same vein, the HBF Award at CineMart also played a key role in discovering and supporting many Asian projects. The project line-ups of CineMart over the decade in question demonstrated Rotterdam's ambition to discover East Asian films.[27] Simon Field, who worked as festival director for eight years (1997–2004) also contributed to the festival's focus on Asian films.[28] These facts illustrate that Rotterdam had self-consciously pursued a platform of East Asian cinema *outside* Asia. In this context, CineMart's support of the PPP and its special partnership with the PPP could be understood as a strategic decision to make the most of both markets.

The intimate collaboration between these two project markets becomes most explicitly articulated in the case of *The Beijing Bicycle* (Wang Xiaoshuai, 2001).

This project was selected at the script stage as one of the official projects at the second PPP in 1999. After a two-year search for funding at the post-production stage, this project turned again to CineMart, which came up with the money. After completion, the film won multiple awards including the Silver Bear at the Berlin Film Festival. Both project markets in Europe and Asia supported this project from its initial stage to completion. In this way, the case of Wang's film and its dual engagement of the two funding bodies can be seen as a typical example that illustrates the way both institutions co-operated in order to brand their product and link with the creators' need to complete their cultural project. It also illuminates how film festivals deal with intensified competition to control risk and manage creativity in the process of decision-making, whom to support, or whom to give up.

In these kinds of decision-making processes at CineMart and the PPP, the role of the cultural intermediaries who engage with and have an impact on the selection process becomes more visible. The issue of evaluating and ratifying arises here. As Howard Becker notes, "[w]ho can confer on something the status of candidates for appreciation, and thus ratify it as art?"[29] Chapter 2 showed that the decision-making process can never be neutral. It depends highly on the current political, economic, and social interests of the institution. Therefore, some people occupy institutional positions which allow them to decide what will be acceptable and what excluded. This group of professionals can be called either "creative managers" or "cultural intermediaries" and they play a significant role as mediators between the interests of filmmakers and those of film institutions.[30] As Julian Stringer argues, "within an overall context of professional standardization of norms, product differentiation is thus one means by which institutional intermediaries articulate and understand their specialized roles."[31] For example, in film institutions such as the PIFF and the IFFR, Kim Ji-seok, who acts as Asian programmer at PIFF, and Simon Field, the previous festival director at the IFFR, take on roles as shapers of a particular trend in Asian cinema each year.

Significantly, the role of intermediaries also ranges across the globe, such as between Rotterdam in western Europe and Pusan in East Asia. Considering the fact that CineMart is a model for the PPP and that it offered its own funding program, HBF, to the PPP from the latter's beginning—as the project of Wang Xiaoshuai demonstrates—decision-making at both markets can be understood to be based on shared information and opinions that are interdependent on each other's interests. As networks shape film festivals according to their mutual interests, these powerful intermediaries influence trends in filmmaking and distribution. Crucially, their role is more significant to the pre-market than to other established film markets, such as the Cannes Film Market. By involving a vital pre-production stage that spans scriptwriting, casting, and budgeting, the interests of institutions—including profits, revenues, and reputation—can be estimated and maximized in advance of the exhibition and distribution stages. Hence, like the international consultants at festivals, the presence of intermediaries in project markets becomes influential because they affect how projects interact with other cultural and non-cultural institutions to build global film culture.[32]

In addition to its close partnership with CineMart, the PIFF has attracted interest from other major Western film institutions, such as the European Film Promotion (EFP), another European partner, by demonstrating its market value through the results of the PPP projects. As briefly mentioned in Chapter 1, the EFP is the umbrella body for all European national promotion and export organizations. With twenty-seven such groups from twenty-eight countries, the EFP included the PIFF as an important Asian associate among partner festivals and markets such as the Berlin International Film Festival, the Buenos Aires Festival of Independent Cinema, Cannes, Karlovy Vary, and the Toronto International Film Festival, as well as the American Film Market. Winning out over the Hong Kong and Tokyo film festivals, the PIFF was chosen as a key partner festival in Asia. The following description clearly shows the high estimation that the EFP had of the PPP:

> European and Asian films take centre stage—European films win over the Korean public during the festival. Directors and actors from Europe introduce their new films at one of the most important Asian film festivals. The event proved to be one of the most energetic film festivals in Asia. With the launch of the new Asian Film Market in 2006, Pusan takes on a new and expanded role in the region—and for the industry in general. The festival is also a partner for the Film Sales Support.[33]

This alliance shows that European cinema's eastward thrust to promote European films in the Asian market encountered Pusan's ambitions to become a nodal point within the Asian market. The successful partnership with CineMart and the EFP accelerated the building of alliances with other institutions. For example, from the fourth PPP in 2001, the Swedish Göteborg International Film Festival joined the PPP awards by organizing the Göteborg International Film Festival Fund Award.[34]

While the PIFF's Asian identity was associated with the PPP's strategy of branding Asian projects, the PPP built up global networks to develop mutual relationships among different institutions, such as CineMart. Through this, a group of agents played a role in the project decision-making process as cultural intermediaries. However, although the PPP is modeled on CineMart, it is noticeable that the PPP sought to use a multifaceted approach to the local, regional, and global markets. It differed from CineMart's relatively inactive relationship with the Dutch and European film industry by employing diverse network strategies that relied more substantially on its market value and active industrial engagement.

As argued in earlier chapters, the establishment of the PIFF and PPP was accompanied by the burgeoning of the Asian film industry. For instance, the success of most PPP projects was helped by increased global interest in Asian films, and the growth and development of Korean film boosted the PPP's prospects of becoming the Asian film market hub. Hence, in terms of its deep engagement with the film industry, the PPP has received more attention than the PIFF itself during the festival period.[35] In this respect, the development and growth of the PPP were related to a broader transformation within the film industry in East Asia. This, in turn, was linked to growing commercial imperatives in international film culture.

Spurred by its early success, the PPP has carved out a major network within Asia's rapidly growing film production sector. Different networks show the direct or indirect economic impact of the PPP and PIFF. Two of the most pertinent are to do with regional development and local government support for the film industry. As demonstrated, the PIFF has continued to actively engage with film industries in Asia by establishing diverse programs. Clearly, this attempt to establish a reputation as the gateway to the Asian film industry was accompanied by a particular approach to networking, centered on establishing its position as an East Asian hub. As argued in Chapter 1, the PPP is the most obvious model for the PIFF to draw on to bolster the Asian regional film network. It aims to attract global capital to the Asian film market and thus facilitate co-financing and co-production of Asian films, as well as generate solidarity among Asian countries. The festival's location in East Asia and the fact that most participants hail from the Asia-Pacific region have been crucial in achieving this. Chapter 1 demonstrated how PIFF adopted an anti-Hollywood stance in establishing networks, as was the case with "Y2K," the first co-production project at the PPP. It also explained how the PIFF embraced this discourse to invigorate the Asian film industry network.

Significantly, since the PIFF has persevered in its efforts to be the hub of the film industry in Asia, it has affected neighboring film industries. In 1999, a year after the first PPP, the Tokyo International Film Festival established the Tokyo Film Creators' Forum, which included a project market to enable young filmmakers to get funding for their new works. The Hong Kong Asia Film Financing Forum (HAF), which is a project market alongside the Hong Kong International Film Festival, was organized in 2000.[36] In this way, the PPP has played a triggering role in East Asia since its inception by attracting a number of international financiers energized by the boom of the local film industry. The presence of rivals in the same region has brought both competitive tensions and collaborative alliances. For instance, when the HAF was not able to host its event due to the SARS epidemic in Southeast Asian countries in 2003, five projects that had been initially submitted to the HAF were co-presented at the PPP that year.

Overall, the PIFF has built up extensive global and regional networks through its industrial drive embodied by the PPP. The festival's growth in this ten-year period has been accompanied by a regional approach in order to co-operate and compete with its regional counterparts through the PPP. This strong drive has affected trends in film festivals and industries in East Asia which will be further discussed in the following chapter. However, the PIFF's case is notable for the way that it has expanded its territory not only in terms of scale but also its exploitation of the possibilities of new functions for the film festival. In addition, the PIFF differed from other festivals in that it used its project market as a means of linking to the local film industry.

Local Networks

While the PIFF forged a relationship with its regional Asian counterparts, its regionalization strategy also had to navigate the anxieties and concerns of the local industry. As argued in Chapter 1, the PIFF was founded partly because the Pusan government and representatives of the local business community desired to gain recognition for the city and rejuvenate the local economy, and were interested in the economic benefits to be had from hosting an international film festival. As the PIFF proved the film industry could revitalize the local economy, it provided a strong incentive for the authorities and business community in Pusan to better support the local film industry. Therefore, a number of film-related institutions were built in Pusan including Cinematheque Busan, the Busan Film Commission (BFC), and the Busan Cinema Studio in the Hauendae area where the PIFF's headquarters are located. Furthermore, the Asia Film Industry Centre and the Asian Film Commissions Network (AFCNet) were subsequently constructed.[37]

In order to understand the PIFF's relationship with the local film industry, it is helpful to examine the case of the BFC, which was founded in 1999 with the support of the Pusan city government. The main purpose of the institution is to provide one-stop support to filmmaking, from pre-production to production to post-production, and to establish the location support system. The city also has plans to construct a base for post-production in the city so as to become a center for the Asian film industry. The following clearly presents their ambitions:

> The Busan Film Commission is building the infrastructure for a new film industry. This includes provision of local human, technological and financial capital to attract national and international films to Busan. Subsequently, it is emerging as a new hub of the Asian film industry, the 'Cine-Port Busan', by maximising its endogenous economic and cultural assets.[38]

In conjunction with the growing scale of the PPP, the BFC forged synergies with the former. In 2003, the BFC and the PPP co-organized the Busan International Film Commission and Industry Showcase (BIFCOM) to highlight the concept of a "one-stop service" wherein everything needed from the start to the finish of the filmmaking process—including sales, purchasing, location research, equipment purchasing and rental, and post-production works—can be sourced at one point.

Apart from the rhetoric of the organization, it should be noted that the founding members of the BFC overlap with those of the PIFF and the PPP. The most distinctive figure is Park Kwang-su, who played a central role in the PIFF founding group. He was appointed the BFC's first commission director after having launched the first PPP in 1998. After successfully establishing the PPP from scratch and leading the PIFF committee to develop the festival's business-oriented position within the global film industry, he was subsequently engaged with launching the BFC as a base of post-production associated with the city of Pusan. Park's presence and role are crucial as they demonstrate the significance of human agency in establishing relationships between the film industry and film festivals. As Stringer asserts:

> The rise of film festivals positively demands expansion in the number of arts administrators required to staff them [...] All of these skill-specific roles constitute part of the network of cooperating specialised intermediaries who need to pick up appropriate knowledge concerning the correct way to do things.[39]

As the principal figure in many of these undertakings, Park contributed to the establishment of the PIFF, PPP, and BFC. He also led the launch of the Asian Film Market in 2006. This suggests the key role played by particular cultural intermediaries in building networks and mediating relationships amongst the diverse interests of different local cultural institutions.

Furthermore, the strong industrial drive in Pusan, propelled as it was by the success of the PIFF and the PPP, had an impact on national goals and imperatives. The Korean Film Council (KOFIC), one of the most important governmental cultural institutions, decided to move its head office from Seoul to Pusan by 2012. KOFIC, initially the Korean Motion Picture Promotion Corporation (KMPPC), was founded in 1999 as a body supported by the Ministry of Culture and Tourism. Like the UK Film Council, the aim of KOFIC is to improve the quality of Korean films and to promote the Korean film industry. Especially since the late 1990s, KOFIC has focused on the international promotion aspect of its mandate to cope with the demands of the global film industry.[40] To promote Korean films at international film festivals, KOFIC co-established the AFIC within PIFF. With KOFIC as the top film policy decision-making institution at the governmental level, the link between the PIFF and KOFIC is distinctive.[41] Although this decision was made with other cities in order to decentralize policymaking from the capital, the shift from Seoul to Pusan (and not to other cities) was clearly affected by the presence of the PIFF, PPP, and BFC. Overall, the PPP's impact on and links with the global economy are related to its dual engagement with the local and regional film industries and are interdependent on this link. In short, the PIFF's ambition to link its local film industry to the global network by attracting co-production and co-financing has been realized by the PPP.

Korean Films and the PPP

The establishment and success of the PPP precisely demonstrates the way the PIFF has set up its brand image as a strongly market-oriented festival. However, it is important to remember that until PPP's launch at the third edition of the festival in 1998, the PIFF had been unable to consolidate this identity even though the festival had consistently emphasized its focus on Asian cinema. Furthermore, in the early stages of the PPP, the local film industry did not pay much attention to this event and few local film production or distribution companies participated in it. This fact suggests that at the time of the launch, the local film industry was not as fully aware of the possible significance of the co-financing and co-production options on offer as was PIFF. For instance, despite the success of the forum in 1997, the PIFF committee clearly states in its own historical documents that "although many Korean producers were absent, the systematic discussions led by a diverse group of experts became the foundation for the following year's PPP."[42]

As many commentators point out, global consumerism has been intensifying, with brand names vying for recognition and attraction. In this respect, the global presence of South Korean cinema is a very recent phenomenon considering Korea has remained a "blank and unimagined space" for the West for a long time.[43] Furthermore, the recent international reception of Korean cinema illustrates that "branding" or establishing a "trademark" is a complex process intertwined with the global distribution system at various levels.

This becomes apparent when observing the recent release of Korean films in the UK. From art to horror to gangster, a range of Korean films have been screened at local cinemas in the UK since 2000, including *Old Boy* (Park Chan-wook, 2003), *A Tale of Two Sisters* (Kim Ji-woon, 2003), *3-Iron* (Kim Ki-duk, 2004), *Sympathy for Lady Vengeance* (Park Chan-wook, 2005) and *A Bittersweet Life* (Kim Ji-woon, 2005). This list shows what kind of Korean films British viewers have favored. Significantly, most of these titles have been released on DVD by Metro Tartan, a major distribution company in the UK, which has also released "Asia Extreme"—a series of popular commercial films from East Asia, including Korea, Japan, and Thailand. As discussed earlier in this chapter, the exhibition and distribution of Asian cinema (including Korean cinema) in the global market has been dependent on and limited by various factors. In this sense, distribution of films on DVD is an important ancillary window that has played a key role in circulating Asian cinema to Britain. However, the method used to categorize and promote Korean cinema is determined and enhanced by the particular distribution channel since the label "extreme cinema" refers to a particular genre: horror films.

Considering the fact that the Korean film industry has had a relatively short history of branding or promoting indigenous cultural products to the global film market, the PPP becomes significant as it aims to engage with the branding and promotion of Korean cinema through programs and events. In this respect, the PPP can be the local film industry's best bet for global/local survival, especially in relation to global distribution systems.

In relation to the PPP's link with the local film industry, the fourth PPP in 2001 marks a turning point. That year saw the launch of an official program for Korean projects, "New Directors in Focus (NDIF)" and the "Industry Center." The number of awards increased from seven to eleven, and four new awards were provided by the local industry to support local projects participating in the NDIF.[44]

It is notable that the PPP has primarily depended on the marketing value and the possibility of commercial success of each project. If not for the concrete results accomplished during the PPP, it would have never got off the ground. Especially as the PPP was a newcomer in this field, the PIFF committee had to choose projects by those directors who had achieved recognition abroad through participation in other film festivals. This reduced the risk of failure and made it possible for a PPP project to receive international recognition during the incubation period. Moreover, since PIFF tried to position itself beyond the Korean nation-state and self-consciously discover Asian films, this tendency was obvious in selecting PPP projects. To justify its Asian focus, especially during the PPP's early stages, the needs of local production had to take a back seat, or at least appear to. Accordingly, the projects that received the most attention from within the festival during the first and second PPP were mainly by non-Korean filmmakers such as Jia Zhangke from the PRC, Fruit Chan from Hong Kong, and Jafar Panahi from Iran.

However, since Korean projects also began to attract international attention during the PPP, and the local film industry became aware of the significance of co-financing/co-production through the PPP, more local projects have benefited from the market's programs. For instance, at the third PPP in 2000, the Korean project *The Trigger* (Park Kwang-su) won both the Kodak Award and the Korean Film-Making Assistant Project (KF-MAP).[45] Another local project, *The Knife* (Song Il-gon), also received USD10,000 cash for the Hanul Award that same year.[46] In 2003, the PPP selection committee decided to support Korean director Hong Sang-soo's *Woman Is the Future of Man*. This project was promptly funded by MK2, a French sales company, which meant automatic distribution in the European film market.

The establishment of the NDIF to support local projects at the fourth PPP was precipitated by the arrival of new sources of sponsorship in the PPP and the success of local projects. This new side initiative within the main selection program was aimed only at local projects. In fact, while the PPP concentrates on relatively well-known Korean and Asian filmmakers for the completion of each project in order to reduce risks, the NDIF to discover talented local directors and is open to prospective Korean directors working on their first feature films, demonstrating how the PIFF has tried to link its industrial functions to the growth of the local film industry. This also shows the way in which the local film industry has responded to the transformation of the local and global markets, including the Western reception of Korean cinema and a rapid shift in trends in film consumption in Korea. The rhetoric used to introduce the new program reveals:

> As the success of PPP has improved, so has the quality of the projects that were submitted. The selection process was near impossible, but finally 19 projects were chosen from around 200 entrants. 2001 PPP will be featuring outstanding projects from China, Hong Kong, India, Indonesia, Iran, Japan, the Philippines, Taiwan, Tajikistan, Thailand and of course, Korea. An equally difficult selection process was required for New Directors in Focus (NDIF). Making its debut this year, a total of 8 projects were chosen to highlight the rising directors of Korea. All of this is designed to meet our goal of providing a convenient meeting place to allow cooperative ties and deals to be made.[47]

Korean directors of all NDIF projects appeal to producers, distributors, and investors in person through pitch presentations during the PPP. Thanks to the enthusiastic response of the local film industry, this section was successful. Several projects were completed and subsequently distributed. For example, the horror film *Into the Mirror* (Kim Seong-ho, 2003) was presented at the first NDIF and after impressing investors at Cinema Service, director Kim Seong-ho was given the opportunity to make the film. Significantly, although this film was not successful at the box office in Korea, it was distributed to the DVD market in the UK and the USA by Metro Tartan.[48] This is another interesting example of the link between local projects at the PPP and the particularities of the Western reception of contemporary Korean films. As Korean projects selected by the PPP targeted global rather than merely local audiences, those projects selected tended to embrace some of the existing perspectives on Korean films within the international film market. For example, there had been a warm reception to the particular genre of horror films via previous DVD releases by Tartan.

Several other projects from the first and second NDIF were completed. This program became increasingly popular by 2003, when sixty young filmmakers applied to the NDIF with their ideas and plot synopses. At the 2004 NDIF, Kim Young-nam's *Don't Look Back* was co-financed by Japan's NHK and completed in 2006. This film received multiple awards at film festivals including Locarno and Taipei. The increasing number of sponsors and special attention to this program for local talent also reflects the rapid transformation of the Korean film industry. As new technologies in the local multimedia industry rapidly develop, the scope of exhibition windows has changed and expanded. New modes of domestic consumption of films have emerged, such as mobiles and Digital Multimedia Broadcasting (DMB), which increasingly need more visual entertainment content.[49]

In the meantime, as the PPP pursued its aim of playing a leading role in Asia, the festival added the Industry Center within the PPP to expand its function within the regional film market. Apart from acting as a project market, the Industry Center, as a small film market, hosts sales agents from Korea and Asia and distribution companies from outside Asia. Although the PIFF operated the PPP as a project market for multiple reasons, as pointed out earlier, the establishment of the Industry Center indicates the PIFF's desire to upgrade its function and expand its project market to a full-scale film market covering the Asian region. This was achieved with the official launch of the Asian Film Market in 2006.

Overall, since the first event in 1998, the PPP has highlighted Asian projects in order to secure its position as a leading project market in the region. However, after its early success it began to support local film projects. On the one hand, a series of processes—incubating and branding indigenous products—shows an attempt to satisfy the demands of the local film industry. On the other hand, this process is closely linked with a response from both the PIFF and the Korean film industry to accommodate Western views on Korean cinema. Furthermore, the PPP's focus on local projects is associated with transformations in the Korean film industry, such as the rapid development of new technologies in the field of multimedia. The PPP has become an important part of the local film industry because its aims have corresponded with the needs of Korean filmmakers and distributors to reach out to the global market.

Conclusion

This chapter has demonstrated how and why the PIFF established the PPP. It has set out to identify how the PIFF's regionalization strategy was achieved in part through the success of the PPP. By charting distinctive features of this project market, the chapter has illustrated how the PPP forged a close relationship with the production arm of the film industry. While the PPP has tried to brand its own products, it also has built networks at the local, regional, and global levels. The PIFF's branding strategy does not seem to be successful since many films funded by the PPP were premiered elsewhere—major Western film festivals. Nevertheless, in seeking a nodal point between festival exhibition and production at the project market, the PIFF and the PPP effectively forged synergies wherein projects become completed products through networks formed with other institutions and cultural intermediaries. Furthermore, the chapter has looked at the NDIF, which supports local projects, and demonstrated that the PIFF equally strove to promote the local as well as regional Asian film industry. Overall, by actively involving itself in film production, the PPP has provided the PIFF with a major justification to grasp a new role for the film festival as a global film producer.

Remapping Asian Cinema: The Tenth Anniversary in 2005

In this final chapter, I consider the tenth PIFF as a significant moment in its history in terms of its overall structure, identity, and position, and specifically examine the events and programs associated with the anniversary festival. Based on my field research in Pusan in October 2005, I will look at this anniversary in a wider context rather than simply provide a snapshot of any particular event. The key to understanding the goals of this anniversary is its varying degrees of "expansionism." The grand scale and scope focusing on Asian identity were used on two fronts. On an industrial side, the festival launched a regional network, the Asian Film Industry Network (AFIN), and announced the inauguration of the Asian Film Market (AFM), a full-scale film market embracing the existing project market. Additionally, the PIFF also sought to gain clear recognition that the festival was not only an industrial but also a "critical" hub of Asian cinema through an extensive list of specifically Asian programs including "Asian Pantheon," "Remapping Asian Auteur Cinema 1," and a "Special Screening for APEC Films."[1] Most importantly, to create a nodal point between these critical and industrial levels, the festival launched a new sidebar workshop—the Asian Film Academy (AFA), an education program modeled on the Talent Campus at the Berlin Film Festival and the Sundance Lab. Finally, the tenth festival created diverse public events to highlight the festival's devotion to local audiences, including a closing party open to the general audience and an increase in the number of festival venues.

This chapter consists of several parts. First, to better understand the PIFF's expansionism, I will look at the recent transformation of the national and global film industry. Second, I will examine the key programs shown in 2005. The chapter then moves on to examine the particularities of the PPP, the AFM, and the AFIN. Finally, I will look at a range of audience-friendly local events.

Above all, the chapter will focus on Asian programming and the Asian Film Academy, as these two undertakings most effectively demonstrate the festival's strategic moves towards its anticipated future directions. By specifically investigating these programs, I aim to provide answers to some of the questions raised by other chapters—for example, why the festival chose expansionism and regionalization as key strategies and how it implemented these choices over the past decade. I will also point out the complexities and contradictions that the PIFF has to face within the rapidly changing local and global circumstances discussed in earlier chapters. The PIFF ostensibly expanded its scale to make this anniversary a turning point in the festival's life, acknowledging the past, present, and future: by collecting Asian classics (past), selecting contemporary Asian films (present), and launching a new education program, AFA (future). The PIFF's emerging priorities, in particular at its tenth event, illustrate how the festival has broadened its roles and diversified its functions in order to effectively cope with the transformations of the global/local economy. In this respect, a close examination of these key programs will provide a new perspective on the ongoing globalization process in the local, national, regional, and global contexts.

"Bigger is Better" to Celebrate a Decade (1996–2005)

To make 2005 a special year, PIFF screened 307 films from 73 countries at its tenth event, including 62 world premieres and 87 Asian premieres, the largest number of films and the greatest number of countries in the festival's history.[2] This dramatic growth may be illustrated by comparing it with the first event in 1996 where 170 films from 27 countries were screened.[3] As the result of extensive media coverage following a huge promotional campaign, PIFF achieved remarkable success in its tenth year, claiming record attendance figures for both festival guests and audience members. Meanwhile, however, there was significant criticism of its growing scale globally and locally. For example, renowned local film critic Cho Hee-moon warned the PIFF of the dangers of its expansionism:

> PIFF seems to be caught in a trap of size. The main concern of PIFF and the media is big figures. Both are emphasizing how many films and how many participating countries and audiences and how quickly films were sold out like a live broadcast. Therefore, their reaction to the decrease in numbers is over-sensitive as if that directly indicates the decline of the festival. Every year it is believed that the more the festival presents, the smoother things go without problems. [...] Although PIFF is called the most dynamic and rapidly growing festival in the world, it is difficult to define PIFF as a creative and distinctive festival in terms of its quality. This is because the scale of the festival does not coincide with improvements in the content or quality.[4]

Variety also described the tenth event as follows: "Scale, scope and celebration, rather than focus and tight selection, appear to be the themes set to dominate the 10th running of the PIFF."[5] Moreover, some local film professionals were skeptical

about the festival's celebratory attitude, pointing out the mutually beneficial relationship between the PIFF and Korean films over the decade. As Kim Hye-joon of
the Korean Film Council (KOFIC) states:

> PIFF should remember that its success has hugely benefited from the
> rise of Korean cinema over the past ten years in many ways. Without
> strong back-up from Korean films, the current powerful position of
> the festival would have not been possible. In this respect, rather than
> to celebrate its tenth anniversary, PIFF should look back at its past in a
> modest way and seek to establish a new role without delay.[6]

All of this poses a question concerning the PIFF's tendency towards continuous
expansion and growth. Despite increasing concern and criticism over its expansionism, why did the PIFF so aggressively pursue such large-scale presentations
on the special occasion of its tenth anniversary? What factors affected the scale
and scope of the event? To unravel the answers to these questions, it will be argued
that rapidly changing festival dynamics in the global market prompted the PIFF's
current tendency towards expansionism.

As discussed in earlier chapters, the worldwide increase in the number of international film festivals over the past two decades has changed the structure of "the
festival world" within a highly competitive global economy. Festivals compete with
each other for the limited number of films produced in the festival calendar. Even
prestigious film festivals such as Cannes, Venice, and Berlin are fighting harder to
obtain new titles. Within the premiere system, more attractive world premieres
provide a clear reason for the media to go to the event and consequently increase the
presence of film distributors and sales agents. In this climate, the smallest changes
seem to have the effect of seismic shocks in the global film industry. For example,
when the Sundance Film Festival (January) announced that it would establish an
international competition section from 2005, several rival festivals held around the
same time of year, such as the Rotterdam (January) and Berlin (February) festivals,
were anxious that competition for premieres would become tougher.[7]

Julian Stringer observes the need for two crucial components to survive in
this competitive festival world: "a sense of stability" and "expansionism."[8] Festivals
self-consciously tend to expand their events to compete with rival festivals, actively
benchmarking themselves against existing big festivals, and claiming to be a
regional cultural hub while operating with dual goals—to be both globally accessible and locally distinctive within the global space economy.[9] In this sense, any anniversary provides a good reason to raise the festival's profile. Even the PyongYang
International Film Festival in North Korea celebrated its tenth anniversary in 2006
by inviting a number of international guests in an effort to upgrade its profile.[10]
The range and scope of events associated with the tenth anniversary of the PIFF
can be understood within this competitive global festival landscape. By selecting an

extensive variety of Asian films and establishing a range of sidebar events focusing on the Asian film industry, the PIFF attempted to reconfirm the festival's identity as an "official" platform for Asian cinema and to differentiate itself from its counterparts in the region, such as the Hong Kong and Tokyo film festivals.

In fact, although this event was the biggest in the PIFF's history, the move towards such a grand scale should not be seen as a sudden or unexpected emergence. The festival had gradually expanded by increasing its number of films, audiences and sidebar events since its inauguration in 1996.[11] In particular, to highlight its brand image as a market-oriented festival, the PIFF had continued to introduce new ancillary events and networks, including the PPP and Asian Film Commissions Network (AFCNet), reinforcing its strong industrial links to the local and regional film industries over the years. In this way, the PIFF's expansion also reflects a recent trend—and substantial transformation—noticeable at many global film festivals that has affected the boundary of the festival's function in relation to the film industry. Festivals have become more influential and their function has expanded at the levels of exhibition, distribution, and even production of films, as clearly shown in the earlier chapter. As film festivals have become a marketing location for the global film business, they have had to provide distributors and sales agents with an attractive place to sell and/or buy their products. This explains why the PIFF also took the opportunity of its tenth anniversary to announce the launch of a full-scale film market, the AFM, to start the following year in 2006.

Moreover, it is worth noting that celebrating an anniversary can provide a film festival with a pretext to receive extra funding from the government and to source new streams of corporate sponsorship.[12] For example, the expanded programs and events of 2005 were made possible by additional funding worth USD1 million from the central and local government to help celebrate the PIFF's anniversary, boosting the total funds the festival received from governmental sources to USD5 million.[13]

The more festivals desire to be fixed in a global festival map, the more they need to stay alert to the rise of new rivals and differentiate themselves from others by reconstructing the host city into a more attractive place and creating new themed programs. In this regard, the PIFF's expansionism is notable, as this tendency has always been incorporated into its strong regional approach. The AFA, as shall be discussed below, is a good example of how festivals broaden their roles and boundaries to become leaders in the regional film industry. While the PIFF has, through the PPP, pioneered a new role for film festivals—that of a producer in the global film market—the inauguration of the AFA suggests that the festival has begun to pursue another linkage between education and industry in order to establish and strengthen regional networks and help mark out the festival's future direction.

It should also be noted that the PIFF's ability to manifest its leading cinematic role in the region is linked to the situation of the national film industry at the time of the tenth anniversary in 2005. There was a celebratory mood in the Korean film industry then, in part because from 2000 the Korean film industry had experienced a remarkable 19 percent average annual growth rate in the number of admissions and of local films produced and screened over the intervening years.[14] For example, at the beginning of 2004, the Korean film industry was buzzing with the surprising success of films like *Old Boy* (Park Chan-wook, 2003), Untold Scandal (E Jae-yong, 2003) and *Memories of Murder* (Bong Joon-ho, 2003). In addition, Korean films were leading local box-office figures following the enormous success of two local blockbusters, Silmido (Kang Woo-suk, 2003) and *Brotherhood* (Kang Je-gyu, 2004). These two titles passed the previously only dreamed of mark of ten million admissions.[15]

Furthermore, prompted by the increased visibility and popularity of the "Korean Wave,"[16] the distribution of Korean films to other countries expanded rapidly over the few years prior to 2005—particularly to Japan, where exports grew by 74.1 percent in the first half of 2005 alone. Alongside increasing national success, Korean films received considerable global attention as many titles had garnered awards at major Western film festivals held earlier in the festival circuit: Park Chan-wook won an award at Cannes with *Old Boy*, while Kim Ki-duk achieved the rare feat of garnering directing prizes at both Berlin and Venice in 2005 with *Samaritan Girl* and *3-Iron*. This "buzz" reached its peak when the PIFF was declared the best film festival in Asia by *Time Magazine* (Asia edition) and Pusan city won its bid to host the APEC Summit.[17]

Overall, all these global and national circumstances further propelled the PIFF's self-generated grandiosity to play on a grand scale and create many new additions to its tenth anniversary program. In this regard, the issue of expansionism at the tenth PIFF should be understood within both the specific global and national contexts. While this event reflects a rapid and visible transformation in global film festivals in recent years, it also mirrors complexities in the national film industry.

A Critical Hub of Asian Cinema: Asian Programming and World Premieres

In this part, I will demonstrate how the PIFF sought to redefine the concept of Asian cinema in order to reconstruct its festival's identity by examining "Asian Pantheon." To illuminate how the festival tried to justify its goal as a showcase of Asian cinema, the notion of a "world premiere" is also discussed, along with some of the problems the festival experienced in selecting contemporary Asian films. Finally, the chapter will reveal the complex and contradictory position of PIFF in the local context by examining the "Special Screening for APEC Films."

The PIFF's consistent focus on Asian films in its program structure reached its peak at the tenth event in terms of the quantity of films shown. Apart from the regular Asian programs—"New Currents" (nine films) and "A Window on Asian Cinema" (thirty-eight films)—PIFF aggressively added extensive numbers of Asian films in special programs: "Remapping Asian Auteur Cinema 1" (eight films), "Asian Pantheon" (thirty films), "Reunion of New Currents" (seven films), and "Special Screening for APEC Films" (twenty films).

Among these, as one of the special programs to celebrate the anniversary, "Asian Pantheon" presented thirty Asian classic masterpieces from seventeen Asian countries. This special section shows how the PIFF tried to both position itself as dedicated to Asian cinema and brand Asian cinema in the name of the PIFF. Embracing an extensive selection of titles, it showcased films from Taiwan, Japan, China, and Hong Kong, as well as from countries whose films are rarely exhibited abroad, such as Kazakhstan, Uzbekistan, Tajikistan, Syria, Sri Lanka, and Mongolia. The list of screened films is as follows:

(1) *The Big Parade*, Chen Kaige, China (1985)
(2) *The Horse Thief*, Zhuangzhuang Tian, China (1986)
(3) *Dragon Inn*, King Hu, Hong Kong (1966)
(4) *Centre Stage*, Stanley Kwan, Hong Kong (1991)
(5) *The Vagabond*, Raj Kapoor, India (1951)
(6) *The Big City*, Satyajit Ray, India (1955)
(7) *A River Named Titash*, Ritwik Ghatak, India (1973)
(8) *Bombay*, Mani Ratnam, India (1995)
(9) *The Face of Man*, Teguh Karya, Indonesia (1972)
(10) *The Cow*, Dariush Mehrjui, Iran (1964)
(11) *Close up*, Abbas Kiarostami, Iran (1990)
(12) *A Moment of Innocence*, Mohsen Makhmalbaf, Iran (1996)[18]
(13) *Late Spring*, Yasujiro Ozu, Japan (1949)
(14) *You Were Like a Wild Chrysanthemum*, Keisuke Kinoshita, Japan (1955)
(15) *Deep Desire of Gods*, Shohei Imamura, Japan (1968)
(16) *Floating Clouds*, Mikio Naruse, Japan (1995)
(17) *The Last Stop*, Serik Aprimov, Kazakhstan (1989)
(18) *The Adopted Son*, Aktan Abdykalykov, Kyrgyzstan (1998)
(19) *Tsogt Taij*, M. Luvsanjamts, Mongolia (1931)
(20) *Manila: In the Claws of Light*, Lino Brocka, Philippines (1975)
(21) *Manila by Night*, Ishmael Bernal, Philippines (1980)
(22) *The Changing Village*, Lester James Peries, Sri Lanka (1965)
(23) *The Leopard*, Nabil El-Maleh, Syria (1972)
(24) *The Terroriser*, Edward Yang, Taiwan (1986)
(25) *Dust in the Wind*, Hou Hsiao-hsien, Taiwan (1986)

(26) *Rebels of the Neon God*, Ming-liang Tsai, Taiwan (1992)
(27) *Kosh ba Kosh*, Bakhtyar Khudojnazarov, Tajikistan (1993)
(28) *Dark Heaven*, R.D. Pestonji, Thailand (1958)
(29) *Tahir and Zühre*, Nabi Ganiyer, Uzbekistan (1952)
(30) *The Girl on the River*, Dang Nhat Minh, Vietnam (1987)

The PIFF defined the purpose of this special selection as such:

> These masterpieces from 17 Asian nations will represent their coun-
> tries, broadening the meaning of 'Asian Cinema.' From some relatively
> unknown works by renowned Asian filmmakers like Hou Hsiao-hsien,
> Mohsen Makhmalbaf, Chen Kaige, Imamura Shohei, and Abbas
> Kiarostami, the programme also covers names who are recognized pri-
> marily domestically within their own countries such as Ishmael Bernal
> from Philippines, Teguh Karya from Indonesia, Keisuke Kinoshita
> from Japan, Rattana Pestonji from Thailand, Nabil El-Maleh from
> Syria, Lester James Peries from Sri Lanka.[19]

As briefly discussed in Chapters 2 and 3, since 1997 the festival had started to systematically showcase Asian films by selecting Asian cinemas in the section entitled "Special Program in Focus." The PIFF's approach to integrating Asian cinema regionally on an industrial level had been synergized by a rapid expansion in how it defined the boundaries of "Asia" both geographically and critically. Following the special program entitled "Central Asian Cinema" in 2000, which featured films from Kyrgyzstan, Turkmenistan, Kazakhstan, Tajikistan, and Uzbekistan, the PIFF included these countries—all traditionally seen as "minorities" in Asia in terms of film production and Western recognition—in the "Asian Pantheon" section of its tenth anniversary. While the festival attempted to show lesser-known titles by regional masters who had already established their reputations, it also tried to rediscover unknown filmmakers in the region, thereby seeking to legitimize its position as a platform for Asian cinema.

The extent to which geography influences programming decisions at the PIFF is also made obvious by the fact that the festival has deliberately continued to screen North Korean films. After several attempts resulted in failure for political reasons, a retrospective of Shin Sang-Ok's films was finally able to be organized at the sixth event, as was discussed in Chapter 4. However, as observed in the case of *Runaway* (1984), which had been withdrawn at the last minute, it has proven difficult to screen North Korean films at the PIFF. At the eighth event in 2003, however, the PIFF was finally able to show seven North Korean films to the public.[20] This is in striking contrast to the PyongYang International Film Festival, Pusan's counterpart in North Korea, which had never attempted to show South Korean films until its tenth event in 2006.

In conjunction with "Asian Pantheon," the tenth anniversary festival added another special program focusing on Asian classics, "Remapping Asian Auteur Cinema 1." Whilst this sidebar event was created to celebrate the anniversary, it was also the first installment of a series aiming to rediscover important Asian directors who have been neglected in world cinema history. It consisted of eight films from three directors: Rattana Pestonji (also called R.D. Pestonji) from Thailand, Teguh Karya from Indonesia, and Sohrab Shahid Sales from Iran.[21] In this program, the "rediscovery" of old Asian films was also highlighted in tandem with "Asian Pantheon." This suggests that the PIFF had actively started spreading its wings as a "critical learning school" with "Remapping Asian Auteur Cinema 1," "a finessing of the Hong Kong Intl. Film Festival's pioneering work during the '80s."[22] While PIFF had gradually increased and enhanced its classic Asian sections ever since its establishment, these two special programs at its tenth anniversary festival clearly articulated its most ambitious and bold approach to the region yet in terms of both the number and range of films.

While the PIFF attempted to play a leading role in the rediscovery of classic Asian films, its Asian programming in general brought several problems, including an "obsession" with premiere titles and the resulting limitations to showcase the whole spectrum of the region's trends. In order to encapsulate the PIFF's self-defined identity as a platform for Asian film, it would be necessary for the festival to showcase the diverse range of Asian cinema being produced. However, as regards the PIFF's contemporary Asian programming, there has been some criticism of a lack of mainstream films, especially from China and Japan. For example, international critics have pointed out that the PIFF's Asian programming favors independent low-budget Chinese films made by new generation directors—the so-called "Sixth Generation" from Mainland China—such as Jia Zhangke, Lou Ye, and Wang Xiaoshuai.[23] Despite this criticism, PIFF has consistently selected a number of independent Chinese films for its main sections highlighting contemporary Asian cinema such as "A Window on Asian Cinema" and "New Currents," and even aggressively established a special 2003 program on independent films from China entitled "Cinema on the Borderline: Chinese Independent Films," showcasing ten films produced over ten years.

Since that time, there has been growing criticism that the PIFF's Asian programming does not portray a wide spectrum of contemporary Asian cinema, instead focusing predominantly on films believed to be suited to western tastes. At the time of the tenth event, *Variety* outlined the success of the PIFF as involving "a combination of lucky timing, canny programming, and quietly aggressive promotion." However, it also sharply points out the limits of the Asian programming at the festival. As Patrick Frater and Derek Elley state:

PIFF officials don't specifically acknowledge their growing role as a fest of record. Still, the bulky Window to Asian Cinema section, which collects films that bowed at other fests throughout the year, certainly takes PIFF in that direction. If an Asian art-house pic doesn't screen at Pusan, it's likely not part of the cream of the year's crop.[24]

Moreover, the PIFF's favoritism towards independent Asian films was also criticized in relation to the festival circuit. Elley further points out:

> Such a tendency was more criticised than so-called 'banana programming' is likely to arouse suspicion that it aims to establish Pusan as the first step in the festival circuit to the prestigious western festival since these type of films—for instance, low budget, small independent, alienated by the mainstream in China, dealing with drugs, gender and political issues—has long been liked by the western film festivals, especially Rotterdam and Berlin.[25]

On the one hand, such a harsh criticism of the PIFF's programming can be attributed to its inability to set its own aesthetic norms at the festival site. As discussed in Chapter 3, PIFF tended to lean on international aesthetics which were already sanctioned by Western film festivals. This inclination has often been criticized both by the local and the global critics as one of the main reasons causing the festival's current limbo in programming.

On the other hand, it is important to note that one possible explanation for this tendency may be the PIFF's inability to premiere mainstream Chinese films. Established (or even new) Chinese directors have tended to premiere their titles at prestigious Western film festivals, and this fact has also been cited as one of the many possible factors in explaining the Hong Kong International Film Festival (HKIFF)'s decline since the 1990s. In addition to the Chinese case, however, it has also become more difficult for the PIFF to stage the world premieres of major local titles since increasing numbers of Korean directors have favored showing their films at major festivals in the West. In this regard, the PIFF's preference for Asian independent films is related to the current global dynamics of film festivals generally —it has simply become more difficult to obtain world premieres. Consequently, the harder it is to win premieres, the more the PIFF has to struggle with finding a "niche" to justify and prove its Asian identity. In short, the PIFF's choice of Asian independent cinema reflects the competitive festival circumstances in regards to obtaining premieres. Like many other international film festivals, the PIFF has sought to screen as many world premieres as possible. In 1999, PIFF enjoyed more world and Asian premieres than any other festival in Asia. For example, whereas the Tokyo International Film Festival staged thirteen world and twenty-four Asian premieres, the PIFF screened twenty-six world premieres and eighty-four Asian premieres.[26]

This obsession with world premieres was most explicitly demonstrated when the PIFF screened Hou Hsiao-hsien's *Three Times* as its opening film at the tenth anniversary festival. It announced the world premiere screening of this film with much fanfare and subsequently boasted that it had completely sold out within thirteen minutes and forty seconds of tickets going on sale. However, the version of *Three Times* screened at the PIFF was, in fact, a revised version of the film which had previously been shown at the Cannes Film Festival earlier that year (the PIFF version being a mere nine minutes longer). Nonetheless, it was important to the PIFF to screen this film for several reasons. Director Hou, often called a part of the "PIFF Family,"[27] had historically been close to the PIFF. Following his win at the previous year's award for "Asian Filmmaker of the Year" and his presentation of a special lecture entitled "Master Class," Hou became dean of the PIFF's new AFA workshop. More importantly, *Three Times* originated as a PPP project in 2002. For all of these reasons, it was extremely important for the PIFF to show his film as a world premiere at its tenth anniversary. The festival's emphasis on "the first" screening of this re-edited version can thus be understood in this context.

A similar case from the previous year of PIFF is also worth noting. The ninth festival screened *2046* (Wong Kar-wai, 2004) as its opening film. Like *Three Times*, this film had also been shown at Cannes earlier that year. Very similarly, the PIFF committee emphasized the "world premiere" status of its screening of *2046* by insisting that the Cannes version was an "unfinished" version and that this "new version" was different from the former as it had been re-filmed and re-edited. As it was the opening film, director Wong and leading actor Tony Leung were invited and highlighted during the festival's glamorous opening gala ceremony. However, there was skepticism about this film's "world-premiere" screening status. For example, one local newspaper criticized the PIFF's choice of *2046* since the film was going to be released across China on September 30, 2004, prior to PIFF's opening date.[28] Furthermore, after the screening, local newspapers also reported on this issue by citing a Western film critic's reaction to it. Ines Cho writes:

> Dutch film critic Peter van Bueren criticised the decision to show the film again in Busan after it had premiered in Cannes in May saying that *2046* didn't need to be reedited and re-shot again, because now the film 'didn't make sense.'[29]

Both cases above precisely reveal the extent of the festival's obsession with world premiere screenings highlighting Asian films. They also illustrate that one of the biggest challenges for any new non-Western film festival is to keep its international profile, as national (regional in this case) "big" films are increasingly premiered at the major festivals in the West rather than at their own neighborhood festivals. Similarly, as many commentators have pointed out, the PIFF's biggest challenge during the next decade will be to avoid the "twin traps" common to many growing festivals: to sustain its international profile as big name national and regional films increasingly premiere their titles at the major Western festivals; and to ride out any future downturn in the Korean film industry initially which helped the festival rise to global prominence.[30]

As the screening of world premieres has become increasingly significant in the fight to sustain a festival's distinctive position, festivals have often co-operated in order to obtain premieres. For instance, the recent launch of the International Film Festival of Rome (Festa Internazionale di Roma) in October 2006, with its convenient location and links to businesses, made organizers at Venice and Pusan very nervous.[31] However, this tense situation was resolved through a negotiated compromise between Rome and Pusan: the two festivals, which were held simultaneously that year, decided to share one simultaneous world premiere, *After This Our Exile* (Patrick Tam, 2006, Hong Kong). Another example is the negotiation between the Berlin and Sundance Film Festivals. When Sundance decided to become a competitive festival, tougher competition to obtain world premieres was then expected. However, this issue was settled by a third party, the FIAPF (International Federation of Film Producers Associations). Before the Sundance and Berlin festivals opened, Dieter Kosslick, director of the Berlin Festival, announced:

> [T]here will be a new regulation in 2004: US productions competing just prior to the Berlinale in the Sundance Film Festival will also be accepted for submission to the Competition stream of the Berlinale International Film Festival. The FIAPF, which supervises the standards of so-called 'A' film festivals, such as Cannes, Berlin and Venice, has given its approval.[32]

Such negotiated settlements, which have arisen in different circumstances in relation to different problems, illustrate the way in which film festivals have striven to remain competitive in these rapidly changing local/global circumstances.

APEC and PIFF in Local/National Context

PIFF's tenth anniversary's focus on Asian cinema is also demonstrated in another context. When it was announced that the APEC Summit was to be held in Pusan, the tenth PIFF committee prepared an event both for the APEC and for the tenth anniversary entitled "Special Screening for APEC Films,"[33] a section dedicated to films from APEC member countries. While this reveals the PIFF's geopolitical approach to Asian programming, it also highlights the festival's contradictory position in the local and global film industries.

Due to the timing of the announcement that Pusan would host the forthcoming APEC conference, it was reported upon and highlighted by local and national media in tandem with the PIFF's tenth anniversary. Hence the promotion of a cultural event (PIFF) became propelled by the meaning and importance of a polit-ico-economic event (APEC). The following passage illustrates some details of the relationship between the two:

> The main theme of the 2005 APEC conference that will be held in Busan is 'Toward One Community', and one of three subtitles is 'Building a Bridge over the Gap', and one of five agendas is 'Respecting Various Cultures.' Cinema can be a perfect tool to materialize these themes and agendas. Pusan International Film Festival (PIFF), recognized as the most prestigious film festival in Asia, will take place from October 6th to 14th this year, a month before APEC. During the festival, PIFF is planning to hold cultural events that mirror the themes and agendas, in part by presenting 'APEC Special Screening'. More specifically, by screening films that can build common ground within various cultures among APEC nations and having a place for constructive discussion, this event will create fruitful results that accord with the main goal of APEC itself.[34]

This special section covered twenty films from countries including Canada, Hong Kong, Indonesia, Australia/Papua New Guinea, Vietnam/Germany/Australia, Singapore, Japan, Russia, Peru, Taiwan, Malaysia, Korea, the Philippines, USA, Thailand, Mexico, Chile/Argentina/France, New Zealand/UK, and China. To match the aim of the APEC meeting, all twenty films dealt with communication and reconciliation between races or nations. According to the PIFF, this would be a chance to stimulate APEC attendees "in considering more universal values for humanity such as antipoverty, war deterrence, and environment protection by recognizing cultural diversity beyond religion and ideologies.[35] The PIFF's engagement with this socio-political event clearly suggests how the festival has attempted to upgrade its position and identity at the regional and global level.

However, importantly, the PIFF's links with APEC gave rise to controversy in the national film industry, as APEC's demands to deregulate and open the film market in Korea so as to "free" trade amongst member economies was contradictory to the perceived interests of the Korean film industry. The Korean screen quota system was the most controversial issue at this time and the local film industry fiercely defended it. Consequently, a group of organizations, including the Coalition for Cultural Diversity in Moving Images,[36] held a number of demonstrations against the agenda of the APEC meeting in front of the APEC Special Program screening venue and organized a separate film screening entitled "No APEC Festival."[37]

The difficult position the PIFF was faced with became more apparent when the Korean film community proclaimed their strong support for the Convention on Cultural Diversity in September 2005. This treaty was ratified by United

Nations Educational, Scientific and Cultural Organization (UNESCO) member nations one month later, in October 2005, and was intended to protect the diverse cultures of nations from the homogenizing effects of globalization. During the festival, approximately five hundred Korean and European film professionals gathered at the Korean Night organized by KOFIC to defend the screen quota system against pressure to reduce or abolish it. This event also focused on revealing problems with the South Korea-US Bilateral Investment Treaty, a pretext for the pressure on the system. Additionally, on the same night and after the event, *Fatal Attraction Vol. 2004* (Lee Hoon-kyu, 2005) was shown at one of the festival venues. This film is a documentary depicting the process through which the US Motion Picture Association of America (MPAA) attempted to pressure the Korean government to abolish the screen quota system. Many in the local film industry, including independent filmmaker Hwang Chul-min, criticized the contradiction whereby the PIFF appeared to support APEC by establishing the "Special Screening for APEC Films," yet had historically claimed to the public that it defended the Screen Quota system.[38] In fact, the PIFF belongs to an organization, "The Committee of the Korean Film Community Opposing the South Korea-US Bilateral Investment Treaty and a Reduction of the Screen Quota System" set up by a broad range of insiders in Korean film circles.[39] This situation reveals the tensions and complexities faced by both the PIFF and the Korean film industry. While defending the screen quota system so as to receive support from the national film industry, the PIFF had to negotiate its position with the central government in order to continue to receive the funding on which it is dependent for running its annual event.

To put it simply, for its tenth anniversary, the PIFF tried to highlight its Asian identity by creating extensive Asian programs focusing on contemporary and classic films from the region. At the same time, this attempt was sometimes at odds with national interests as illustrated by the controversy surrounding the APEC Screening.

It is worth comparing the scale and scope of the tenth PIFF with that of the same anniversary of the HKIFF. When the tenth HKIFF was held in 1986, Hong Kong did not mount a huge event, screening only 120 feature films, including twenty-two Asian films.[40] Established in 1977, the HKIFF maintained its prominent international profile as a platform for Asian cinema during the 1980s. Several big names such as Chen Kaige were "discovered" there. By the time of its tenth anniversary in 1986, the HKIFF was clearly aware of its status and identity as a premier film festival in East Asia. In the foreword to the 1986 program, festival coordinator Albert Lee states:

> Over the decade, the festival, apart from presenting recent European and American films, has also put much effort into showcasing Asian and Hong Kong cinema. This has given the HKIFF its uniqueness among film festivals all over the world.[41]

Significantly, the PIFF asserts a surprisingly similar rhetoric with its tenth event in 2005, with program notes including such phrases as "to become a center of cultural exchange in Asia and to further promote cultures of visual arts worldwide' and "serving Asian cinema as a stepping stone into the world market" with "Pusan a hub city for the Asian film industry."[42] This suggests that the use of a regionalization strategy to promote an Asian film festival both locally and globally is not unique to PIFF.

As pointed out in earlier chapters, since the late 1980s, the HKIFF had slowly begun to decline as many new Asian titles were premiered instead at major Western film festivals.[43] Moreover, due to the relatively unstable funding environment with censorship problems since the 1990s, it was less likely to regain its reputation as a prime showcase for Asian cinema.[44] Artistic director Li Cheuk-to notes:

> Compared to the generally unfriendly social climate to arts and culture here, our efforts are destined to be regarded as trivial and ineffectual. But do we really have a choice? Perhaps wait for the West Kowloon Cultural District to materialise seven years later? If we take this option, I believe that other cities in the region will leave us so far behind that it would be impossible to even catch up. We have no choice but to get to work ... now.[45]

It is noticeable that fifteen years later, to celebrate its 25th anniversary in 2001, the HKIFF evaluated its achievements and redefined its festival identity by focusing on integrating three types of ethnic Chinese cinema: that from Mainland China, from Taiwan, and from Hong Kong. Specifically, it published a special catalog entitled *A Century of Chinese Cinema: Look Back in Glory*, which featured twenty-five Chinese classics of the past century.[46] Attempting to redefine Chinese cinema, the HKIFF states:

> Chinese cinema covers productions originating in Mainland China, Hong Kong, and Taiwan, created by ethnic Chinese on subject matters that are historically and culturally distinctive of the Chinese race; this would seem a more appropriate definition than merely 'Chinese language films.'[47]

Contrasting with the PIFF's strong regional focus on Asian cinema as a whole in celebrating its ten-year achievement, the HKIFF's emphasis on the notion of Chinese cinema in particular suggests there has been an ongoing struggle between the two festivals for pre-eminent regional status and festival identity, and this seems to be the latest solution to their complex relationship.

Whilst the twenty-fifth anniversary of the HKIFF presented this event as a special occasion, the atmosphere was not entirely celebratory as there was huge criticism of "political or administrative interference" in the selection process.[48]

For example, writing under the title "Anniversary Blues," journalist Jeremy Hansen reported on the HKIFF's bureaucracy and political meddling by pointing out:

> [t]he festival opened April 6 against a backdrop of infighting, protest resignations by key staff members, and previously heard recriminations that Hong Kong's annual cinema celebration is being upstaged by a younger and more dynamic counterpart in Pusan, South Korea.[49]

As a result of this situation, after its twenty-fifth event, the HKIFF became more aware of and felt threatened by PIFF's new success.[50] Furthermore, as briefly mentioned in Chapter 4, the 26th HKIFF in 2002 deleted the section "Asian Vision" which had previously showcased fourteen to sixty contemporary Asian films. Instead, films produced in Asia were now allocated to the "Global Vision" section in general and the festival separately created a new section entitled "Age of Independence: New Asian Film and Video, Asian Digital Competition." This development also illustrates how the HKIFF has consciously tried to differentiate itself from the PIFF's aggressive Asian-focused programming.

In sum, while the PIFF's extensive regional approach focusing on Asian programming reveals the festival's complex relationship with the national film industry, it also shows that this aggressive drive severely affects the identity and position of its regional counterpart in Hong Kong.

Asian Film Academy (AFA): Education and Industry

Alongside a wide range of programs operating at a critical level, the tenth PIFF launched a new training scheme, the AFA. Closely modeled on the "Filmmaker's Lab" at Sundance and "Talent Campus" at Berlin, the AFA aims to provide young Asian young directors with film education, as well as production experience and skills.[51] It helps them learn about film production, produce their work, and establish networks that can be drawn upon in their future careers. Upon launching the AFA in 2005, festival director Kim Dong-Ho announced:

> Successful film festivals have their own strengths but they need to keep trying to come up with new programs to compete with other festivals, not just merely try to maintain the status quo [...] AFA is the result of 10 years of Pusan International Film Festival. PIFF will be reborn as a productive festival through a new program, Asian Film Academy, which will find and support young filmmakers from all over Asia.[52]

Such comments testify to the festival's intention to continue to sustain its firm position in the future, in part through this regional training scheme. As argued in the introduction, such an education program aiming to produce talent in the region is closely linked with the notion of creative migration, as suggested by

Michael Curtin. To become a center of cultural production, maintaining access "to reservoirs of specialized labour that replenish themselves on a regular basis" is required.[53] By establishing education programs, festivals can act as a powerful attraction to those who aspire to make films in the region and around the world. Thus, to remain sustainable, increasingly more and more film festivals make effort to maintain their infrastructure for organizational learning, even with massive infusions of capital or government subsidies.[54]

As mentioned, the AFA adopted specific know-how from two Western counterparts: firstly, the training workshop methods from Talent Campus; and secondly, the production system which supports the works of candidates at the Sundance Lab. However, the PIFF has differentiated the AFA from other existing workshops in several important ways.

First, while its Western counterparts do not put geographic restrictions on where applicants can come from, the AFA strictly limits applicants to those living in Asia, thus manifesting its aim to support specifically the Asian film industry.

Second, the PIFF claims that the AFA is not only for experienced filmmakers, but also for Asians who have not had the opportunity to obtain a proper film education and so discover his or her cinematic potential.[55]

Third, the AFA provides all participants with full-expense reimbursement including travel, accommodation as well as any visa fees. This is in consideration of the fact that many Asian participants are still unlikely to be able to afford the initial financial outlay required for participation in the AFA. This is similar to the Cannes Film Festival's Résidence du Festival, which provides young international directors working on their first or second fictional feature film project with a place of residence in Paris, a personalized program accompanying the writing of their scripts, and a collective program of forums with film industry professionals.[56]

Fourth, unlike other festival-associated workshops, the AFA is not considered a one-time event, as support continues after the workshop itself has finished. This ongoing assistance aims to help participants persist in filmmaking as well as to establish networks to enable them to do so. The PIFF, Dongseo University in Pusan, and the Korean Academy of Film Arts were linked through this program and work together to make this continuous support for future filmmakers possible.[57] In order to allow the existence of this extended training course, extra funding programs were created.[58] In terms of funding sources, it is noticeable that funding for the AFA is provided at the national level, from the Korean government, while other festival-aided workshops in Europe receive funds from regional associations such as the European Union.[59] In this regard, the AFA is the first program targeting the regional film industry in Asia created by an individual film festival and financially supported solely by the host country.

The decision by the PIFF to create this training program apart from the PPP, whose aim is also to incubate potential Asian talent, has often been seen as controversial because it required extra funding and a separate budget and organizational infrastructure. However, as demonstrated in Chapter 4, the PPP has tended to select and support projects by those directors who have already achieved recognition abroad at other film festivals. This has been done in order to reduce the risk of failure as it is believed that prior success by a director would make it more likely for a PPP project to receive international recognition during its incubation period. The PIFF felt that this limitation in the PPP necessitated the launch of the AFA which, in the name of "education," can actually discover and nurture young Asian film students or novice filmmakers who have yet to prove themselves but who possess much potential. The most explicit statement of this aim came when PIFF Director Kim Dong-Ho contended, "If PPP has led PIFF by linking film directors to investors over the last decade, AFA will allow PIFF to leap forward into the next decade."[60]

At the first AFA in 2005, renowned Asian filmmaker Hou Hsiao-hsien participated as school dean while two established filmmakers from Asia and another two from Korea played a key role in presenting the course program.[61] One hundred and sixty-four applicants from Asia applied to this workshop and twenty-eight were selected in 2005. For the short film project, the filmmakers (two directors and two cinematographers) formed two groups with AFA participants and each made fifteen minutes of short film in HD or 35 mm.[62] Their completed projects were filmed and edited in Pusan during the festival and the finished projects were officially screened at a PIFF venue.

Like the PPP, the AFA is understood as resulting from the PIFF's strong drive to boost the film industry in Asia and create its brand name: "made in Pusan." In this sense, PIFF's expansionism and new additions are used through a wide range of strategies; while the festival draws on and finetunes several ideas originating in the West, it tries to do so in a way that will create successful examples of creative localization.

Industry and the Regional Network: the PPP, Asian Film Market (AFM) and AFIN (Asian Film Industry Network)

The PIFF's consistent industry-oriented approach to the regional film industry was at its height at its tenth anniversary. Following the successful establishment of PPP in 1998, PIFF was able to boast that a number of projects had been completed and showcased in 2005, including the opening film *Three Times*, six films shown in "A Window on Asian Cinema," four films shown in "New Currents," and two films in other sections. This testifies to PIFF's ability to provide solid proof that PIFF is functioning as a productive market place and providing leadership to the regional film industry. By selecting thirty-three projects—the largest number ever and ten more than the previous year—the eighth PPP, taking place at the tenth festival also demonstrated the festival's continuing inclination towards growth and expansionism.[63]

Alongside this, the dominant issue in relation to the PPP at the tenth event was the announcement of the inauguration of a full-scale film market, AFM, by city mayor Hur Nam-sik at the end of the festival. The proposed market, heavily subsidized by Pusan city, would be part of a plan to turn Pusan into a film and multimedia hub.[64] For example, PIFF would have a purpose-built theater complex in 2008 and both KOFIC and the Korea Media Rating Board had decided to relocate to Pusan. In fact, before this announcement, the festival had from the ninth PIFF established separate "market screenings" for those Asian companies participating in the PPP. The PIFF stated that the AFM, co-organized with the Busan Film Commission, would be the biggest and most comprehensive film market in Asia.[65] Housed at the Busan Exhibition and Convention Centre (BEXCO) and the ten-screen Megabox multiplex in Haeundae, the market would also feature programs and about two hundred market screenings.

After this announcement, popular opinion was divided. On the one hand, the festival committee claimed an urgent necessity for the full-scale market alongside the festival, as the PPP was unable to deal with completed works including those produced under its auspices. Furthermore, being aware of recently increasing rivalries in the region, the PIFF had to take a further step towards distinguishing itself from its counterparts. Hence, it was believed that the launch of the market was the only way for the festival to move on to the next stage to survive in the global film economy.[66]

On the other hand, there was some doubt expressed about the necessity and potential for success of this market, as it takes place shortly after similar ad hoc markets at the Venice and Toronto film festivals and just weeks before the American Film Market in November. As argued in earlier chapters, timing is significant for the success of any market as much as for the main festival. For example, since 2004 when the American Film Market rescheduled its annual event from February to November, the Cinema and Television, International Multimedia Market (MIFED) in Italy, also held in November, had already declined. In the wake of the PIFF's announcement, tension had already been generated among its counterparts in the region: the Hong Kong International Film and Television Market (FILMART), an already established film market in the region; TIFFCOM, another film market associated with the Tokyo International Film Festival; and smaller markets at the Bangkok and Shanghai film festivals.[67]

Apart from the expansion shown by the PPP and AFM, the tenth PIFF also inaugurated the Asian Film Industry Network (AFIN) in conjunction with KOFIC. Its aim was to advocate for the concept of a "Pan-Asian" film network, following the previous year's launching of the Asian Film Commissions Network (AFCNet), an umbrella of organizations in Asia that provides production support services. Initially proposed at the seventh PIFF in 2002, AFIN seeks to promote Asian film through co-promotion activities at international film festivals and markets, exchanging research and film-related data, and facilitating international co-productions. The network's four founding members include the Korean Film Council, UniJapan, the Vietnam Media Corporation, and the Federation of National Film Association of Thailand. Two additional organizations—China Film Promotion International and the Singapore Film Commission—joined this network as official observers with a view to joining at a later date.

Thus, a trio of industry-oriented undertakings—the PPP, AFM, and AFIN— at the tenth anniversary event illustrate how the PIFF has forged synergies through linking industrial activities. In particular, the tenth festival attempted to provide evidence of its ability to provide the regional market with varying degrees of industrial support by initiating the full-scale market and regional network. These activities also reveal the extent to which the festival can take an active role in the film industry at local, regional, and global levels. While such industry-oriented expansion shows how the PIFF has pursued a more self-reliant structure by establishing a large scale industrial base in Pusan, these multiple activities conversely testify to the festival's struggle for its position in the global festival calendar, which in recent years has become unexpectedly changing and increasingly competitive.

Public Events for Local Audiences

As well as embracing an expansive industry-oriented and critical approach aimed at the regional level, the tenth PIFF also paid special attention to emphasizing its dedication to local audiences by organizing a series of public events. These included the opening up of the closing night party to the public and increasing the number of screening venues from seventeen in the previous year to thirty-one, to make this anniversary more service-oriented and easier to access.[68]

This increase in the number of audience-oriented events suggests that the PIFF has attempted to reconstitute local audiences' attention and foster a sense of community to compensate for some of the negative side effects of the previous decade's expansionist projects. It also testifies to the festival's efforts to negotiate its changing role and position in the global and local film markets. In short, all these arrangements aim to facilitate good community feeling by offering opportunities "to partake of exclusive and differentiated pleasures" and to assure the local community of an important role in the festival.[69]

As discussed above, the fast growth and success of the PIFF has propelled the "professionalization" of the festival and enhanced its business-oriented function. As a result, there has been a tendency for the festival to concentrate on building up its international profile rather than devoting itself to the interests of the local community. In other words, the PIFF and local audiences had to be ready to embrace outsiders (mostly international professionals) as guests to the festival, rather than expecting merely the presence of those belonging to the city and nation. This welcoming atmosphere has been facilitated by the economic benefits of the festival, including those brought about by tourism. However, it is also true that the PIFF's establishment and success relied on the strong local support of Pusan, as explained in Chapter 1. In this context, while the PIFF has achieved its global goals and established a solid reputation over the years, the local/national film industry and audiences have tended to be skeptical of the festival's links with them. As film journalist Han Sun-hee comments:

> I agree with the fact that PIFF has played an important role in boosting Asian cinema. However, Korean cinema? I know that some local film professionals consider PIFF's role in relation to promoting Korean films abroad to be important, but others don't agree that PIFF directly influenced the growth and development of the domestic film industry itself.[70]

Alongside this skepticism, the larger scale of the festival also began to affect the ability of the local population to participate in the festival, as it became harder and harder for the general public to get tickets. As soon as the festival opens online ticket sales each year, most screenings become quickly sold out. As briefly described in Chapter 1, PIFF relocated from Nampo-dong, the city center of Pusan, to Haeundae, a newly built suburban area, in 2002 and increased the number of festival venues alongside the previously existing screening locations in Nampo-dong. Despite this, however, and due to the growing number of films screened every year, the public—and even film professionals and international guests—began to gripe about the difficulty of getting tickets. Therefore, the question of "Whose festival is it?" has been raised. *Variety* complained:

> As the number of films at PIFF grows ever larger—a giant 170-plus features this year, excluding retros—it's developing a rep as one of the hardest fests at which to actually see them. Even invited guests, shipped in and housed at the fest's expense, face a daily scramble for press and guest tix at booths that open at 8.a.m. but hang up the "sold-out" sign at 8.01.[71]

Moreover, for professionals who attend the festival, the PIFF became a more difficult festival to get access to. For instance, like the Cannes Film Festival, the PIFF has started to restructure its accreditation system and classify it into more than four categories. This restructuring towards a more complex accreditation system in order to make itself look like a prestigious film festival actually makes it difficult for audiences to get access to films. Being self-consciously aware of these problems, PIFF made a special effort to resolve them on the occasion of its tenth anniversary. Specifically, to prevent early ticket sell-outs and provide more opportunities to watch films, the number of theaters rose to thirty-one—fourteen more than the previous year—and the number of seats rose to 300,000. In addition, following a pilot midnight screening at the ninth event, the PIFF introduced some special midnight screenings for younger audiences.[72]

Although funds from the central government and Pusan city are the major source of revenue for the annual budget, ticket sales have also been important to the PIFF, making up approximately 20 to 30 percent of its annual budget each year.[73] Therefore, in addition to invited international guests, local festival audiences who purchase their own tickets are important consumers and sources of revenue for the PIFF. Furthermore, aside from actual profits from ticket sales, the high rate of occupancy in seats is significant for the PIFF as local support and enthusiasm can help the festival sustain its distinctive position in the global market.

It is apparent that the effects of these audience-friendly events are maximized through various forms of tie-ins. This was most explicitly articulated by the closing night event at the tenth festival. As previously mentioned, unlike in previous years, the PIFF opened its tenth closing night gala to the public. With a special ticket package including entrance to both the closing ceremony and closing party, this event was entitled "Closing Reception with Lotte" and allowed general audience members to gather together with film professionals and invited guests.[74] Not surprisingly, tickets for the closing film, *Wedding Campaign* (Hwang Byung-kuk, 2005) were quickly sold out.

It is noticeable that the PIFF's choice of a world premiere screening of *Wedding Campaign* helps explain the excitement that arose in conjunction with these public events. This film is the story of two men from the countryside in Korea who go to Uzbekistan to search for wives. The pair meet a series of different girls—a refugee from North Korea, as well as women from Uzbekistan and Kazakhstan—as they search for the right mate. Festival Director Kim Dong-Ho asserts that the tenth festival chose this film to wrap up the festival "as part of efforts to make the festival more widely available and enjoyable."[75] Programmer Hur Moon-yung also comments, "[W]e looked for something a little more commercial in order to finish with a sensation of festivity."[76] Obviously, unlike previous closing films, such as *The Scarlet Letter* (Daniel H. Byun, 2004) and *Acacia* (Park Ki-hyung, 2003), which were both critically well-received, this film was described as "a heart-warming melodrama" which could be enjoyed by "audiences of all ages."[77] In short, this process reveals how the notion of the "festival audience" can be justifiably incorporated into film programming at a major festival.[78]

Overall, the rapid growth of the festival and its accompanying response from local audiences, in conjunction with successive transformations in the local and global markets, prompted the PIFF to turn more to local audiences in its tenth year. Through multiple appeals to this audience, it is obvious that the PIFF attempted to negotiate its role and position to effectively cope with a changing film festival landscape.

Conclusion

In this chapter I have looked at the tenth PIFF and examined the various expressions of expansionism associated with the event. In doing so I have suggested that its range and scale present an example of how film festivals can broaden the range of their roles within rapidly changing local and global circumstances. The PIFF's case, in particular, illustrates how a festival's expansionism may be linked to a regionalization strategy.

Specifically, the chapter has focused on Asian programming in order to illustrate the PIFF's ambition to be a critical hub as well as an industrial hub of Asian cinema. While the "Asian Pantheon" and "Remapping Asian Auteur Cinema 1" sections were crucial instruments for reconstructing Asian identity by allowing for the incorporation of a massive selection of Asian classics, the sometimes problematic relationship between the world premiere system and contemporary Asian programming at PIFF demonstrates the way in which the festival attempted to cope with an increasingly competitive global film festival economy.

Most importantly, by launching the AFA, the PIFF attempted to synergize the existing regional network by linking education and industry in a new way. This decision reflects a larger trend amongst global film festivals which have begun to concentrate on boosting the festival's industrial function by establishing sidebar training programs to discover and nurture potential young filmmakers. Moreover, following the success of the PPP, the PIFF's strong regionalization drive was furthered when, at the tenth festival, it launched the AFIN alongside its announcement of a full-scale film market the following year—the AFM. This ambitious approach suggests the way in which the PIFF perceived its role and responded to the demands of the local and global film markets.

It is instructive to consider what has emerged over the first ten years of the PIFF's existence. This period coincided with rapid changes across East Asia, both economically and culturally, and also with the dramatic growth and transformation of the Korean film industry as a whole. In this regard, the massive scale and scope of the tenth PIFF should be understood as occurring in conjunction with a rapidly changing local and global film industry, rather than being regarded as a single event's celebration of its success. Whilst the jubilant tone of the tenth anniversary was propelled by the growing importance of the Korean film industry in local and global markets, it also revealed some of the contradictions and complexities experienced by PIFF within the local/global context. Specifically, the PIFF's special program in tandem with the APEC conference and the festival's relation to the screen quota system provides a clear example of some unresolved political tensions within the organization. Furthermore, I have illustrated how the PIFF's extensive program of regional initiatives directly affects the identity and position of other regional film festivals. Finally, the strategic arrangement of diverse audience-friendly public events demonstrates that the PIFF is aware of its changing relationship with local audiences and has sought to renew its links with the local film culture. In all of these ways, the priorities and decisions that the PIFF has made, such as struggles over the definition of a self-proclaimed "Asian" identity, have to be observed within particular political, economic, and historical contexts.

In sum, this chapter has illustrated how the dominant trend of expansionism can cause contradictions and complexities for a film festival while still providing opportunities for the PIFF to distinguish itself from its counterparts in Asia. A close examination of the varying degrees of expansionism and regionalization evidenced by this specific case study enables us to broaden extant perspectives on the complex phenomenon of international film festivals.

Conclusion: Toward a New Channel

This book has brought the discussion of film festivals into an East Asian context by exploring how the PIFF in South Korea has actively positioned itself within the rapidly changing global film economy. By investigating the establishment and development of the festival between 1996 and 2005, I have demonstrated how and why the PIFF has used the Asian identity as its most visible marketing strategy. The book has thus brought to light a series of self-definition processes that the festival used to differentiate itself from its regional counterparts, such as the Hong Kong and Tokyo film festivals.

This project has analyzed this regional approach which was synergized with the festival's strong regional industrial drive. It has also considered the complexities brought by the rapid transformation of the South Korean film industry which has sought to reach out to the global film market since the late 1990s. The key objective of this study was to show the ways in which film festivals in East Asia are now moving from a focus on the national to the regional as they aim increasingly to influence the global market. However, this trend does not mean that the notion of the national is not valid in observing the global phenomenon of film festivals. Rather, this research has suggested how film festivals have begun to negotiate their roles and identities between the national, the regional, and the global by examining the PIFF's programming politics, its own project market—the PPP—and the tenth anniversary as a clear landmark in its history.

Focusing on the PIFF's position between the national and the regional, I have argued that film festivals illustrate this tension between these two contradictory but interlinked and often overlapping forces. Film festivals have played a significant role in exhibition for national cinemas and nationalistic agendas, and their function has been multiplied and amplified on the national level. Meanwhile, the regional force is also permeated throughout the contemporary dynamics of film festivals as they operate within the forces of economic globalization. Within this context, this book has put the PIFF into a discursive space wherein the ambivalences of the inter-relation between the national and the regional appears in conjunction with the impact of economic and cultural globalization in this region. As demonstrated, the PIFF's self-determined conceptualization and manipulation of a regional identity as a means of approaching the global market are unique and not to be found among any prestigious film festivals in the West including Cannes, Venice, and Berlin. This study therefore broadens our perspective on the specificities of individual film festivals and helps us to comprehend the institutional and conceptual complexities of researching film festivals in national and regional contexts.

The value of this research lies in its analysis of the diverse sides of contemporary film festivals, such as their economic viability and their unique relations to national and regional film industries. Moreover, the book has showed how the festival's spatial aspect—cities—is intertwined with its temporal dimension such as the festival's non-competitive system and scheduling of dates within the hierarchical map of festivals. By linking these two key aspects of festivals, I have sought to situate discussion of film festivals within current understandings of global cities, urbanism, and global networks as a complex response to ongoing cultural and economic globalization.

It cannot be emphasized enough that existing Western perspectives on film festivals are not sufficient to comprehensively explain either the complexities of non-Western film festivals such as PIFF or the multi-dimensional nature of film festivals whose importance has been rapidly growing in the global economy. By placing the discussion of film festivals into a non-Western perspective, this empirical study on a particular film festival in South Korea can offer an accessible map to researchers navigating the complexities of film festivals in non-Western regions within many different sociocultural contexts. It is important to note, however, that this does not simply mean that this book deals with a single festival geographically located outside of the West. Rather, by looking at the PIFF as a case study, this book is more than solid empirical research on one particular film festival; it is also a reflection on the shifting dynamics of cultural industries in an era of economic and cultural globalization. Ultimately, this project aims to answer the key question: how does the successful establishment of the PIFF help us understand the interaction among local, national, regional, and global forces? More specifically, how do the PIFF's unique formulation of regionalization and its complex relationship with Korean and Asian cinema reflect the changing tendencies and patterns of cultural industries to reach out to the global market more broadly, not only in East Asia but also in the rest of the world? I have sought to provide readers with a discursive site through which to understand the tensions and negotiations among cultural and economic forces nationally, regionally, and globally.

As highlighted in Chapter 5, I have observed that the PIFF's regionalization strategy as cultural and industrial practice is combined with the festival's rapid expansion. This provides a useful basis from which to address the gap in understanding film festivals in different regions—between the West and the non-West, in particular. It is worth noting that the PIFF has recently attempted to add a venue in Los Angeles to its expanding roster. In 2006, its organizing committee announced that, from 2007, the festival would launch a new program called "PIFF in LA" that would screen about twenty to thirty Asian and Korean films in Los Angeles annually, with the number of films gradually increasing. Although this project has not yet been achieved at the time of writing this book, PIFF boasted that this was one of the most ambitious attempts to extend the festival's actual boundary and to "upgrade the global role and position of the festival" in the international film industry.[1] This is a clear example of the recent trend of expansionism that many film festivals have shown. In addition, this example is closely linked to the festival's effort to build up its global networks as discussed in detail in Chapter 1. Interestingly, the ways in which film festivals extend their networks seem to be similar to various diasporic networks which operate in the form of the film festival, such as the Kurdish Film Festival in London, Greek Film Festival in New York, and Korean Film Festival in Los Angeles.[2] Likewise, film festivals today have become one of the significant new channels of global cinema, transitioning between the global and the national in particular.

One of the strongest findings in this research is that film festivals today have escaped the boundaries of their previously understood functions in diverse ways. International film festivals have played a key role in introducing world cinema to the West for the past few decades. Among the global film industry's three conventional modes—production, exhibition, and distribution—festivals have, up until now, been known as important centers only of exhibition and distribution. However, one of the most distinctive features of the PIFF is its establishment of a project market, the PPP. By forging a close relation with the production arm of the film industry, the PPP has tried to brand its own products and hence build networks at the national, regional, and global levels. By actively involving itself in film production, the PPP has provided the PIFF with a major justification to grasp its new role as global media producer. This aspect of the film festival has never before been critically explored with specific case studies.

PIFF since 2005 and Future of Film Festivals

As argued in the previous chapter, the tenth PIFF in 2005 marked the most crucial moment in the PIFF's history in many ways. Since then, given the ongoing globalization process, the circumstances under which film festivals operate have continued to change. In particular in South Korea, significant changes took place over the past few years.

Apparently, the proliferation of film festivals seems unstoppable. Following the remarkable success of PIFF and its firm position in the national and global film industry, a number of different kinds of film festivals have been inaugurated. For example, the Korean Film Commission recently reported that there are around seventy film festivals that officially registered.[3] Apart from the PIFF, the most noticeable local player is Jechon International Music & Film Festival (since 2005) which receives warm reception from both the local and national audiences, while Chungmuro International Film Festival in Seoul (since 2007) is distinctive in its strong support from City of Seoul. Several festivals also deserve mentioning, as they reflect the political and social trends in Korea. DMZ Korean International Documentary Festival held in Paju (since 2009) and Migrant Worker Film Festival (since 2006) are just two examples. However, as Kim Soyoung points out, many film festivals in South Korea whose local governments had excessively engaged with programming and organizing seem to have lost their strong drive that they had in the beginning.[4] While festivals continue to increase and develop in a diverse way in Korea, there are a range of issues to be seriously considered in the festival context: standardization and human resources, budget problems, ideological back-lash, new technologies, and audiences. Firstly, as demonstrated earlier, a festival's "identity" for differentiation has become a key issue in recent years. As festivals are bigger and their operation becomes professionalized, they tend to resemble each other more and more in organization, programming, and promotion. As a result, standardization and similarities have emerged and thus prevent the public audience from differentiation. Among various reasons and factors, this is particularly related with the issue of human resource in Korea. As most people who work in the festivals are temporary workers, the same group of people tend to migrate from one festival to another in search of work. Following the festival calendar, they move to work from Jeonju (April) to Puchon (July) and finally to Pusan (October). Aside from a lack of audience research in relation to festivals, it should be mentioned that film festivals do not know very much about people who are involved with their own events, and who play a significant role in shaping trends, making decisions, and differentiating one event from another in various ways. This is a significant topic since it can be extended from cultural intermediaries such as festival directors and programmers, as discussed in Chapter 4, to the broader issue of a "creative class" and migration.[5]

Secondly, despite their growing global position, film festivals in Korea have continued to suffer a fall in state funding, particularly since the change of the government in 2008. It provoked public controversy when the state decided to decrease the budget for the nation's six annual international film festivals, including PIFF.[6] In 2010, for example, film festival organizers staged a joint protest against a government plan to further cut their funding. The Ministry of Culture, Sports and Tourism allocated KRW2.5 billion (around USD2.2 million) in its proposed 2011 budget, down from KRW3.5 billion in 2010.[7] This situation is in striking contrast to the previous administration's positive attitude toward PIFF, which was evident in the exceptional financial support that it provided for the event's tenth anniversary just five years ago, as shown in Chapter 5. The government's decision then was the economic logic prevalent in Korea at that time; culture was generally considered a profitable product to rejuvenate the local and national economy. According to this logic, economic profit generated by each festival became of great importance in the evaluation criteria for funding from central and local governments, often threatening the existence of some festivals.

Another further factor is the current situation at the national level. Apart from its prevalent economic logic, the current governmental cultural policy has been criticized for being overly ideological. Following the recent government's audits, major cultural and educational institutions, including the PIFF, that were considered left-leaning had to change their heads or leave their own offices (being fired or dismissed), as well as be deprived of financial support. It is noticeable that public funding for independent filmmaking has been on the wane as clearly shown in the cases of Indie Space and the Media Center (better known as *Midiact*).[8] These situations have caused worries and controversy because it may be a symptom of a wider affliction that has wreaked havoc on Korean cultural policy for decades.[9] Most recently, Kim Soyoung laments: "Even when a movie is successful globally, locally, or in its subject, emphasis is placed on its financial success, to enforce an ideological backlash." Kim further states that "it's more absurd than difficult. Anyone in the cultural and film industry is subject to public inquiry, as though we live in a time of war or emergency."[10] She goes on to conclude:

> Even though public funding of independent and artistic film diminishes or is altogether cancelled, so long as there exists support of the audience and society, the making of movies that explore the possibility of different lives will not cease. In fact, film festivals are important strongholds that can call for such social support. Why should the public funding made up of taxes have to be shaken at its core by a handful of people who keep changing the rules at whim?[11]

As mentioned in the introduction, her analysis of film festivals provides important insights into the cultural politics in South Korea in the 1990s. A decade later—in the current era of neo-liberalism—she considers film festivals as a new channel to link people with social support. Could this new role address the challenges and difficulties that film festivals and other cultural institutions currently face in Korea? She further contemplates the ways in which film festivals in Korea—such as Jecheon—have been established within particular social, political, and cultural circumstances and points out a significant transformation in their directions: moving closer to their "local" roots. As she states:

> Watching the harmony between the local people and the singers and directors who brought their movies from abroad to sing in the theater scene, I felt that the international film festivals that had started in the

late 1990s have come closer to their local roots. The film festivals that had started with the encounter of cinephilia and globalphilia, have now formed a topophilia. For instance, where there exists a platform like the Pusan International Film Festival, and a place to showcase social issues like the Indieforum and Seoul Independent Film Festival, there is also forums to celebrate different genres like the Puchon Film Festival and the Women's Film Festival in Seoul that focuses on the female and minority issues. Then there are also festivals like that in Jecheon, a mainly farming town, which spread cultural education through movies (I am aware that there is much controversy about the future direction of this festival based on the shifts of its market, and do not find it agreeable).[12]

Apart from major film festivals held in big cities such as the PIFF, many festivals in small towns in Korea are now shaping the "trans-local" network which is a tendency that has emerged in recent years.[13] While this research on the PIFF focuses particularly on the tension and negotiation between the national and the regional in the light of globalization, it is equally significant to note that the role of trans-local connector that Korean film festivals are playing currently might be one of the solutions to address their difficulties.

Another important change over recent years is the impact of new digital technologies on film festivals. It is widely observed that film festivals are confronted with rapidly changing digital developments. The screening of all films will be done digitally at some point and film festivals will have to adapt to the transformations related to digitization and its unpredictable consequences.[14] However, the most severe challenge to film festivals today seems to be their "audiences." Marijke de Valck seeks to find an answer to this question in the ways festivals engage with their audiences. She asserts that festivals have more advantages over digital environments because the new generation of cinephiles who use digital technology more directly and share experiences through channels such as YouTube can play a more proactive role as a "stakeholder" of film festivals. For this, she pays particular attention to the festival's role of "gatekeeper" (judge and guide, in other words).[15] By offering opportunities for special audience participation in both online and offline space, a festival can lead audiences to express their voices and needs. It is significant that this "empowerment of audience" also can be the key to addressing the significant issues surrounding festivals today.[16] By doing this, film festivals are able to play another new role in connecting and networking with a new kind of audience who comes in and out between virtual space and actual festival space in different ways and times. Aside from the spatial and temporal aspects of film festivals discussed in this book, an important topic for future studies is the new virtual dimension of film festival space—a permanent online presence—which academics are now beginning to consider.

As illustrated in this book, many film festivals around the globe are in the process of extending their networks to survive the highly competitive film industry under a diverse range of strategies. In such circumstances, the future of film festivals, including the PIFF, is in many respects uncertain. Apart from the decline of public funding and other difficulties over the past years, PIFF remains the most successful film festival at both the national and regional levels. However, it is noticeable that the PIFF's tendency towards continuous expansion and growth seems stable but less strong since its tenth anniversary in 2005. For example, audience figures remain stagnant even though the budget has increased.[17] In addition, the PIFF's relationship with the Korean film industry, which initially helped the festival rise to global prominence, has substantially changed. As shown in Chapter 2, filmmakers in Korea who seek to establish an international reputation for their artistic achievements have directly approached the global market by entering the competition sections of major festivals such as Cannes, Berlin, and Venice, without the institutional support of the PIFF. I have demonstrated that as the PIFF was unable to premiere Korean films in Pusan, the festival has begun to seek a new way through its strategic Asian programming to discover new Asian names. Furthermore, the PIFF currently seems to face another crucial stage in terms of its direction and further development since the resignation in 2010 of the founding director Kim Dong-Ho who had far-reaching impact on the Korean and Asian film industries for fifteen years.

At this moment, it is worthwhile to ponder on the prospects of the PIFF on the basis of the outcome of this research. It may provide a guide to the prospects of other film festivals because the PIFF can be seen as a representative case study of film festivals in Asia. As observed in earlier chapters, the current limbos of the PIFF can be partly explained by the festival's reliance on world premieres and its inability to establish its own aesthetics. From this view, one of the keys to future success of the festival may depend on whether it can attract creative labor in the region and make effective use of it. As pointed out in our earlier discussion on standardization and human resources, it is important for film festivals to understand people who are involved with their own events. From this context, attracting and managing talent is now one of the most difficult challenges that cultural industries face. Being aware that creativity is a core resource for a festival to survive in the competitive global cultural economy, film festivals are trying to produce talent as discussed in Chapters 4 and 5. I have argued that the PIFF has established a project market, the PPP, and tried to brand its own products since 1998. However, it is less likely that this branding strategy was successful, as many Asian film directors decided to premiere their films at major Western film festivals rather than the PIFF, which had provided funding and support in completing their products. In this respect, creative capacity can help the PIFF's long-term branding strategy by building and supporting a creative community in the region.

In this concluding chapter, I have paid particular attention to people involved with film festivals, and sought to provide further evidence of how film festivals can remain as a significant new channel in the future. Despite the changes and difficulties surrounding film festivals, there is still much room for them as long as they play a proactive role as a connector: between audiences and festival spaces in different dimensions; between the local, national, regional, and global; and, finally, between the local and local in the Korean context.

This book aims to give a full account of the PIFF in terms of its history, development, and transformation of strategies and programming by situating them in a wider context of globalization. I hope I have shown how an individual film festival in a non-Western country has worked to position itself within the rapidly changing global film economy. Its empirical investigation of one single event, which has to date been little studied before, will hopefully serve to draw further academic attention to this long-neglected but important topic and to encourage the study of different film festivals in different regions. Furthermore, this book aspires more broadly to be a significant academic contribution to other fields, in particular our understanding of globalization and cultural industries in the region.

Appendix 1. Film Festivals in East Asia (1999)

City (dates)	Founded	Number of Films	Total Attendance	World Premiere	Asian Premiere
Hong Kong (April, 2 weeks)	1977	250	103,000	8	0
Tokyo (November, 9 days)	1988	146	116,400	13	24
Yamagata (October, 1 week)	1989	67	20,000	24	27
Fukuoka (July, 9 days)	1991	53	15,700	3	6
Pusan (October, 10 days)	1996	171	180,900	26	84

Figures for the year 1999. Source: *Asian Wall Street Journal*, April 20, 2000.

Appendix 2. PIFF over 15 Years (1996–2010)

Year		Countries (No)	Films (No)	Budget (1000 $)	Audience (1000 Persons)
1st	1996	31	169	1955	184
2nd	1997	33	163	2177	170
3rd	1998	41	211	2221	193
4th	1999	53	207	2355	181
5th	2000	55	207	2443	182
6th	2001	60	201	2621	143
7th	2002	57	226	2888	167
8th	2003	61	243	3287	165
9th	2004	63	262	3510	166
10th	2005	73	307	4842	193
11th	2006	63	245	6575	163
12th	2007	64	271	6930	199
13th	2008	60	315	7979	199
14th	2009	70	355	8974	174
15th	2010	67	308	8885	182

Source: The Official Website http://www.piff.org (accessed 8 Jan, 2011)

Appendix 3. Main Program Sections of PIFF

Sections		Contents
1	A Window on Asian Cinema	A showcase of brand new and/or representative films by the talented Asian filmmakers with their diverse point of views and style
2	New Currents	The only international competition section featuring the first or the second feature films by the future leading directors of Asian cinema
3	Korean Panorama	A presentation of latest outstanding Korean films that will help grasping the current trends in Korean cinema
4	Korean Cinema Retrospective	Re-shedding on the history of Korean cinema by spotlighting the films by a certain notable director or a significant subject matter
5	World Cinema	A presentation of new works by world's renowned filmmakers along with the year's best films that will help in understanding of the recent trend in world cinema
6	Wide Angle	A section dedicated in showing the outstanding short films, animation, documentary and experimental films presenting different and distinct vision via broader cinematic viewpoints
7	Open Cinema	A collection of new films, combining both art and mass popularity, along with internationally acclaimed works, are shown at the unique outdoor screening venue
8	Critic's Choice	Screening of films chosen by four renowned critics in an attempt to discover new film artists and engage in sincere aesthetic discourse with new cinema generation
9	Special Program	A retrospective and/or a special showcase of films by a certain notable director or a genre

The order of the section's title in this table follows its original form.

Source: The Official Website http://www.piff.org/english/html/info_02.asp (accessed February 10, 2006)

Appendix 4. An Overview of the Tenth PIFF (October 6–14, 2005)

• Opening Film: *Three Times* (Hou Hsiao-hsien)	
• Closing Film: *Wedding Campaign* (Hwang Byung-kuk)	
• Invited guests: 6,088 from 55 countries (excluding PPP & Press)	
• New Currents Award: *Grain in Ear* (Zhang Lu, China)	
• Korean Cinema Award: Dieter Kosslic (director of the Berlin Festival) and Thierry Fremaux (Artistic Director of the Cannes Festival)	
• Asian Filmmaker of the Year: NHK (Japan Broadcast) Korean Cinema Retrospective; Lee Man-hee, the Poet of the Night	
• Special Programmes	Re-mapping Asian Auteur Cinema 1; APEC Special Programme; Reunion of New Currents; Spotlight on British Cinema; Critics Choice; Industry Screenings; PIFF's Asian Pantheon.
• The first Asian Film Academy (September 24–October 14):	Co-hosted by the Korean Academy of Film Arts and Dongseo University (Director of AFA: Hou Hsiao-hsien)

The 8th PPP: October 10–12, 2005

1,100 participants from 320 companies of 30 countries; 27 official projects; 6 NDIF projects. Total of 600 official meetings

PPP Project Awards	NDIF Project Award
• Busan Award: Lee Kwang-mo's *Fairy Tale of a Picture Tree*; Thunska Pansittivorakul and Sompot Chidgasornpongse's *Heartbreak Pavilion* • Kodak Award: Park Chan-ok's *Paju* • MBC Movies Award: Hong Ki-seon's *Broken Piece of Mirror* • Cineclick Asia Award: Siddig Barmak's *Opium War* • BFC Award: Djamshed Usmonov's *To Get to Heaven First You Have to Die*	• LJ Films Award: Park Eun-young's *A Girl from 4th Dimension* • Barunson Award: Chung Hee-sung's *Stay with Me*

Source: The 10th PIFF official website (accessed September 12, 2007)

Appendix 5. PPP Project Accomplishments (1998–2005)

(Project title / Director / Country)

The 1st PPP (1998): 7 projects completed
The Student Spy / HWANG Chul-min / Korea
Thousand Dreams Such As These / Sudhir MISHRA / India
The Road Taken / HONG Gi-sun / Korea
The Camel(s) / PARK Kiyong / Korea
Gojoe / ISHII Sogo / Japan
Lagarista / Mel CHIONGLO / Philippines
Platform / JIA Zhangke / China

The 2nd PPP (1999): 12 projects completed
Unni / Murali NAIR / India
The Monkey / Aktan ABDYKALYKOV / Kyrgyzstan
Little Cheung / Fruit CHAN / Hong Kong
The Poet / Garin NUGROHO / Indonesia
Address Unknown / KIM Ki-duk / Korea
Betelnut Beauty / LIN Cheng-sheng / Taiwan
The Ballad of Love / Farhad MEHRANFAR / Iran
The Circle / Jafar PANAHI / Iran
The Paper / DING Jiancheng / China
The Face / SAKAMOTO Junji / Japan
The Unforgettables / SHINOZAKI Makoto / Japan
The Beijing Bicycle / WANG Xiaoshuai / China
Paradise in the City / TANG Danian / China

The 3rd PPP (2000): 9 projects completed
Rice Rhapsody / Kenneth BI / Hong Kong
The Summer Palace / LOU Ye / China
Uniform / Yinan DIAO / China
There Was Once A Time When / Viet Linh NGUYEN / Vietnam
Resurrection of the Little Match Seller / JANG Sun-woo / Korea

All About Lily Chou-Chou / IWAI Shunji / Japan
Weekend Plot / ZHANG Ming / China
Mask de 41 / MURAMOTO Taishi / Japan
The Road / Darejan OMIRBAEV / Kazakhstan

The 4th PPP (2001): 11 projects completed
The Moon Also Rises / LIN Cheng-sheng / Taiwan
Living Fish / Bakhtiar KHOUDOINAZAROV / Tajikistan
One Summer With You / XIE Dong / China
My Right to Ravage Myself / JEON Soo-il / Korea
One Night Husband / Pampika TOWIRA / Thailand
Monrak Transistor / Pen-ek RATANARUANG/ Thailand
Cry Woman / LIU Bingjian / China
Oasis / LEE Chang-dong / Korea
Border Line / LEE Sang-Il / Japan
Nothing to Lose / Danny PANG / Hong Kong
The Bow / KIM Ki-duk / Korea

The 5th PPP (2002): 11 projects completed
Story Undone / Hassan YEKTAPANAH / Iran
Woman is Man's Future / HONG Sangsoo / Korea
Coal Mine (Day and Night) / Wong Chao /China, France
Let the Wind Blow / Partho SEN GUPTA / India
The Floating Landscape / Carol LAI / Hong Kong
Osama / Sedigh BARMARK / Afghanistan, Iran
Three Times / HOU Hsiao-hsien / Taiwan
The Texture of Skin / LEE Sung Gang /Korea
Gie / Riri RIZA / Indonesia
Dam Street / LI Yu / China
Starfish Hotel / John WILLIAMS / Japan, USA

The 6th PPP (2003): 4 projects completed
The Buffalo Boy / Minh NGUYEN-VO / Vietnam
Waiting for Nike / PANG Ho-cheung / Hong Kong
Loft / KUROSAWA Kiyoshi / Japan
The Aggressives / JEONG Jae-eun / Korea

The 7th PPP (2004): 4 projects completed
Grain in Ear / ZHANG Lu / China, Korea
0430 / Royston TAN / Singapore
Big River / Atsushi FUNAHASHI / Japan
Poet of the Waste / Mohammad AHMADI / Iran
Magdalena / Laurice GUILLEN / Philippines

The 8th PPP (2005): 6 projects completed
Raised from Dust / GAN Xiao'er /China
Pure Coolness / Ernest ABDYJAPAROV / Kyrgyzstan
Tireless Mountain / KIM So-yong /Korea
Sakai's Happiness / Mipo O /Japan
3 Days Forever / Riri RIZA / Indonesia
Butterfly / CHANG Tso-chi / Taiwan

Source: *The 8th PPP Projects* (Pusan: 10th PIFF, 2005), 16–9. PPP, http://ppp.asianfilm-market.org/eng/main.asp (accessed April 27, 2008).

Notes

Note to Reader

1. Although I have tried to provide the exact page number(s) of newspaper reports, this has not always been possible because of complicated research processes.

2. KOFIC published this book in order to establish and promote the consistent listing of Korean film titles and names of directors and actors in English. The system used in this publication is identical with the rules of the Revised Romanization in 2000.

Introduction: Film Festivals between the National and the Regional in the Age of Globalization

1. Hereafter abbreviated to PIFF. Following the revision of the Korean Romanization system in 2000, "Pusan" became "Busan." However, the festival committee decided to retain "Pusan," hence "PIFF" rather than "BIFF." Since February 24, 2011, when this book has been finalized, the official festival name was finally changed to "Busan International Film Festival" from "Pusan International Film Festival." The festival explained it is because there has been constant confusion with the names between the city and the festival. Upon the decision, "Pusan Promotion Plan" was also changed to "Asian Project Market."

    In this book, however, "Pusan" is used for two reasons. Firstly, this book focuses upon a decade (1996–2005) when this festival was PIFF. Secondly, it is significant to this research that the festival tried to keep its own name under any (political) circumstances for ten years after the revision. This point closely links to the key argument of this book. Therefore, I use Pusan (name of the city) and PIFF to be consistent. Apart from this, "Busan" is used when referring to other relevant organizations that changed their names following the revision in 2000, such as the Busan Film Commission (BFC).

    Source: http://www.biff.kr/artyboard/mboard.asp?Action=view&strBoardID=96 11_05&intPage=1&intCategory=0&strSearchCategory=|s_name|s_subject|&strSea rchWord=&intSeq=9407 (accessed July 12, 2011).

2. In particular, the Cannes Film Festival has been the most frequently studied subject and is often positioned as representative of all the others. Kieron Corless and Chris Darke's book, *Cannes: Inside the World's Premier Film Festival* (London: Faber and Faber, 2007), also focuses on the politics of the Cannes Film Festival.

3. The PPP is a co-financing and co-production market for Asian films established in 1998 as a sidebar event of the third PIFF. Each year the festival showcases a select number of Asian film projects in the development or production stages, giving out cash awards and providing an opportunity for these filmmakers to meet with prospective financiers. The PPP will be discussed in Chapter 4. As explained earlier, this book uses the Pusan Promotion Plan (PPP) although the festival changed "Pusan Promotion Plan" to "Asian Project Market" since February 2011.

4. This figure includes overseas-guests. In the same year, the Tokyo Film Festival attracted around 116,000 people. John Krich, "Asia's Upstart Film Festival," *Asian Wall Street Journal*, April 20, 2000, 6.

5. As a political term, "region" usually means an integrated area beyond the nation-state, such as East Asia and Western Europe. I will explain this term in detail in Chapter 2.

6. Jeeyoung Shin, "Globalisation and New Korean Cinema," in *New Korean Cinema*, eds. Chi-Yun Shin and Julian Stringer (Edinburgh: Edinburgh University Press, 2005), 54–5; Darcy Paquet, "The Korean Film Industry: 1992 to the Present," in ibid., 49.

7. The term "Korean cinema" here designates films made in South Korea, not North Korea.

8. Stuart Hall, "The West and the Rest: Discourse and Power," in *Formations of Modernity*, eds. Stuart Hall and Bram Giebens (Cambridge: Polity, 1992), 276–95.

9. Stringer, 2003, 12.

10. See bibliography for a list of interviewees.

11. Dorothy E. Smith, "Institutional Ethnography," in *Qualitative Research in Action*, ed. Tim May (London: Sage, 2002), 17–9.

12. Ibid., 28.

13. This was to: 1) examine the film festival-related marketing and distributing system through the PPP; 2) understand how Korean and Asian cinema are perceived internationally; 3) acknowledge the way in which the PIFF organized these special events in a different direction (i.e., critically or industrially).

14. One of the rare materials is *The 10th PIFF Documentary* DVD (D&D Media, b/w, 60 min., 2005) that is not for sale. I was able to get this DVD title through an executive producer of this DVD, Dong-jin Oh, who previously worked for film magazine *Film 2.0*.

15. Thomas Elsaesser, *European Cinema: Face to Face with Hollywood* (Amsterdam: Amsterdam University Press, 2005), 83–5.

16. Janet Harbord, *Film Cultures* (London: Sage, 2002), 60–7.

17. Mitsuhiro Yoshimoto, "National/International/Transnational: The Concept of Trans-Asian Cinema and Cultural Politics of Film Criticism," in *The First Jeonju International Film Festival Symposium*, ed. Soyoung Kim (Jeonju: JIFF, 2000), 61–9.

18. Julian Stringer, "Global Cities and the International Film Festival Economy," in *Cinema and the City*, eds. Mark Shiel and Tony Fitzmaurice (Oxford: Blackwell, 2001), 143.

19. Film trade magazines such as *Variety* and *Screen International* often use the term "festival calendar." The meaning is attributed to the fact that many film festivals are usually annual events held for a limited time. It also implies a similar term, "festival circuit," which characterizes close links and interdependency among festivals. For further discussion, see ibid., 134–44.

20. See festival reports in *Framework* between 1976 and 1983. Richard Allen, "Pesaro 1: Festival Review," *Framework*, no. 22/23 (Autumn 1983): 74; Don Ranvaud, "Italian Festivals," *Framework*, no. 21 (1983): 54; Ian Christie, "Rendezvous a Bruxelles," *Framework*, no. 14 (Spring 1981): 55; Paul Willemen, "Pesaro," *Framework* (Summer 1981): 96–8; Paul Willemen, "Rotterdam," *Framework*, no. 20 (1983): 41–4.

21. Marijke de Valck discusses the international film festival circuit and cinephile culture based on her research on four major European film festivals in her Ph.D. thesis. Marijke de Valck, "Film Festivals: History and Theory of a European Phenomenon that Became a Global Network," (Ph.D. thesis, University of Amsterdam, 2005).

22. Thomas Elsaesser, "Images for Sale: The 'New' British Cinema," in *Fires Were Started: British Cinema and Thatcherism*, ed. Lester Friedman (London: UCL Press, 1993), 52–69.

23. Bill Nichols, "Discovering Form, Inferring Meaning: New Cinemas and the Film Festival Circuit," *Film Quarterly* 47, no. 3 (Spring 1994): 16, 21.

24. Ibid., 20.

25. Stringer, "Global Cities and the International Film Festival Economy," 137.

26. Dudley Andrew, "Waves of New Waves and the International Film Festival," in *Asia/Cinema/Network: Industry, Technology, and Film Culture*, Tenth PIFF symposium booklet (Pusan: PIFF, 2005), 256.

27. Ibid.

28. Yingjin Zhang, *Screening China: Critical Interventions, Cinematic Reconfigurations, and the Transnational Imaginary in Contemporary Chinese Cinema* (Ann Arbor: University of Michigan Press, 2002), 33.

29. Ibid., 28.

30. Ibid., 35.

31. Chris Berry, "Introducing 'Mr. Monster': Kim Ki-Young and the Critical Economy of the Globalized Art-House Cinema," in *Post-Colonial Classics of Korean Cinema*, ed. Chungmoo Choi (Irvine: Korean Film Festival Committee at the University of California, Irvine, 1998), 39–47.

32. Ibid., 42.

33. Ibid., 46.

34. Ibid., 40.

35. Liz Czach, "Film Festivals, Programming, and the Building of a National Cinema," *The Moving Image* 4, no. 1 (2004): 82. http://muse.jhu.edu/journals/the_moving_image/v004/4.1czach.html (accessed September 19, 2006).

36. Czach employs the term "critical capital" to refer to the value that a film accrues through its success on the festival circuit. For instance, critical capital is accrued and often determined through the film's placement within the festival structure as well as through being screened at prestigious festivals such as Cannes.

37. "Taiwan Trilogy" is composed of three films: *A City of Sadness* (1989), *The Puppetmaster* (1993), and *Good Men, Good Women* (1995).

38. Chris Berry, "From National Cinema to Cinema and the National: Chinese-Language Cinema and Hou Hsiao-hsien's 'Taiwan Trilogy,'" in *Theorising National Cinema*, eds. Valentina Vitali and Paul Willemen (London: British Film Institute, 2006), 148.

39. Ibid., 155.

40. Ibid., 149.

41. Soyoung Kim, "'Cine-mania' or Cinephilia: Film Festivals and the Identity Question," *UTS Review* (*Cultural Studies Review*) 4, no. 2 (1998): 183.

42. Ibid., 178.

43. *Segyehwa* is the Korean term for globalization, first formally introduced by President Kim Young-sam in 1994. *Segye* means "world" and *hwa* is "becoming" in Korean. President Kim's *Segyehwa* campaign was an economically oriented project, focusing on equalizing national development in every sector to the level attained by developed nations. Kim, "'Cine-mania' or Cinephilia": 185; Shin, "Globalisation and New Korean Cinema," 54–5.

44. Kim, "'Cine-mania' or Cinephilia," 176.

45. Ibid., 175.

46. Ibid., 183.

47. Arjun Appadurai, *Modernity at Large: Cultural Dimensions of Globalization* (Minneapolis and London: University of Minnesota Press, 1996), 37.

48. Stringer, "Global Cities and the International Film Festival Economy," 139.

49. Ibid., 138.

50. Ibid.

51. Michael Curtin, *Playing to the World's Biggest Audience: The Globalization of Chinese Film and TV* (Berkeley, University of California Press, 2007), 10–28.

52. Ibid., 19.

53. Ibid., 9.

54. Ibid., 10–1.

55. Film festivals' education programs that aim to produce talents will be introduced in Chapter 5.

56. Curtin, *Playing to the World's Biggest Audience*, 14–7.

57. Ibid., 14.

58. Ibid., 17.

59. Stringer, "Global Cities and the International Film Festival Economy," 138.

60. Harbord, *Film Cultures*, 60.

61. Ibid., 60–1.

62. Ibid., 68.

63. De Valck, "Film Festivals," 155. For further discussion of the role of the media in festivals, see ibid., 135–75.

64. Hyuk-sang Lee, ed, *10 Year's PIFF History* (Pusan: PIFF, 2005), 277.

65. Ashis Nandy, "A New Cosmopolitanism: Toward a Dialogue of Asian Civilizations," in *Trajectories: Inter-Asia Cultural Studies*, ed. Kuan-Hsing Chen (London and New York: Routledge, 1998), 142.

66. Leo Ching, "Yellow Skin, White Masks," in *Trajectories: Inter-Asia Cultural Studies*, ed. Kuan-hsing Chen (London and New York: Routledge, 1998), 70.

67. Ibid.

68. Koichi Iwabuchi, *Recentering Globalization: Popular Culture and Japanese Transnationalism* (Durham and London: Duke University Press, 2002), 169–70.

69. Chris Berry, Jonathan D. Mackintosh, and Nicola Liscutin, eds. *Cultural Studies and Cultural Industries in Northeast Asia: What a Difference a Region Makes* (Hong Kong: Hong Kong University Press, 2009), 8.

70. Ibid., 8.

71. Leo Ching, "Globalizing the Regional, Regionalizing the Global: Mass Culture and Asianism in the Age of Late Capital," *Public Culture* 12, no. 1 (Winter 2000): 244.

72. Ibid., 237.

73. Ibid., 236.

74. Ibid., 236.

75. Ibid., 257.

76. Berry, Mackintosh, and Liscutin, *Cultural Studies and Cultural Industries in Northeast Asia*, 10.

77. Iwabuchi, *Recentering Globalization*, 199.

78. Ibid., 18.

79. Ibid., 157, 193–9.

80. Berry, Mackintosh, and Liscutin, *Cultural Studies and Cultural Industries in Northeast Asia*, 4–5.

81. Ibid. For further discussion on the regionalism in Northeast Asia, see introduction to ibid.

82. Kim, "'Cine-mania' or Cinephilia," 183.

83. The term indicates the sudden influx since the late 1990s of Korean popular culture, ranging from television dramas to popular music and films, throughout East Asia including Hong Kong, Taiwan, Singapore, Vietnam, Japan, as well as Mainland China. In discussing *Hanryu*, it is generally agreed that Korean film boom in Asia was followed by the popularity of TV drama and music as the last runner of this phenomenon.

84. Iwabuchi, *Recentering Globalization*, 200.

85. Manuel Castells, "The Reconstruction of Social Meaning in the Space of Flows," in *The Informational City: Information Technology, Economic Restructuring and the Urban Regional Process* (Oxford: Blackwell, 1989), 348–53.

86. Ching, "Globalizing the Regional, Regionalizing the Global": 242.

87. Arif Dirlik, "Culture against History? The Politics of East Asian Identity," *Development and Society* 28, no. 2 (December 1999): 188.

88. Kuan-hsing Chen, ed. *Trajectories: Inter-Asia Cultural Studies* (London and New York: Routledge, 1998), 2.

89. Stringer, "Global Cities and the International Film Festival Economy," 140.

90. Elsaesser, *European Cinema*, 98.

91. Ibid., 83, 487.

92. In this book, Elsaesser describes the relations between Europe and Hollywood as being like a two-way mirror. He contends that it is no longer possible to speak of the European/Hollywood stance in terms of confrontation; transatlantic exchange has often shown that the relationship is mutually beneficial and not always a question of asserting economic or aesthetic superiority.

93. Ibid., 17.

94. Ibid., 83.

95. Since its establishment in 1969, FESPACO, Africa's largest film festival, has been mostly focusing on African film and African filmmakers. It has been sponsored by European countries such as Germany, France, and Denmark.

96. Elley has written about a range of topics related to this book in both the international trade magazine *Variety* and the Korean film magazine *Cine21*. It is noticeable that while many popular writings praised the success of Korean cinema at major Western film festivals from the late 1990s, Elley consistently pointed out the negative impact of the festival circuit on the Korean film industry. He also asserts that the Korean film industry should not assume that success on the festival circuit will alter the industry as a whole, and that it should bear in mind that the success of Taiwanese filmmakers in international film festivals was not connected to subsequent development in national filmmaking. On the other hand, as Elley's position as a Western-based critic with twenty-five years' insider knowledge of the global film industry suggests, his observations on the Korean film industry and international festival circuit do accurately reflect the way the Korean film industry perceives itself and responds to the reception it has received to date in the West.

97. His account of ten "misunderstandings" of the international film circuit includes: film festivals are truly international events; winning a prize is the most important thing; festival heads are experts in world cinema; Cannes is the ultimate pinnacle to aspire to; Cannes showcases the best of world cinema every year; Toronto and Sundance are the gateways to the North American market; being in competition is the most important thing; the director knows best; South Korean cinema is "hot," so the festival circuit is its oyster; local success = festival invitations. Derek Elley, "Korea, Beware! Ten Myths

about the International Film Festival Circuit," *Cine21*, February 6, 2004. http://www.
cine21.com (accessed October 10, 2006).

98. Ibid.

Chapter 1 Why Pusan?: The Political Economy of a Film Festival

1. In this book, "region" usually means an integrated area beyond the nation-state, such
as East Asia or western Europe.

2. For a comparison of the PIFF with other film festivals in Asia around the late 1990s,
see Appendix 1. For example, according to *Asian Wall Street Journal*, April 20, 2000,
world premieres at the PIFF outnumbered ones in Hong Kong. In addition, in terms
of attendance, 102,000 attendees visited HKFF for two weeks in 1999 whereas PIFF
had 180,900 for ten days in the same year 1999.

3. For the figures related to the development of the PIFF between 1996 and 2005,
see Appendix 3. The rating of A-category for film festivals is determined by the
International Federation of Film Producers Associations (FIAPF). According to
the FIAPF, besides Tokyo, there are twelve A-category festivals, including Cannes,
Berlin, Venice, San Sebastian, Moscow, Karlovy Vary, Cairo, Mar del Plata, Shanghai,
Locarno, and Montreal.

4. Bill Nichols, "Discovering Form, Inferring Meaning: New Cinemas and the Film
Festival Circuit," *Film Quarterly* 47, no. 3 (Spring 1994): 68.

5. Soyoung Kim, "'Cine-mania' or Cinephilia: Film Festivals and the Identity Question,"
UTS Review (*Cultural Studies Review*) 4, no. 2 (1998): 182. In the late 1990s, a number
of local film festivals were organized: the PIFF, the Seoul Human Rights Watch Film
Festival, and the Indi-forum in 1996; as well as the Puchon Fantastic Film Festival, the
Seoul Women's Film Festival, and the Seoul Queer Film Festival in 1997.

6. The term *Segyehwa,* the official version of globalization and economic liberaliza-
tion, was further explained in the introduction. Kim, ibid.: 185; Jeeyoung Shin,
"Globalisation and New Korean Cinema," in *New Korean Cinema*, eds. Chi-Yun Shin
and Julian Stringer (Edinburgh: Edinburgh University Press, 2005), 52–6.

7. Kim, "'Cine-mania' or Cinephilia," 183. Kim emphasizes the differences in every
sector of Korean society between the two periods since the mid-1990s. For example, it
includes a shift of regime and a financial crisis.

8. Julian Stringer, "Global Cities and the International Film Festival Economy," in
Cinema and the City, eds. Mark Shiel and Tony Fitzmaurice (Oxford: Blackwell,
2001), 134.

9. Ibid., 143. The term, "global city" here follows the work of Saskia Sassen who has illustrated how global cities such as London, New York, and Tokyo have become an important node point in the global economic system according to a hierarchy of importance
to the operation of the global system of finance and trade. This argument is also closely
linked to Manuel Castells' work that points out the flows of transnational capital and
information in a highly technological society into a global space as stated in the second
section of the next chapter. In this context, Pusan is positioned as a global city in the
global economy which "expands and incorporates additional cities into the various

networks." That is, as Stringer considers cities as a nodal point of the film festival economy beyond the nation-state, this book illustrates how Pusan (not South Korea) interacts with the forces of cultural economy of globalization and forges its network between other film festivals and related cultural industries at the local, regional, and global levels through PIFF and the PPP. Saskia Sassen, *The Global City: New York, London, Tokyo* (Princeton and Oxford: Princeton University Press, 2001), 2nd ed., preface xix, 3–15, 90–126.

10. Ibid., 142.

11. Michael Curtin, *Playing to the World's Biggest Audience: The Globalization of Chinese Film and TV* (Berkeley: University of California Press, 2007), 10–28.

12. Rob Wilson, "Melodrama of Korean National Identity: From *Mandala* to *Black Republic*," in *Melodrama and Asian Cinema*, ed. Wimal Dissanayake (Cambridge: Cambridge University Press: 1994), 90–104.

13. The Japanese government required all foreign and domestic features to be submitted to a government censorship board for approval, and police were present at cinemas for all screenings. From 1930, censorship became much stricter, so that melodramas, costume dramas, and pro-Japanese films were the only genres approved by the government. Finally, in 1942, Korean-language films were banned outright. Young-il Lee, *The History of Korean Cinema: Main Current of Korean Cinema*, trans. Richard Lynn Greever (Seoul: Motion Picture Promotion Corporation, 1988), 75–82.

14. The key points of the law were that each production company must produce a minimum of fifteen films per year; all production companies were required to be licenced, dependent on fulfillment of strict conditions; and each licenced film company was given a special quota for the import of foreign films.

15. Myung-goo Kang, "Decentralisation and the Restructuring of Regionalism in Korea: Conditions and Possibilities," *Korean Journal* (Summer 2003): 81–108.

16. *Minjung* literally means "mass of people" but in the Korean context its connotation is "oppressed, exploited people." Although *Minjung* indicates the working class as well as the rural poor, the *Minjung* movement was a coalition across different strata, including the working class, intellectuals, and even the middle class at some point. In the wake of this movement, college filmmakers such as *Yallasung* and Seoul Cine Group produced several films with antigovernment themes, shown at university lecture theaters and factories. Eung-jun Min, "Political and Sociocultural Implications of Hollywood Hegemony in the Korean Film Industry: Resistance, Assimilation, and Articulation," in *The Globalization of Corporate Media History*, eds. Lee Artz and Yahya R. Kamalipour (Albany: State University of New York Press, 2003), 245–64.

17. Soon after Park Chung Hee's death, General Chun Doo Hwan took control of the government in a silent coup. Students at Jeonnam National University, Gwangju, demanded the release of Kim Dae Jung, the opposition leader who had been imprisoned for political activities, and the removal of Chun. Shocked by the brutality of the suppression ordered by Chun, ordinary citizens joined the demonstration. Gwangju citizens controlled the city for five days before Chun deployed Special Forces to the city on May 27, 1980. Thousands of people were indiscriminately slaughtered. Because

this crime was committed with the United States' connivance, the Gwangju Uprising did not receive as much attention from the global media as did China's Tiananmen Square. As clarified in the introduction, unlike Pusan, "Gwangju" is used here (not "Kwangju", the old name of the city) according to the Revised Romanization System.

18. The oppressed left-wing political Kim Dae Jung (who is from Honam) became symbolically associated with Honam Province after the uprising, as a great number of the people killed during the massacre were originally from there.

19. Isolde Standish, "Korean Cinema and the New Realism: Text and Context," in *Colonialism and Nationalism in Asian Cinema*, ed. Wimal Dissanayake (Bloomington: Indiana University Press: 1994), 65–89; Tony Rayns, *Seoul Stirring, 5 Korean Directors A Festival of Korean Cinema*, (London: Institute of Contemporary Arts, 1994), 4–5; Hyo-in Yi and Chong-ha Lee, eds., *Korean New Wave: Retrospectives from 1980 to 1995* (Pusan: PIFF, 1996), 32–8.

20. In addition, domestic film production was separated from foreign film importation and a license system was changed to a registration system. However, the law included a "screen code" designed to protect domestic films. The number of days which Korean films had to be shown at cinemas was set at 146.

21. Standish, "Korean Cinema and the New Realism," 65.

22. Mark Jancovich and Lucy Faire, with Sarah Stubbings, *The Place of the Audience: Cultural Geographies of Film Consumption* (London: British Film Institute, 2003), 16–7.

23. Ibid., 18.

24. This began with pirates periodically ravaging costal villages; the Imjin Wars at the end of the sixteenth century involved a brutal invasion. In 1592, the Japanese warlord Hideyoshi dispatched 150,000 troops in an ambitious assault on the Chinese Empire. When Korea refused to grant the Japanese free movement across its frontiers, they proceeded to fight their way through. After six years of war, they finally retreated, failing to conquer China, but devastating Korea.

25. The Russians demanded coal mining rights, trade, and diplomatic relations, but were turned down in 1866. In the same year, nine French Catholic priests and thousands of Korean Christian converts were executed. The French Asiatic Squadron with seven warships was sent to seize Ganghwa Island. In 1871, the American minister to China accompanied five warships to Korea to try to open trade links. After a clash, the Americans occupied Ganghwa but withdrew following resistance. In 1875, the Japanese determined to force the Koreans to abandon their policy of seclusion.

26. Kang, "Decentralisation and the Restructuring of Regionalism in Korea," 102.

27. In 1991, the KMPPC organized the first public seminar/forum on establishing an international film festival, with Jeju in mind as hosting city (at that time, the director of the KOFIC was Kim Dong-Ho, the current director of the PIFF). In 1995, Seoul Metropolitan city tried to organize a Seoul international film festival but it failed at the final stage. Moon-sup Lee, "PIFF," *Busan Ilbo*, August 13, 1996, 5.

28. Kim, "'Cine-mania' or Cinephilia," 176.

29. Ibid., 178.

30. Kyung-sup Chang, "Compressed Modernity and Its Discontents: South Korean Society in Transition," *Economy and Society* 27, no. 1 (February 1999): 30–55. The first PIFF was held on September 13, 1996 and the financial crisis hit East Asia, including South Korea, in 1997. However, this book largely considers the symptoms of the financial crisis in Korea which had already appeared in the mid-1990s.

31. Ibid., 31.

32. Ibid.

33. Ibid., 47.

34. Ibid., 35.

35. Ibid., 47.

36. Jancovich and Faire, with Stubbings, *The Place of the Audience*, 25.

37. Kim, "'Cine-mania' or Cinephilia," 176.

38. Yung-ho Im, "The Media, Civil Society, and New Social Movements in Korea 1985–93," in *Trajectories: Inter-Asia Cultural Studies*, ed. Kuan-Hsing Chen (London: Routledge, 1998), 330–45.

39. After the PIFF's initial success, however, the central government began to contribute about one third of the festival's annual budget, making up for the decrease in corporate donations, which had slipped 40 percent due to the International Monetary Fund crisis. See Krich, *Asian Wall Street Journal*, April 20, 2000, 6.

40. Recently, Puchon (Buchon) city removed festival director Kim Hongjun, one of Korea's most renowned film directors, due to a conflict between Kim and the mayor of Puchon. Jeonju city also dismissed the founding intellectuals after conflicts developed and restructured the committee just before the second festival in 2001.

41. Jin-woo Lee, "PIFF Opens in September," *Kukje Shinmun*, February 2, 1996, 21.

42. However, the Asian Week event did not receive much attention due to the spotlight on the PIFF. Ji-tae Jang, "Asian Week and PIFF Open in the Same Day," *Busan Ilbo*, August 28, 1996, 29.

43. Most national newspapers reported this as well as local newspapers. They include: Myung-Hwan Kim, "PIFF Opens," *Chosun Ilbo*, May 20, 1996, 19; "PIFF Count Down," *JoongAng Ilbo*, June 6, 1996, 21.

44. Kim, "'Cine-mania' or Cinephilia," 175.

45. The third category includes the Human Rights Film Festival, the Labor Film Festival, and the Queer Film and Video Festivals in Korea.

46. Kim, "'Cine-mania' or Cinephilia," 176.

47. Ibid., 182.

48. In 1983, Gyeongseong University in Pusan established a film department, the first specialized film course in Pusan. Most teaching staff came from Seoul and were actively involved in the PIFF's establishment in the 1990s. All three main programmers at the PIFF were involved in local film education.

49. The Buil Film Award had a strong reputation in Korean film history but was discontinued as the local film industry in Pusan declined. Since the PIFF was based in Pusan, the committee tried to revive this traditional local film award and absorb it into the PIFF's own program. These attempts failed, however, partly because the name "Buil" literally meant the event was fully sponsored by a private local newspaper, *Busan Ilbo*. Pusan Jikhalsi Sa Pyeonchan Wiwonhyoe, *History of Pusan City: Pusan-si Sa*, vol. 4 (Pusan: Pusan Jikhalsi, 1991), 514–6.

50. Tony Rayns was involved in the Vancouver and the Hong Kong Film Festivals as a festival advisor. As a specialist on East Asian cinema and a foreign festival consultant, Rayns played a key role in the establishment of PIFF. Paul Yi worked at the San Francisco Film Festival, while Wong Ainling had been previously involved in the Hong Kong Film Festival. Their experience and networks enormously contributed to the initial organizing stage in many ways.

51. *Chungmuro* is the name of a district in Seoul synonymous with Korea's film industry because of the high concentration of film production companies there.

52. After the successful launch of the PIFF, Park subsequently started another important sidebar event, the Pusan Promotion Plan (PPP), a project film market in 1997. Then, he moved on to the Asian Film Market (AFM) in 2005, a full-scale international film market in Pusan.

53. Hyuk-sang Lee, ed., *10 Years' PIFF History* (Pusan: PIFF, 2005), 137. Following Park's leadership, the PIFF was structured into two parts: programming and administration. Lee Yong-kwan, a Seoul-based film professor, became Korean cinema programmer and Jay Jeon, world cinema programmer. Two natives from Pusan were also appointed: Kim Ji-seok handled Asian cinema and Oh Seuk-keun was general manager.

54. *Jaebol* (*Chaebol*) in Korean means "giant conglomerates usually owned by family groups." KRW300 million is approximately USD320,000.

55. It was apparent that Kim was well aware that he is not from Pusan, as he often mentioned that he was honored to be appointed director of PIFF even though he was not a native. In addition, there was a news report that he was self-consciously not present at some sensitive meetings in the initial stage before the PIFF was firmly announced as he did not want to give rise to unnecessary tension among the local communities. Eun-young Kim, "PIFF Opens," *Busan Ilbo*, February 15, 1996, 1; Eun-young Kim, "From Preparation to Opening," *Busan Ilbo*, September 13, 1996, 18.

56. Stringer, "Global Cities and the International Film Festival Economy," 134.

57. Jancovich and Faire, with Stubbings, *The Place of the Audience*, 21.

58. Sang-kon Shim, "Editorial: Film Festival in Pusan," *Kookje Shinmun*, February 6, 1996, 6.

59. In 1995, the Paradise Hotel in Pusan was supposed to be the main sponsor of the first PIFF by providing funding of KRW500 million but withdrew it in the same year. Left in the lurch at the last minute, the PIFF asked the Pusan government for financial support. Finally, the local government decided to commit KRW300 million from its budget to the festival. Lee, *10 Years' PIFF History*, 132–3.

60. Jin-kyung Kim and Jung-ho Lee, "PIFF Square," *Busan Ilbo*, September 21, 1996, 31.

61. Ibid. During the first PIFF period, the removal was temporary and then open-air markets returned soon after the PIFF. However, after the huge success of the festival, public opinion to reconstruct the market square permanently and to remove the old shabby stalls poured in. Thus, the local council had to hold a public hearing several times to discuss this issue.

62. Lee, *10 Years' PIFF History*, 142.

63. Ibid., 141.

64. For instance, on October 4, 1996, the Constitutional Court overturned pre-screening censorship in favor of a ratings system. Michael Baker, "Having It Both Ways: Korea Promotes and Censors Films," *Christian Science Monitor*, October 22, 1996. n.p.

65. The PIFF pursued this policy with no official permission from the state. However, because this was the first international film festival in South Korea, the central government was relatively generous and flexible about screenings.

66. This ban was relaxed in the interests of bilateral relations between Japan and Korea, especially in the wake of President Kim Dae Jung's visit to Tokyo in 1998. Jonathan Watts, "Korea to Lift Ban on Japan," *Hollywood Reporter*, October 6–12, 1998. n.p.

67. Andrew Hindes, "First Korean Pic Fest an Artistic, Popular Success," *Variety*, September 23–29 1996, 29.

68. Ibid.

69. The National Security Law was promulgated in 1948 to restrict anti-state acts that endangered national security and to protect the nation's safety and its people's life and freedom. Since the Anti-Communism Law was merged into the National Security Law during the 1980s, this law is acknowledged by many South Koreans as a symbol of the anti-communism of South Korea's First Republic and its dictatorial period of 1964–87; yet this law still exists.

70. In 2001, the PIFF finally organized a retrospective of the work of Shin Sang-Ok, who had been kidnapped and taken to North Korea where he was held captive until his escape in 1986. Banned from public screening by the South Korean government, these titles were exclusively presented to festival guests at the PIFF. This topic will be argued in detail in Chapter 3.

71. Dina Iordanova, "Showdown of the Festivals: Clashing Entrepreneurship and Post-Communist Management of Culture," *Film International* 4, no. 23 (October 2006): 36; interview with Derek Elley in London (March 14, 2007).

72. Mark Shiel, "Cinema and the City in History and Theory," in *Cinema and the City*, eds. Mark Shiel and Tony Fitzmaurice (Oxford: Blackwell, 2001), 1–2.

73. Julian Stringer, "Global Cities and the International Film Festival Economy," 140.

74. Ibid., 138–9; Thomas Elsaesser, *European Cinema: Face to Face with Hollywood* (Amsterdam: Amsterdam University Press, 2005), 86–93.

75. Stringer, "Global Cities and the International Film Festival Economy," 139.

76. Ibid., 141.

77. Lee, *10 Years' PIFF History*, 133.

78. Iranian cinema is categorized as Asian cinema in the PIFF's programs. Iran, officially the Islamic Republic of Iran, is a Southwest Asian country located in the geographic territories of the Middle East and Southern Asia. Dong-Ho Kim, foreword to *The First Pusan International Film Festival*, program booklet (Pusan: First PIFF, 1996), 10.

79. This award was established in 2003. Given to the individual or organization who contributed significantly to the advancement of the film industry and cultural exchanges in Asia, the first recipient of this award was director Mohsen Makhmalbaf.

80. Maarten A. Hajer, "Rotterdam: Redesigning the Public Domain," in *Cultural Policy and Urban Regeneration: The West European Experience*, eds. Franco Bianchini and Michael Parkinson (Manchester and New York: Manchester University Press, 1993), 62.

81. Paul Swann, "From Workshop to Backlot: The Greater Philadelphia Film Office," in *Cinema and the City*, eds. Mark Shiel and Tony Fitzmaurice (Oxford: Blackwell, 2001), 88.

82. "Movie Lovers Get a Chance to Tour Pusan and Attend the Film Festival," *Korea Herald*, September 11, 1998, 10.

83. Sang-keun Cha, "Five-Star Hotels in Pusan are Fully Booked," *Busanmaeil Shinmun*, September 23, 1998, 18.

84. Joo-young Kim, "Festivals' Impact on Local Economy," *Maeil Kyungje Shinmun*, December 23, 1999, n.p. KRW25 billion is around USD2.6 million. Since then, every year the statistic figure of the PIFF's impact has been announced. In 2004, the economic impact of the PIFF was reported as approximately KRW5.2 million, for example. Chang-bae Kim, "PIFF's Economic Impact Is 5.2 Million Won," *Hankook Ilbo*, October 7, 2004. http://news.hankooki.com/lpage/society/200410/h2004100721170043400.htm (accessed June 4, 2007).

85. Director Park Kwang-su has been appointed the head of the BFC.

86. Established in Pusan in 2003, AFCNet is a network of Asian film commissions and organizations whose aim is to provide a convenient filming environment in the region. Board members include Japan, China, Malaysia, Indonesia, Russia, as well as Korea. AFCNet, http://www.afcnet.org/ (accessed August 12, 2007).

87. Interview with Kim Hye-joon, previous General Secretary of KOFIC, in Seoul (October 8, 2005); Byung-won Jang, "Can Busan Be a Cinema City?" *Film 2.0*, November 28, 2005. http://www.film2.co.kr (accessed May 18, 2005).

88. Manuel Castells, "The Reconstruction of Social Meaning in the Space of Flows," in *The Informational City: Information Technology, Economic Restructuring and the Urban Regional Process* (Oxford: Blackwell, 1989), 348–53.

89. NETPAC is an international, non-profit foundation, which was registered in Manila in December 1994. With representatives throughout Asia and the world, NETPAC is a pan-Asian film cultural organization involving critics, filmmakers, festival organizers, curators, distributors, exhibitors, and film educators. The genesis of NETPAC lies in the first conference in New Delhi in 1990, "Promoting Asian Cinema," organized by

Cinemaya, the Asian film quarterly, in collaboration with UNESCO, to address a felt need to promote Asian films within Asia and around the world. To facilitate interaction and exchange regionally and globally, it was decided at this conference to set up a network of Asian film centers in Asian countries, with international associate members.

90. NETPAC, http://net-pac.net/ (accessed September 20, 2006).

91. "Objectives of the ASEAN," Association of Southeast Asian Nations, http://www.ase-ansec.org/64.htm (accessed July 10, 2007).

92. Hollywood dominance of the local film market in the 1980s had spurred local intellectuals and workers to create resistant film discourses. "National cinema resists Hollywood dominance in the international market and the government's monopoly and control over film distribution." Eung-jun Min, "Political and Sociocultural Implications of Hollywood Hegemony in the Korean Film Industry: Resistance, Assimilation, and Articulation," in *The Globalization of Corporate Media Hegemony,* eds. Lee Artz and Yahya R. Kamalipour (Albany: State University of New York Press, 2003), 253–4.

93. Lee, *10 Years' PIFF History,* 137.

94. Seung-hyun Cho, "PIFF Seminar," *Kukjeshinmun,* June 7, 1996, 15.

95. Maureen Sullivan, "Pusan Focuses on Holding Back H'wood Onslaught" *Variety,* Oct 10–26, 1997, n.p.

96. The screen quota system is a kind of trade barrier to protect local films. The strictly enforced system, introduced in 1966, requires Korean cinemas to screen local films for between 106 and 146 days each year. It is widely presumed that the screen quota system has helped local films to secure screen space and to survive in the highly competitive global film industry. However, this system has been challenged by Hollywood and put under pressure by the dramatic growth of the local film industry since the late 1990s. As a result, controversy has emerged with some advocating a reduction of the quota or the abrogation of the entire system. Korean filmmakers have vigorously fought to protect the system through continuous protest against its abolition. Recently, however, as a result of the Free Trade Agreement between Korea and the United States on April 2, 2007, the screen quota has been reduced from 146 to 73 days.

97. Quoted in Jonathan Watts, "Korea to Lift Ban on Japan," *Hollywood Reporter,* October 6–12, 1998, 143.

98. WTO is an acronym of the World Trade Organization. Together with this conference several programs, such as The Future of the Asian Film Industry Network (AFIN), were organized in relation to the WTO issue during the 2002 PPP.

99. The PIFF has closer ties with Western Europe than with North America, especially with France, which shares its strong anti-Hollywood stance. In fact, the majority of Korean art-house films have been officially released in France since the late 1990s. Furthermore, *Cahiers du Cinema,* one of the most prestigious film journals in France, set up an annual screening event in Paris devoted solely to Korean cinema. Interview with Charles Tesson, previous editor-in-chief of *Cahiers du Cinema,* in Paris, June 10,

2003. The line-up has included *Choonhyang* and *Chiwaseon* by Im Kwon-taek, and the majority of Hong Sang-soo's films. Considering that Korean films enjoyed relatively few opportunities to be screened at European venues at the time, such cases appear to reflect the PIFF's efforts to forge links with Europe.

100. Due to the absence of an exclusive festival venue, the PIFF has to rent cinema venues in Pusan. Local cinemas in Pusan show blockbuster movies during the peak *Chusuk* (Korean Thanksgiving Day) season generally for four-weeks at least. This means that every year the PIFF can start the event only after this traditional holiday. Since 2003, with support from the Pusan council, an exclusive venue for the PIFF has been constructed in the suburban area of Haeundae which should be completed by 2009.

101. Janet Harbord, *Film Cultures* (London: Sage, 2002), 68.

102. According to the International Federation of Film Producers Association (FIAPF), there are four categories of festivals: competitive feature film festivals, competitive specialized feature film festivals, non-competitive feature film festivals, and documentary and short.

103. As detailed in note 4, FIAPF operates this kind of hierarchical relationships among international film festivals around the world. For further reading of the rules of FIAPF, see FIAPF, http://www.fiapf.org.

104. Dina Iordanova, "Showdown of the Festivals": 28. In this article, Iordanova argues about Karlovy Vary's case and its relation to the rules of competition operated by FIAPF. For example, FIAPF's rules include that no more than one festival per country can have an A-category status and no more than two A-festivals can exist per region.

105. CineMart ran the Hubert Bals Fund Award (a cash prize of EUR10,000) during the PPP event to discover a new talented Asian director as a sponsorship program. It largely shows how two project markets in different regions cooperate for their mutual interests.

106. Dina Iordanova, "Editorial Issue 34," *Film International* 6, no. 4 (2008): 4.

Chapter 2 Negotiating a Place Between Korean Cinema and Asian Cinema: Programming Politics

1. Jeeyoung Shin, "Globalisation and New Korean Cinema," in *New Korean Cinema*, eds. Chi-yun Shin and Julian Stringer (Edinburgh: Edinburgh University Press, 2005), 54–5; Darcy Paquet, "The Korean Film Industry: 1992 to the Present," in ibid., 49.

2. Julian Stringer, "Global Cities and the International Film Festival Economy," in *Cinema and the City*, eds. Mark Shiel and Tony Fitzmaurice (Oxford: Blackwell, 2001), 139.

3. Interview with Derek Elley in Karlovy Vary (July 23, 2003).

4. The whole program and the entry criteria are explained in Appendix 2.

5. Liz Czach, "Film Festivals, Programming, and the Building of a National Cinema," *The Moving Image* 4, no. 1 (2004): 82. http://muse.jhu.edu/journals/the_moving_image/v004/4.1czach.html (accessed September 19, 2006).

6. Ibid.

7. Ibid., 85.

8. Since the first event, however, these categories have slightly changed—"Open Cinema" was added in 1997 at the second event, and "Critic's Choice" in 2002 at the seventh event.

9. Interview with Park Kwang-su in Seoul (January 6, 2006).

10. Unlike the PIFF, other festivals in East Asia have tended to select an international— most often, a Hollywood—title that has already gained a distribution deal. This is because a festival screening prior to a theatrical release could add box-office value to the film. For example, the Tokyo International Film Festival in 2000 presented *The 6th Day* (Roger Spottiswoode, 2000) and *Charlie's Angels* (McG, 2000) as the opening and closing films respectively.

11. Yong-kwan Lee, "Opening Film," *The Fourth Pusan International Film Festival,* program booklet (Pusan: Fourth PIFF, 1999), 21.

12. Dong-jin Lee, "To Get the Innocent Dream back, 'About-Turn,'" *Chosun Ilbo,* October 15, 1999, 35.

13. The film attracted over 300,000 admissions in Seoul alone. This means that it received relatively handsome box-office returns especially in Seoul, considering that the average admissions for Korean blockbusters was over one million nationwide. www.kofic. or.kr/statistics (accessed June 18, 2007).

14. It should be noted that one of the key members of the programming committee at the PIFF played an influential role in this film's smooth entry to some of the European film festivals such as Cannes and Karlovy Vary. Jay Jeon, programmer of the World Cinema section, was associate producer of this film.

15. Kyung-moon Jung, "Peppermint Syndrome Changed Cinema Culture," *Hankook Ilbo,* February 11, 2000. http://www.hankooki.com/ (accessed February 20, 2007).

16. Ibid.

17. The official website of this film is http://www.peppermintcandy.co.kr/.

18. Interview with Lee Yong-kwan in Seoul, Korea (January 4, 2007).

19. Moon-yung Hur, "Opening Film," *The Seventh Pusan International Film Festival Catalogue* (Pusan: PIFF, 2002), n.p.

20. David Martin-Jones, *Deleuze, Cinema and National Identity* (Edinburgh: Edinburgh University Press, 2006), 205–21.

21. Chris Berry, "'What's Big about the Big Film?': 'De-Westernizing' the Blockbuster in Korea and China," in *Movie Blockbusters*, ed. Julian Stringer (London: Routledge, 2003), 226.

22. Hye-jin Jung, "'The Last Witness' Fail to Deliver," *Korea Times,* November 17, 2001, 16.

23. Yoon-mo Yang, "This Year's Programming," *Busan Ilbo,* November 17, 2001, 26.

24. Eun-ju Park, "The Last Witness," *Hankook Ilbo,* November 13, 2001, 36.

25. Frank Segers, "Hae-an-seon," *Moving Pictures* (November 2002), n.p.

26. Soo-kyung Kim, "Hae-an-seon," *Dong-A Ilbo*, November 21, 2002. http://www. donga.com/fbin/output?code=Q__&n=200211210301 (accessed March 8, 2007).

27. Tony Rayns, "Sexual Terrorism: The Strange Case of Kim Ki-Duk," *Film Comment* (November/December 2004): 51. In this article, Rayns particularly uses this expression to describe the striking scene of fishhooks in the woman's vagina and down the protagonist's throat in Kim's *The Isle* (1999).

28. In Venice, *The Isle* (1999) and *Unknown Address* (2001) were nominated in the competition and *3-Iron* (2004) received the Best Director Award. *Bad Guy* (2002) was shown in the competition and *Samaritan Girl* (2003) received the Best Director Award at the Berlin Film Festival.

29. Rayns, "Sexual Terrorism," 50.

30. Kenneth Turan, *Sundance to Sarajevo: Film Festivals and the World They Made* (Berkeley: University of California Press, 2002), 27.

31. Czach, "Film Festivals, Programming, and the Building of a National Cinema," 84.

32. Yong-kwan Lee, "Program Note," *The First Pusan International Film Festival*, program booklet (Pusan: PIFF, 1999), 42.

33. Ibid., 54.

34. Paquet, "The Korean Film Industry," 44–6.

35. Hyangiin Lee, "South Korea: Film on the Global Stage," in *Contemporary Asian Cinema*, ed. Anne Ciecko (Oxford·New York: Berg, 2006), 184.

36. Chris Berry, "Full Service Cinema: The South Korean Cinema Success Story (So Far)," in *Text and Context of Korean Cinema: Crossing Borders*, ed. Young-Key Kim-Renaud et al., Sigur Center Asia Paper, no. 17 (2003): 7–16. www.gwu.edu/~eall/special/ berry-hms02.html (accessed June 20, 2003).

37. Czach, "Film Festivals, Programming, and the Building of a National Cinema," 85.

38. *Shiri* was released in February 1999 to the public and the new director's cut was screened at the "Open Cinema" section in the same year at the fourth PIFF.

39. Although his theoretical approach is different from mine, David Martin-Jones also points out the importance of UniKorea (see note 20) in his analysis of *Peppermint Candy*. See Martin-Jones, *Deleuze, Cinema and National Identity*, 205–21.

40. "Mainstream" here indicates films intentionally targeted to be box-office hits such as *The Gingko Bed* (Kang Je-kyu, 1996), *The Letter* (Lee Jung-gook, 1997), *A Promise* (Kim Yoo-jin, 1998), and *Shiri* (Kang Je-kyu, 1999). From the late 1990s, Korean cinema entered a boom period with the unprecedented box-office success of many of its films. The key factors explaining this rapid growth are new sources of film finance, increased standards of film production, and governmental film policy prompted by Korean globalization. See Paquet, "The Korean Film Industry," 32–50.

41. UniKorea Culture & Art Investment Co. Ltd, an investment firm made up of actors and filmmakers, was launched in January 1999 with an initial operating budget of KRW3 billion (USD2.5 million). The owner of the company is Yeom Tae-soon who runs an enterprise named Aizim, a fashion brand for young consumers. Its key

members are Lee Chang-dong, Moon Sung-keun, and Myung Kae-nam. UniKorea and Aizim were one of the key sponsors of the 1999 PIFF.

42. Martin-Jones, Deleuze, Cinema and National Identity, 208.

43. The Korean Film Council was established on May 28, 1999 through the restructuring of the Korean Motion Picture Promotion Corporation (KMPPC) by the new regime of President Kim Dae Jung (1998–2003). The KMPPC was founded on April 3, 1973 under the military regime. President Park Chung Hee's government (1961–79) enforced a strict political and ideological agenda that stifled the film industry, as discussed in Chapter 1. For example, the KMPPC enacted the Motion Picture Law and frequently revised it to keep the film industry under tight control.

44. Following the revision of the Film Promotion Law in 1999, the reform of film policy by KOFIC changed the structure of the industry. For example, claiming "cultural diversity," KOFIC has supported art-house cinema as well as commercial cinema and tried to restructure the distribution system.

45. *Oasis* was one of the Korean projects of PPP in 2001 with *Bow* (Kim Ki-duk, 2005), receiving Mybi Award (cash prize KRW 10 million).

46. Jonathan Watts, "Japan-Korea Team at Pusan," *Hollywood Reporter*, September 17–19, 1999, 16.

47. Screen Quota system is a kind of trade barrier to protect local films. The strictly enforced system, introduced in 1966, required Korean cinemas to screen local films for between 106 and 146 days each year. It is widely presumed that the Screen Quota system has helped local films to secure screen space and to survive in the highly competitive global film industry. However, this system has been challenged by Hollywood and put under pressure by the dramatic growth of the local film industry since the late 1990s. As a result, controversy has emerged, some advocating a reduction of the quota or the abrogation of the entire system. Korean filmmakers have vigorously fought to protect the system through continuous protest against its abolition. Recently, however, as a result of the Free Trade Agreement between Korea and the United States on April 2, 2007, the Screen Quota has been reduced from 146 to 73 days.

48. Czach, "Film Festivals, Programming, and the Building of a National Cinema," 82.

49. Ibid., 78.

50. Dong-Ho Kim, foreword to *The First Pusan International Film Festival*, program booklet (Pusan: PIFF, 1996), 10.

51. Ibid.

52. For the entry criteria of this section, see Appendix 3.

53. Stephen Cremin, "Pucheon Set to Fill Regional Niche," *Hankyureh 21*, August 2, 2006. http://english.hani.co.kr/arti/english_edition/e_entertainment/146041.html (accessed October 8, 2006).

54. Derek Elley, "Pusan Pumps Korean Pic Profile," *Variety*, November 1–7, 1999, 19 However, responding to those criticisms, the PIFF established an extra section in 2004 named "Industry Screening" for guests who attend the PPP to show more Korean films.

55. Su-yun Kim, "British Film Critics Pleased with Improved Facilities at PIFF," *Korea Times*, October 22, 1999, 12.

56. Cremin, "Pucheon Set to Fill Regional Niche."

57. Another interesting example would be the Karlovy Vary Film Festival in the Czech Republic, one of the most important international venues within the Eastern bloc, which was put at risk by an attempt to replace it with a new festival in Prague between 1995 and 1996. See Dina Iordanova, *Cinema of the Other Europe: The Industry and Artistry of East Central European Film* (London and New York: Wallflower Press, 2003), 30.

58. PIFF, http://www.piff.org/english/html/info_02.asp (accessed July 27, 2005).

59. Ibid.

60. The preceding chapter briefly discussed the roles and influences of the International Federation of Film Producers Associations (FIAPF) to explain the rules of competition and the premiere system.

61. For IFFR's Asian-focused programs, see Chapter 4.

62. For example, in 2004, 95 films were in the program. The winners of this section included Kore-eda Hirokazu (*Maborosi*, Japan, 1995), Hong Sang-soo (*The Day the Pig Fell into the Well*, Korea, 1996), Zhang Ming (*Rainclouds over Wushan*, China, 1996), Lee Chang-dong (*Green Fish*, Korea, 1997), Jia Zhangke (*Xiao Wu*, China, 1998), and Liu Jiayin (*Ox Hide*, China, 2005). http://www.viff.org/viff05/index05. html (accessed June 22, 2006).

63. Thomas Elsaesser, *European Cinema: Face to Face with Hollywood* (Amsterdam: Amsterdam University Press, 2005), 85.

64. Kim, foreword, 10.

65. According to Derek Elley, specialist in the Asian film industry, there was a kind of "vacuum" period after Hong Kong and before the PIFF around the mid-1990s, and PIFF aggressively took over at this moment (Interview in London, October 6, 2006). For a more detailed and in-depth discussion of the relationship between the HKIFF and PIFF, see Chapter 5.

66. For an in-depth analysis of "branding" and "made in Pusan," see Chapter 5.

67. Kim, foreword, 10.

68. Iordanova, *Cinema of the Other Europe*, 14.

69. Stringer, "Global Cities and the International Film Festival Economy," 138. Stringer observes two crucial components: "a sense of stability" and "expansionism."

70. A close examination of varying degrees of expansionism in relation to a regional approach is discussed in Chapter 5 through the specific case of the PIFF's tenth anniversary in 2005.

71. At the previous event (2004) there had been 17 screens, and 266 films from 63 countries.

72. Elsaesser, *European Cinema*, 85.

73. *A Century of Chinese Cinema: Look Back in Glory*: The Twenty-fifth Hong Kong International Film Festival (Hong Kong: Hong Kong Critics Society, 2001).

Chapter 3 Re-Imagining the Past: Programming Retrospectives

1. Young-shin Park, "Why Bong Joon-Ho Jumped Up from the Chair to Say Something", *Ohmynews*, November, 18, 2006. http://www.ohmynews.com/articleview/article_view.asp?at_code=374048 (accessed November 28, 2006). This article reported on the second Korean cinema and music festival (2eme festival de cinéma et musique coréenne) in Strasbourg, France held from November 7 to 12, 2006. This festival screened contemporary Korean films including Bong Joon-ho's *The Host* (2006) as the opening film. It also organized a retrospective of Yu Hyun-mok's films: *An Aimless Bullet* (1961), *Daughters of the Pharmacist Kim* (1963), and *Rainy Days* (1979).

2. The full titles of the Korean Retrospective section are as follows: "Korea's New Wave" (1996); "Kim Ki-Young, Cinema of Diabolical Desire and Death" (1997); "Beautiful Cinematographer Yoo Young-Kil" (1998); "The Pathfinder of Korean Realism Yu Hyun-Mok" (1999); "Everlasting Scent of the Classic: Choon-Hyang Jeon" (2000); "Shin Sang-Ok, Prince of Korean Cinema, Leading the Desire of the Masses" (2001); "Kim Soo-Yong, An Aesthete Bridging Tradition and Modernism" (2002); "Chung Chang-Wha, the Man of Action" (2003); "Rediscovering Asian Cinema Network: The Decades of Co-Production between Korea and Hong Kong" (2004); and "Lee Man-Hee, the Poet of Night" (2005). Korean and Asian retrospectives were included together in the "Special Program in Focus" section until the seventh PIFF (2002), but since 2003, the PIFF has split Korean retrospectives from this section and created an independent section entitled "Korean Cinema Retrospective."

3. Both "old" and "classic" Korean films in this chapter generally indicate films made before the 1980s, including films of the colonial period and Golden Age Korean cinema. I avoid the terms indicating specific historical periods in Korean cinema history in order to effectively reveal and focus upon the festival's institutional working in organizing retrospectives. In the same vein, these terms are used for Asian cinema and Hollywood cinema through this chapter.

4. Dudley Andrew, "Waves of New Waves and the International Film Festival," in *Asia/Cinema/Network: Industry, Technology, and Film Culture*, Tenth PIFF Symposium Booklet (Pusan: PIFF, 2005), 255–65.

5. Julian Stringer, "Raiding the Archive: Film Festivals and the Revival of Classic Hollywood," in *Memory and Popular Film*, ed. Paul Grainge (Manchester: Manchester University Press, 2003), 81–96.

6. Ibid., 82.

7. Ibid., 83.

8. Ibid., 81–96.

9. Ibid., 85.

10. Ibid., 95.

11. Barbara Klinger, *Beyond the Multiplex: Cinema, New Technologies, and the Home* (Berkeley: University of California Press, 2006), 102; Roberta Pearson, "A White

Man's Country: Yale's Chronicles of America," in *Memory and Popular Film*, ed., Paul Grainge (Manchester: Manchester University Press, 2003), 25.

12. Edmund Lee, "Pusan Power," *Village Voice*, October 29, 1996, n.p.

13. Eun-young Kim, "Interview with Kim Dong-Ho," *Busan Ilbo*, August 16, 1996, 6. According to a local newspaper interview with PIFF festival director Kim Dong-Ho, the festival committee had desperately looked for this film since it had never been shown to the public. They failed to negotiate with Abe, the Japanese owner of this film, as this person had placed some difficult conditions on lending it to the PIFF. However, Kim Dong-Ho asserted that the PIFF would not give up efforts to screen this historic film in the future.

14. KOFA, "History," http://www.koreafilm.org/kofa/history.asp (accessed December 2, 2006).

15. Haidee Wasson, *Museum Movies: The Museum of Modern Art and the Birth of Art Cinema* (Berkeley: University of California Press, 2005), 6.

16. For a discussion of some of the specific cases of ancillary markets in East Asia, see Darcy Paquet's report on the "PPP Seminar: Advanced Window Marketing" held at the tenth PIFF in 2006. http://www.koreanfilm.org/piff05.html (accessed November 29, 2006).

17. Stringer, "Raiding the Archive," 85.

18. *South Korean Golden Age Melodrama: Gender, Genre, and National Cinema*, eds., Kathleen McHugh and Nancy Ablemann (Detroit: Wayne State University Press, 2005), 3.

19. Hannah McGill and Andrew Pulver, "World Cinema Special—Is Nigeria the New Japan?" *Guardian*, March 30, 2007, 9.

20. Ibid., 9.

21. Ibid., 10.

22. Dong-Ho Kim, foreword to *The First Pusan International Film Festival*, program booklet (Pusan: PIFF, 1996), 10.

23. Julian Stringer, introduction to *New Korean Cinema*, eds., Chi-yun Shin and Julian Stringer (Edinburgh: Edinburgh University Press, 2005), 2.

24. Song-hyun Cho, "Special Programmes and Korean Retrospective," *Kookje Shinmun*, September 13, 1996, 13.

25. Steven D. Lavine and Ivan Karp, "Introduction: Museums and Multiculturalism," in *Exhibiting Cultures: The Poetics and Politics of Museum Display*, eds., Ivan Karp and Steven D. Lavine (Washington and London: Smithsonian Institution Press, 1991), 2.

26. Cho, "Special Programmes and Korean Retrospective," 13.

27. Tony Rayns, "Korea's New Wave," *Sight and Sound* 4, no. 11 (1994): 21–5.

28. Andrew, "Waves of New Waves and the International Film Festival," 256.

29. Tony Rayns, 1996: 22–5; Rayns, *Seoul Stirring: 5 Korean Directors* (London: Institute of Contemporary Arts); Stringer, introduction, 6; Isolde Standish, "Korean Cinema and the New Realism: Text and Context," in *Colonialism and Nationalism in Asian*

Cinema, ed., Wimal Dissanayake (Bloomington: Indiana University Press, 1996), 65–89.

30. Stringer, introduction, 6. Stringer defines "New Korean Cinema" by period: the post-authoritarian, post-political period of the post-1990s, and post-*Sopyonje* era. He also emphasizes specific elements which define the commercial film industry in defining New Korean Cinema.

31. Hyo-in Yi, "A Turning Point: The New Wave (1988–1991)," in *Korea's New Wave*, eds., Hyo-in Yi and Jung-ha Lee (Pusan: PIFF, 1996), 35.

32. Hyo-in Yi, "The New Beginning of Korean Cinema," in ibid., 9.

33. Kim, foreword, 10.

34. Lee, "Pusan Power," n.p.; Aruna Vasudev, "Pusan's Enthralling Show," *The Pioneer*, October 3, 1996, 11; Andrew Hindes, "First Korean Pic Fest an Artistic, Popular Success," *Variety*, September 23–29, 1996, 27.

35. Sang-do Jung and Jin-woo Lee, "World Cinema Is the Most Popular Section at PIFF," *Kookje Shinmum*, September 21, 1996, 13.

36. "What PIFF Left Behind," *JoongAngilbo*, September 23, 1996, 6. This editorial emphasizes the importance of cinema as an industry which can provide enormous profits to the national economy by citing the huge box-office blockbuster of *Jurassic Park* (Steven Spielberg, 1993).

37. "Exhibition of Historical Material of Korean Cinema Is Empty and Quiet," *Kookje Shinmum*, September 21, 1996, 13.

38. Yong-kwan Lee, *The First Pusan International Film Festival*, program booklet (Pusan: PIFF, 1996), 118.

39. Ibid.; Chris Berry, "Introducing 'Mr. Monster': Kim Ki-Young and the Critical Economy of the Globalized Art-House Cinema," in *Post-Colonial Classics of Korean Cinema*, ed. Chungmoo Choi (Irvine: Korean Film Festival Committee of University of California, Irvine, 1998), 39–47; Soyoung Kim, "Modernity in Suspense: Translation of Fetishism," in *The First Jeonju International Film Festival Symposium*, ed. Soyoung Kim (Jeonju: JIFF, 2000), 83–90.

40. Berry, "Introducing 'Mr. Monster,'" 41.

41. Ibid., 39–41.

42. Richard James Havis, "A Star Is Born—Aged 78," *Moving Pictures MIFED* 1997 Special (November 1997), n.p.

43. Chuck Stephens, "Pusan the Envelope: Film-Festival Fever Seize South Korea's 'Hermit Kingdom,'" *LA Weekly*, November 7–13, 1997, n.p.

44. Berry, "Introducing 'Mr. Monster,'" 39; Havis, "A Star Is Born"; Stephens, "Pusan the Envelope."

45. Soyoung Kim, "'Cine-mania' or Cinephilia: Film Festivals and the Identity Question," in *UTS Review (Cultural Studies Review)* 4, no. 2 (1998): 183. Before the retrospective in 1997, it was widely known that some local critics and journalists appreciated the distinctiveness of Kim Ki-young's films and that his films were circulated by on VHS

tapes. However, their recognition of Kim's films failed to further develop to a focused critical study of his work. Thomas Jong-suk Nam, former festival coordinator at PIFF 1997–2004, e-mail, August 10, 2007.

46. Hai Leong Toh, "Postwar Korean Cinema: Fractured Memories and Identity," *Kinema* (Fall 1996). http://www.kinema.uwaterloo.ca/article.php?id=296&feature (accessed June 10, 2006).

47. "'Festival for the Public,' Korean Cinema Spotlighted: Interview with Soyoung Kim," *Kookje Shinmun*, September 23, 1996, 21. At the first PIFF, a number of international guests were invited, including Laurence Kardish, senior curator of MoMA; Erica Gregor and Dorothee Wenner from the Berlin Film Festival; Adriano Apra, the festival director of Pesaro Film Festival; Simon Field, the director of Rotterdam Film Festival; Alain Jalladeau from the Nante Film Festival; and representatives from the Pompidou Centre and the Cannes Film Festival. Eun-ha Oh and Hong-joo Sohn, "Pleased to See Korean Film Festival," *Hankyeorye Shinmun*, September 29, 1997, 15–7.

48. For example, *Korea Herald*, a major English language newspaper reported: "However, Korean films were on the whole, neglected by fans and foreign distributors. With a few exceptions like 'Motel Cactus' and 'Green Fish,' local productions weren't well received for their conventional subjects and lack of quality." "Pusan Film Fest: Huge Success with Foreign, Local Movie Fans," *Korea Herald*, October 20, 1997, 11.

49. Dong-jin Lee, "Toward the New Centre in Asia," *Chosun Ilbo*, November 10, 1997, 14.

50. Berry, "Introducing 'Mr. Monster,'" 46.

51. Ibid., 44.

52. Ibid., 45.

53. Ibid., 44–6.

54. Richard Allen, "Pesaro 1: Festival Review," *Framework*, no. 22/23 (Autumn 1983): 74.

55. Cheong-sook An, "Shedding a Light on Asian Cinema: Closing the Second PIFF," *Hankyureh Shinmun*, Oct 18, 1997, 16.

56. Interview with Lee Yong-kwan in Seoul, Korea (January 4, 2007).

57. A retrospective on Kim Ki-young was held at the Busan Cinematheque from February 20 to March 4, 2007.

58. Sang-jun Han, "The Cinematic World of Shin Sang-Ok," in *Shin Sang-Ok: Prince of Korean Cinema, Leading the Desire of the Masses*, eds. Sang-jung Han and Jeong-hwa Yang (Pusan: PIFF, 2001), 6; Young-jin Kim, "Fantastic Shin Sang-Ok: A Legend in Korean Film in the '60s and '70s" in *Tenth Puchon International Fantastic Film Festival*, program booklet (Puchon: PiFan, 2006), 148.

59. John Gorenfeld, "Producer From Hell," *Guardian*, April 4, 2003. http://film.guardian.co.uk/print/0,,4640432–3181,00.html (accessed December 1, 2006).

60. For instance, an article on his death also began clearly by indicating the existence of Kim Jong-il by exemplifying his notorious terrorist image presented in *Team America: World Police* (Trey Parker, 2004), the recent Hollywood animation film, taking up a large part of the story. "Obituary: Shin Sang-Ok, Film Director and Abductee, Died

on April 11th, Aged 79," *The Economist*, April 27, 2006. http://www.economist.com/people/displayStory.cfm?story_id=6849979 (accessed December 2, 2006).

61. Jung-in Sohn, "Art or Law?" *Kukje Shinmum*, November 15, 2001, 3.

62. For example, programmers from Berlin, as well as Cannes' artistic director Thierry Frémaux and newly appointed Critics' Week head Claire Clouzot were present.

63. Sang-jun Han, "Korean Cinema Retrospective," in *The Sixth PIFF*, program booklet (Pusan: PIFF, 2001), 226.

64. Derek Elley, "Korean Pix Primp at Pusan Fest," *Variety*, November 20, 2001. http://www.variety.com/toc-archive (accessed August 11, 2006). It was believed that the Shin's retrospective was delayed at the PIFF. According to Han Sang-jun, it was supposed to run in the previous year but the PIFF committee changed the initial plan and announced *Choon Hyang* instead of Shin. Interview with Han Sang-jun (Seoul, January 8, 2007).

65. Jung-in Sohn, "Runaway Was Banned," *Kukje Shinmun*, November 15, 2001, 1.

66. Yingjin Zhang, *Screening China: Critical Interventions, Cinematic Reconfigurations, and the Transnational Imaginary in Contemporary Chinese Cinema* (Ann Arbor: University of Michigan Press, 2002), 31–9.

67. *Korea Herald* reported that "'Hermes Night for Korean Filmmakers' will take place at the Paradise Hotel at 10 p.m., said officials of the sponsor firm, Hermes Korea." Yong-shik Choe, "Director to Be Honoured at PIFF," *Korea Herald*, November 15, 2001, 16.

68. Ibid. KRW20 million is approximately USD21,000.

69. Young-jin Kim, "Fantastic Shin Sang-Ok," 148.

70. Ibid. However, it should be mentioned that although Kim Young-jin co-ordinated this second retrospective program at the PiFan, Han Sang-jun was deeply engaged with it. As programmer of Korean cinema at the PIFF in 2001, Han was in charge of Shin's first retrospective. After he quit the PIFF in 2002, he took over the new position as senior programmer at PiFan in 2006 and became festival director from 2007.

71. Ibid., 148.

72. Han, "The Cinematic World of Shin Sang-Ok", 7.

73. Dong-Ho Kim, preface to *The Second PIFF*, program booklet (Pusan: PIFF, 1997), 119.

74. Ji-seok Kim, "Celebrating 20th Century Asian Cinema: 20th Century Masterpieces," *The Fourth PIFF*, program catalog (Pusan: PIFF, 1999), 198.

75. The FIAF, founded in 1938 in Paris, France, is an international body consisting of organizations and institutions that preserve and manage moving image materials from all over the world as cultural heritage as well as historical material. Members cover more than 140 institutions from over 77 countries. http://www.fiafnet.org/uk/ (accessed June 28, 2007).

76. Dong-Ho Kim, "The Past, the Present and the Future of Asian Cinema," in *FIAF 58th Congress Symposium in Seoul: Asian Cinema—Yesterday, Today and Tomorrow*, ed. KOFA (Seoul: KOFA, 2002), 158.

77. Ibid., 156–60.

78. Young-jung Cho, "Programme Note of Korean Cinema Retrospective" in *The Ninth Pusan International Film Festival*, program booklet (Pusan: PIFF, 2004), 112.

79. Moon-yung Huh, "For Greater and Deeper Dialogue—Reflections on the Cultural Significance of Co-Production," in *Rediscovering Asian Cinema Network: The Decades of Co-Production between Korea and Hong Kong*, eds. Lee Yong-kwan, Huh Moon-yung, Cho Young-jung, and Park Dosin, The Ninth PIFF (Pusan: PIFF, 2004), 9.

80. "Budget for Special Program and Retrospective (2000–2007)," Ji-seok Kim, Asian Programmer of PIFF, e-mail, June 28, 2007.

Chapter 4 A Global Film Producer: The Pusan Promotion Plan

1. Hereafter abbreviated to PPP. As explained in the Introduction, although Pusan became Busan in 2000 following the revision of the Romanization system, the festival committee decided to retain Pusan and thus the acronym is PPP rather than BPP. However, Busan is used in other relevant organizations that changed their names following the revision, such as Busan Award, Busan Film Commission (BFC), and Busan Cinematheque.

2. Derek Elley, "Savvy Moves Boost Pusan Fest Fortunes," *Variety*, October 8, 2006, A1/A4.

3. Julian Stringer, "Global Cities and the International Film Festival Economy," in *Cinema and the City*, eds. Mark Shiel and Tony Fitzmaurice (Oxford: Blackwell, 2001), 135.

4. Yingjin Zhang, *Screening China: Critical Interventions, Cinematic Reconfigurations, and the Transnational Imaginary in Contemporary Chinese Cinema* (Michigan, Ann Arbor: Center for Chinese studies in University of Michigan, 2002), 40.

5. Stringer, "Global Cities and the International Film Festival Economy," 142.

6. The first PPP was held in 1998, two years after the establishment of the PIFF in 1996. This chapter deals with the eight festivals held from 1998 to 2005.

7. The IFFR launched the Hubert Bals Fund (HBF) within the CineMart in 1988 to support the completion of talented projects from developing countries. The HBF is also organized in partnership with CineLink, a co-production market of the Sarajevo Film Festival. This fund was awarded at the PPP between 1998 and 2003 and has since been transferred to the Hong Kong-Asia Film Financing Forum (HAF) in the HKIFF. The principal financier of the fund is the Dutch Ministry of Foreign Affairs.

8. Sponsors have varied and every year since its launch in 1998 new awards have been established. Apart from the main awards, there were other funding awards such as the UniKorea Award (1998, KRW10 million), the Ilnshin Award (1998–2001, USD10,000), and the Hanul Award (2000–2001, USD10,000), which were sponsored by the local film industry.

9. For a detailed list of projects presented to the PPP between 1998 and 2005, see PPP, http://ppp.asianfilmmarket.org/eng/03database/list_2006_project.asp. For the PPP projects completed up to the year 2005, the 8th PPP, see Appendix 5.

10. Within the film production process, there typically are the pre-production, production, and post-production stages. The pre-production stage is concerned with the development and revision of the script. Budgeting and financing decisions are made in this period. The production stage is when the actual filming takes place. This is the phase of principal photography with the director of the film overseeing the operations. During the post-production stage, film editing and the addition of visual effects are completed. Also, sound editing, musical scoring, and sound effects are completed during this stage.

11. Dong-Ho Kim, *The Second PIFF*, program booklet (Pusan: PIFF, 1997), 137.

12. Ibid., 139.

13. Julian Stringer, "Putting Korean Cinema in Its Place: Genre Classifications and the Contexts of Reception," in *New Korean Cinema*, eds. Chi-yun Shin and Julian Stringer (Edinburgh: Edinburgh University Press, 2005), 105.

14. Stringer, "Global Cities and the International Film Festival Economy," 136.

15. According to the PIFF's official record, 659 professionals from twenty-five countries were invited to the PIFF and the PPP in 1998. PIFF proudly reported the outstanding number of international participants. In that year, international guests numbered 419 while Korean guests were 240. PIFF, http://www.piff.org (accessed April 18, 2006).

16. Jonathan Watts, "Pusan Festival Perseveres," *The Hollywood Reporter*, October 2–4, 1998. n.p.

17. Derek Elley commented that "there's still a perceptible feeling both at PIFF headquarters and in the South Korean industry as a whole that the good times could end tomorrow." Derek Elley, "10th PIFF," *Cine 21*, October 27, 2005. http://www.cine21.com/Article/article_view.php?mm=001001002&article_id=34493 (accessed August 25, 2007).

18. As well as director Wayne Wang, Daniel Marquet (Le Studio Canal Plus, France) and Yoshizaki Michiyo (NDF International, UK) also attended the roundtable to discuss the co-production process in 1997.

19. Kim, *PPP Project: Fourth PPP* (Pusan: Sixth PIFF, 2001), 10.

20. For example, the Busan Award, the most prestigious fund, was given from 1999 onwards.

21. Kim, *PPP Project*, 10.

22. It should be noted that it was not always film directors who made this decision. Producers or distributors, for instance, closely (often financially) involved with the film also did. However, this chapter largely considers film directors as key decision-makers.

23. Hyuk-sang Lee, "The Third PIFF," *10 Years' PIFF Moments*, Photo Collection, (Pusan: PIFF, 2005), n.p.

24. Watts, "Pusan Festival Perseveres."

25. David Hesmondhalgh, *The Cultural Industries* (London: Sage, 2002), 2.

26. IFFR, http://www.filmfestivalrotterdam.com/eng/about/profile_iffr.aspx (accessed May 9, 2006).

27. For the full list of projects selected by CineMart, see CineMart, http://professionals. filmfestivalrotterdam.com/eng/cinemine/cinemart_awards.aspx (accessed July 20, 2007).

28. Jan Brussels, "Asian Films Getting Popular in Europe," *Kyodo News International*, January 29, 2004. http://findarticles.com/p/articles (accessed August 24, 2007).

29. Howard S. Becker, *Art Worlds* (Berkeley: University of California Press, 1982), 150.

30. Hesmondhalgh, *The Cultural Industries*, 53.

31. Julian Stringer, *Regarding Film Festivals* (Ph.D. thesis, Indiana University, 2003), 20.

32. Stringer, "Global Cities and the International Film Festival Economy," 138.

33. EFP, http://www.efp-online.com/cms/overview/overview_p_festivals_markets.html (accessed July 20, 2007).

34. To be used for project development, this fund supports a total sum of SEK150,000 for travel and accommodation costs of eight to ten directors and/or producers of selected projects. It also provides a SEK25,000 cash award to the best pitched project.

35. Derek Elley, "Pusan Mart Hits Bull's Eye," *Variety*, Oct 5–11, 1998, 21–2.

36. HAF is co-organized by the Hong Kong Trade Development Council and Hong Kong, Kowloon and New Territories Motion Picture Industry Association Ltd. The past HAF took place in 2000, 2005, and 2006.

37. The AFCNet was explained in Chapter 2.

38. BFC, http://www.bfc.or.kr/eng/01_about/overview.php (accessed June 29, 2006).

39. Stringer, *Regarding Film Festivals*, 44.

40. On May 28, 1999, the KMPPC was renamed the Korean Film Commission and changed its organizational structure in conjunction with the launch of Kim Dae Jung's government.

41. As a non-governmental cultural organization, the PIFF played a leading role in the promotion of Korean films by establishing international networks before KOFIC started it full-scale international marketing business in 1999. Since then, the two organizations have worked in close collaboration, promoting Korean films to the global market.

42. Hyuk-sang Lee, ed. *10 Years' PIFF History* (Pusan: Tenth PIFF, 2005), 175.

43. Rob Wilson, "Melodramas of Korean National Identity: From *Mandala* to *Black Republic*," in *Melodrama and Asian Cinema*, ed. Wimal Dissanayake (New York: Cambridge University Press, 1994), 90.

44. The new awards for the NDIF are Zemiro, Movie Zemiro, Muhan, and the BFC Award. *The PPP Project Guide Book* (Pusan: Fourth PPP, 2001), 17. Zemiro is a Korean multimedia entertainment company.

45. The Kodak Award provides negative film or services from Cinesite valued at USD20,000. The Korean Film-Making Assistant Project (KF-MAP) was sponsored by Japan's SONY PCL to support the post-production of the project.

46. This award was sponsored by the local film company Hanul Cine, providing a USD10,000 cash prize.

47. Tae-sung Jeong, *Introduction of the PPP Project* (Pusan: Fourth PPP, 2001), 6.

48. The total number of spectators of this film was approximately 240,000. KOFIC, http://www.kofic.or.kr/b_movdata/b_02bstatis.jsp (accessed July 15, 2007).

49. In recent years, mobile and DMB markets in Korea have become increasingly competitive. The links between these new media and films have become significant. For example, the first Mobile and DMB Film Festival was held in 2005 within the fifth Seoul Net Film Festival (SeNef), the online international film festival in South Korea. Mobile & DMB Fest, http://senef.net/senef_2006en/dmb/dmb_info.php (accessed July 22, 2007).

Chapter 5 Remapping Asian Cinema: The Tenth Anniversary in 2005

1. APEC (Asian Pacific Economic Cooperation) comprises twenty-one members including Australia, New Zealand, Brunei Darussalam, Canada, and the United States. APEC brands their members "economies" since the APEC co-operative process is predominantly concerned with trade and economic issues.

2. For an overview of the 10th PIFF, see Appendix 4.

3. For comparison, fifty-two films were shown as world premieres in the main sections of the 65th Venice Film Festival from August 27 to September 6, 2008. Of all films screened at the festival, only 12 films from Asia (three from China; one from India; two from Iran; four from Japan; and two from the Philippines) were invited. La Biennale di Venezia, http://www.labiennale.org/en/cinema/festival/en/77920.html (accessed August 29, 2008). See also Appendix 3.

4. Hee-moon Cho, "Forum: PIFF's Achievement for Ten Years and Assignment for Future." *Munhwa Ilbo*, October 15, 2005, 23.

5. Patrick Frater, "Pusan Unveils Bumper Crop," *Variety*, September 9, 2005. http://www.variety.com/article/VR1117928571.html?categoryid=19&cs=1 (accessed September 6, 2005).

6. Interview with Kim Hye-joon, general secretary of KOFIC, in Pusan (October 8, 2005).

7. Derek Elley, "How Things Have Changed in the World of Film Festivals during the Past 20 Years!" *Cine 21*, no. 525, October 27–November 1, 2005. http://www.cine21.com/Article/article_view.php?mm=001001002&article_id=34493 (accessed September 10, 2007).

8. Julian Stringer, "Global Cities and the International Film Festival Economy," in *Cinema and the City*, eds. Mark Shiel and Tony Fitzmaurice (Oxford: Blackwell, 2001), 139.

9. Ibid.; Thomas Elsaesser, *European Cinema: Face to Face with Hollywood* (Amsterdam: Amsterdam University Press, 2005), 86.

10. The tenth PyongYang International Film Festival was held in PyongYang, the capital city of North Korea between September 13 and 22, 2006. PyongYang International Film Festival (PIFF), which shares the same acronym as the South Korean Pusan International Film Festival, showcased seventy-two films including forty-two features,

documentaries, shorts, and animation. It started in 1987 bi-annually since its second edition in 1990. For its tenth anniversary in 2006, the PyongYang Festival invited international guests, including representatives from the Cannes Festival; Dieter Kosslick, director of the Berlin Film Festival; and journalists from the UK. However, Americans were still barred from attending and no US films were screened. For further information, see Derek Elley, "In North Korea, Serenity Is Surreal", *Variety* Oct 2–8, 2006, 10 and 16; Elley, "N. Korean Festival Draws Int'l Crowd" *Variety*, September 25–October 1, 2006, 7 and 12.

11. For an overview of the decade between 1996 and 2005, see Appendix 3.

12. Elley, "How Things Have Changed in the World of Film Festivals during the Past 20 Years!".

13. The PIFF is the first film festival in South Korea able to use the occasion of its tenth anniversary to leverage resources from the central government. Unlike PIFF, PiFan, the second biggest festival in Korea, failed to receive financial support for its tenth anniversary in the following year, 2006. This was widely attributed to the festival's unstable status stemming from the collision between the local film community and the festival committee since the mayor of Puchon dismissed festival director Kim Hong-joon the previous year.

14. "A Review of Korean Film Industry during the First Half of 2005," *Korean Film Observatory*, no. 16 (Summer 2005): 2–3.

15. Ibid. In the first half of 2005, the market share of domestic films was 50.4 percent.

16. Ibid.

17. Ilya Garger, "Best Film Festival," *Time Asia*, November 15, 2004. http://www.time.com/time/printout/0,8816,501041122–782192,00.html# (accessed September 7, 2007).

18. This was the opening film at the fourth PIFF.

19. Tenth PIFF press release, PIFF, September 29, 2005, http://press.piff.org/kor/index.asp (accessed June 1, 2006).

20. In 2003, PIFF announced the screening schedule for North Korean films at its press conference and stated, "The selection consisted of a range of seven films made between independence in 1945 and the 1990s, including *Beyond Joy and Sadness, Newly-Weds,* and *Snow Melts in Spring*. For three days starting the seventh PIFF, October 2003, the North Korean films were shown free of charge at two cinemas." Hyuk-sang Lee, ed. *10 Years' PIFF History* (Pusan: PIFF, 2005), 256–7.

21. The screening list of this section was as follows: *Ballad of the Man* (Teguh Karya, Indonesia, 1972), *Behind the Mosquito Net* (Teguh Karya, 1983), *Black Silk* (R.D. Pestonji, Thailand, 1961), *Country Hotel* (R.D. Pestonji, 1957), *Dark Heaven* (R.D. Pestonji, 1958), *A Simple Event* (Sohrab Shahid Sales, Iran, 1973), *Still Life* (Sohrab Shahid Sales, 1974), and *Sugar is Not Sweet* (R.D. Pestonji, 1965). In the following year (2006), fourteen films, made by Iran's Amir Naderi, India's Rajaram Vankudre Shantaram, and China's Cui Zi'en were highlighted. 2007, the third year of this special program, focused on Iranian director Dariush Mehrjui's films.

22. Derek Elley, "Savvy Moves Boost Pusan Fest Fortunes," *Variety Daily*, Oct 14, 2006, A1/A4.

23. In particular, a couple of journalists who wrote for the international trade magazines— *Variety* and *Screen International*—such as Patrick Frater and Derek Elley were critical about the scope of the PIFF's Asian programming.

24. Patrick Frater and Derek Elley, "Pusan Fest Balloons: Record Films, Attendance Marks 10th Year," *Variety*, October 3–9, 2005, B4.

25. "Banana programming" is a term used to describe Asian programming that deliberately reflects Western taste. This is a festival term informally well-known to festival professionals, particularly journalists who write for the industry magazines. The origin of this term can be traced back to the Hong Kong film *Banana Cop* (Po-Chih Leong, 1984), the story of a British-born Chinese cop who is sent to Hong Kong but cannot speak or read Chinese at all. In this film, "banana" specifically refers to someone who is "yellow" on the outside and "white" on the inside. Interview with Derek Elley in London (October 6, 2006 and September 13, 2007).

26. See Appendix 1.

27. Ji-seok Kim, "PIFF Family," *Cine21*, October 7, 2005. http://piff.cine21.com/2005/ article_view.php?article_id=33980&mm=006005001 (accessed September 10, 2007).

28. Eunjung Lee, "Selection of Opening Film," *Kookje Shinmun*, September 14, 2004, 21.

29. Ines Cho, "Bright Light on for PIFF Opening," *JoongAng Daily*, October 11, 2004. http://joongangdaily.joins.com/article/view.asp?aid=2479244 (accessed September 6, 2007).

30. Elley, "Savvy Moves Boost Pusan Fest Fortunes," A1/A4.

31. This festival was established as a strong market-based film festival in downtown Rome. The dates it ran in its first year were October 14–21, which overlapped with the PIFF's festival period in that year.

32. Festival director Dieter Kosslick further stated, "For American productions, especially for independent productions, this new procedure offers a unique chance within a very short period to position a new film not only on the market in America, but also worldwide at the Berlinale—and testifies once more to the good relationship between Germans and Americans." "The Berlinale 2004: February 5 to 15, 2004," press release, Berlinale, March 5, 2003. http://www.berlinale.de/en/archiv/jahresarchive/2004/08_pressemitteilungen_2004/08_Pressemitteilungen_2004-Detail_708. html (accessed June 13, 2011).

33. Here the concept of Pacific Rim or Asia Pacific is often related to socioeconomic processes and patterns of migration rather than geographic definition.

34. Tenth PIFF, press release, PIFF, September 29, 2005. http://press.piff.org/kor/index. asp (accessed June 1, 2006).

35. "Introduction of the APEC Screening," *Ticket Catalogue*, The Tenth PIFF (Pusan: PIFF, 2005), 126.

36. For instance, this organization claimed: "We object to the conspiracy of mercantilists who use the yardstick of neoliberalistic economics in the area of culture, and we do not think the cultural area should be subject to negotiations in a bilateral investment treaty, free trade agreement, and World Trade Organization." http://culturescope.ca/ev_en.php (accessed September 14, 2007).

37. Sooman Jegal, "Dark Clouds over PIFF," *Jeongookmael Shinmun*, October 10, 2005, 8.

38. Joon-sang Kang, "Defending Screen Quota but Supporting APEC?" *Prometheus*, October 13, 2005. http://www.prometheus.co.kr/articles/107/20051013/200510131 92600.html (accessed September 10, 2007).

39. The members include a range of film community organizations and insiders, including Busan Film Commission, PiFan, Seoul Film Commission, Council of Professors of Motion Picture Departments in Korean Universities, JIFF, Korean Film Directors Association, The Korean History of Motion Pictures Association, The Korean Movieman Association, The Association of Korean Movie Producers, Korean Motion Pictures Assistants Association, Korean Film Critics Association, and Korean Motion Pictures Institute.

40. Elley, "How Things Have Changed in the World of Film Festivals during the Past 20 Years!".

41. Albert Lee, foreword to *The Tenth Hong Kong International Film Festival*, program booklet (Hong Kong: Urban Council, 1986), 8.

42. Dong-Ho Kim, foreword to *The Tenth PIFF*, program booklet (Pusan: PIFF, 2005), 5.

43. Interview with Derek Elley in London (October 6, 2006).

44. First sponsored by the Urban Council, then, after 1997, by the Leisure and Cultural Services Department, the HKIFF was privately organized for the first time in 2005 with the incorporation of the Hong Kong International Film Festival Society, relying more than ever on private sponsorship. Charles Leary, "Hustle with Speed: The 29th Hong Kong International Film Festival March 22–April 6, 2005," *Senses of Cinema*, no. 36 (June 2005). http://archive.sensesofcinema.com/contents/festivals/05/36/hong_kong2005.html (accessed March 20, 2010).

45. Li Cheuk-to, foreword to *29th Hong Kong International Film Festival Catalogue* (Hong Kong: Hong Kong International Film Festival Society, 2005).

46. Films include *Spring River Flows East* (Cai Chushen, Zheng Junli, 1947) from the PRC; *The Beauty of Beauties* (Li Hanxiang, 1965) and *A Touch of Zen* (King Hu, 1971) from Taiwan; *Laugh, Clown, Laugh* (Li Pingqian, 1960) and *Boat People* (Ann Hui, 1982) from Hong Kong; and *Crouching Tiger, Hidden Dragon* (Ang Lee, 2000), a co-production of Taiwan/Hong Kong/US/PRC.

47. *A Century of Chinese Cinema: Look Back in Glory*, The 25th Hong Kong International Film Festival (Hong Kong: Hong Kong Critics Society, 2001), 5.

48. Jeremy Hansen, "Anniversary Blues: Bureaucracy and Political Meddling Threaten Hong Kong Film Festival," *Asia Week* 27, no. 14 (April 13, 2001). http://www.pathfinder.com/asiaweek/magazine/life/0,8782,105407,00.html (accessed August 15, 2007).

49. Ibid.

50. In addition to this situation, it is widely believed that frequent changes to the nature of its funding body can be understood as another factor in the decline of the HKIFF. It was initially funded by the Urban Council and Leisure and Cultural Services Department from 1977 to 2001, and then by the Hong Kong Arts Development Council from 2001 to 2004. In 2006, after completing its twenty-eighth edition, the HKIFF became officially incorporated as an independent, charitable organization—the Hong Kong International Film Festival Society Limited.

51. Talent Campus is a training program wherein about 500 new directors from almost seventy countries are invited to attend seminars and meetings at the festival. Since 2003, this has taken place in tandem with the Berlin Film Festival and attracted many talented young filmmakers from all over the world. In addition, it was recently expanded to include Talent Abroad, an identical program taking place in locations outside of Berlin such as India, South Africa, and Argentina.

52. AFA, http://afa.piff.org/eng/index.asp (accessed on September 3, 2007).

53. Michael Curtin, *Playing to the World's Biggest Audience: The Globalization of Chinese Film and TV*, (Berkeley, University of California Press, 2007), 14.

54. Ibid., 17.

55. Twenty candidates and eight teaching assistants from Asia are selected through both open admissions and a recommendation process.

56. This Paris-based residency program is a part of the Cinefondation which was created in 1988 as a Cannes festival selection category for short films. Each year since 2000, twelve participants are selected and invited to live in Paris for four and a half months. The residents all receive a EUR800-grant per month, free access to a large number of Paris cinemas, optional French lessons, and the opportunity to attend the Cannes festival during their stay.

57. When the AFA launched in 2005, it was hosted by Dongseo University and Korean Academy of Film Arts (KAFA), the national film school, which was first established in 1984 as the Korean Film Council's affiliation to nurture professional resources. The KAFA officially co-hosted the AFA until 2009, although the funding program provided by the KAFA lasted until 2006. Busan Film Commission joined co-host since 2010.

58. As a part of the post-AFA program, AFA is planning for the selected participants to continue their studies in filmmaking in the long term through KAFA's KASP (KAFA Asian Scholarship Program) and Dongseo University's DASP (Dongseo University Asian Scholarship Program). DAF (Dongseo University Asian Fund) was created in order to form a budget to support continuous production for the selected participant. In 2010, DASP, Technicolor Post-Production Fund, and Showbox Fellowship Fund were provided.

59. For instance, as well as Talent Campus at the Berlin Film Festival, there have been several similar workshops including Interactive Film Lab in Utrecht Academy of Arts in Netherlands, which all were supported by the Media Plus program in the European Union.

60. Jae-hyuk Yoo, "PIFF Has Surpassed Thirty Years' Tokyo Film Festival in Just Ten Years," *The Korean Economy Daily (Hankook Kyungje Shinmun)*, September 25, 2005, 26.

61. The dean of the second AFA was Korean director Im Kwon-taek, and the third in 2007 was Mohsen Makhmalbaf, an Iranian director. Among the many training programs run by film festivals, only the PIFF has this "dean" system. While the dean, who is usually a renowned Asian filmmaker, plays a key role in promoting the AFA by creating the image of a "real school," the PIFF may experience some difficulty in finding suitable deans in Asia in coming years as the dean has to be changed every year.

62. AFA takes place in two cities in Korea—Pusan and Seoul—over a three-week period: the first half in Seoul and the second half in Pusan. In the first part, participants get to make a short film after practical and individual training on HD and 35 mm while various programs, including master workshops, individual mentoring, seminars, interviews, and intensive lectures, are held in the second part.

63. This drive towards growth and change was also obvious when the PPP started including non-Asian projects from 2006. That same year, with the purpose of embracing a wider range of recent trends in the film industry, the PPP selected forty projects, including, for the first time, projects with a more commercially oriented nature, moving beyond but not forsaking its traditional preference for low-budget or independent films. This significant change of direction came alongside the launch of the Asian Film Market.

64. The AFM benefits from a six-fold budget increase, in comparison to a budget of USD500,000 for the PPP in 2005.

65. The AFM is structured around market booths, with room to accommodate three hundred companies from forty countries, the BFM-TV multimedia contents market and exiting events PPP and the BIFCOM locations showcase.

66. Jung-in Sohn, "Tokyo, Hong Kong Tensed, Pusan Is Going to Be a Mecca of Cinema," *Kookje Shinmun*, October 12, 2005, 21.

67. Patrick Frater, "Beyond Borders: Pusan Pumps Market Plans", *Variety*, Oct 11, 2006. http://www.variety.com/article/VR1117951695.html?cs=1&s=h&p=0 (accessed July 14, 2007).

68. In addition, to strengthen links with the local audience, the festival added an event called "Actors' Choice Troopers (AC Troopers)," in which selected audiences are joined by a group of Korean actors to watch films together. The AC Troopers joined the "Directors' Choice Troopers (DC Troopers)" which had been established at the ninth festival.

69. Julian Stringer, *Regarding Film Festivals* (Ph.D. thesis, Indiana University, 2003), 266.

70. Interview with Han Sun-hee in Pusan (Oct 11, 2005). Han was ex-online chief editor of *FILM2.0* and was in charge of reporting from the PIFF between 1998 and 2005.

71. Derek Elley, "Fest's Big Ticket Thicket," *Variety Daily*, Oct 19, 2006, 6.

72. PIFF finally decided to establish another special section entitled "Midnight Passion" in 2006.

73. For instance, according to the festival's official records, the fifth PIFF in 2000 gained KRW648,188,600 (approximately USD698,103) from paid admission of 148,733 for the ticket sales (the whole budget is USD3.5 million) and the sixth in 2001 sold 657,149,000 KRW (USD707,753) from 143,106 paid admissions (the whole budget is USD3.9 million). The sold tickets were KRW604,490,000 (USD651,039) from 165,102 admissions at the eighth PIFF in 2003 (the budget USD4.6 million). PIFF Organizing Committee, *A Report on Final Accounts*, unpublished material (Pusan: Fifth PIFF, 2000), 26; (Pusan, Sixth PIFF, 2001), 28; (Pusan: Eighth PIFF, 2003), 20.

74. Lotte Entertainment has begun to invest in and distribute local films since 2004. With a remarkable multiplex cinema chain running across the nation (more than 206 screens in twenty-six cities), this *jaebol* (*chaebol*) corporation has aggressively increased its domain in the film business and emerged as one of the forerunners, alongside Showbox and CJ Entertainment/Cinema Service, in the Korean film industry. Furthermore, it is worth noting that the sponsor of this spectacular event at closing night event was Lotte Entertainment, both the distribution company of the closing film and one of the premiere sponsors of the tenth PIFF.

75. Sung-jin Yang, "Pusan Film Festival to Strengthen Leading Position in Asia," *Korea Herald*, September 8, 2005. www.koreaherald.co.kr/archives (accessed September 8, 2007).

76. Lina Yoon, "On Parade at Pusan," *The Wall Street Journal*, www.wsj.com (accessed September 30, 2006).

77. Sung-jin Yang, "Quality Asian Films Await Movie Buffs" *Korea Herald*, October 1, 2005. http://www.koreaherald.co.kr/archives (accessed September 2, 2007).

78. For an extended discussion of the "festival audience" and "festival communities" in a European context, see Stringer, *Regarding Film Festivals*, 239–82; Marijke de Valck, "Drowning in Popcorn at the International Film Festival Rotterdam?: The Festival as a Multiplex of Cinephilia," in *Cinephilia: Movies, Love and Memory*, eds. Marijke de Valck and Malte Hagener (Amsterdam: Amsterdam University Press, 2005), 97–109.

Conclusion: Toward a New Channel

1. Jin-kwon Kang, "Pusan Film Fest to Add Los Angeles as a Venue," *Joongang Daily*, October 18, 2006. http://joongangdaily.joins.com/article/view.asp?aid=2829609 (accessed February 17, 2009). This event was also organized to celebrate the fortieth anniversary of the sister city relationship between Pusan and Los Angeles. This new joint-project was announced when Antonio Villaraigosa, the mayor of Los Angeles visited Pusan in October 2006.

2. Dina Iordanova, "Editorial Issue 34," *Film International* 6, no. 4 (2008): 7.

3. Korean Film Commission, http://www.kofic.or.kr/cms/132.do (accessed July 17, 2010)

4. Soyoung Kim, "'Cinemania' or Cinephilia: Film Festival and the Identity Question" in *International Film Festival Development Seminar: The Status of Researches and the Role of "International Film Festivals."* (Pusan: PIFF, 2010), 44.

5. Thomas Elsaesser, a paper presented at the *International Film Festival Development Seminar: The Status of Researches and the Role of "International Film Festivals."* (Pusan: PIFF, 2010).

6. It includes the Puchon International Fantastic Film Festival, Jeonju International Film Festival, Jecheon International Film & Music Festival, the Women's Film Festival in Seoul, and Seoul International Youth Film Festival. In the PIFF's case, most of its budget relies on corporate sponsors and the local government of Pusan. Of the PIFF's budget of KRW8.8 billion (USD8 million) in 2010, only KRW1.5 billion came from the central government, down from 1.8 billion in previous year. Although this is relatively small amount, the financial support from the state is critical to the festival.

7. Yonhap News, "Film Festival Organizers Protest Planned State Funding Cut," *Korea Joongang Daily*, November 23, 2010. http://joongangdaily.joins.com/article/view.asp?aid=2928702

8. Indie Space and the Media Center had been managed by the Association of Korean Independent Film and Video. This article reports that the Korean Film Council fired the association and determined the new operators—new right wing in 2009. The following article explains the background of the recent cultural and political affairs and criticizes a new conservative leadership. For further information, see Sung So-young, "In War Over Cultural Policy, Artists Lose," *Korea Joongang Daily*, July 1, 2010. http://joongangdaily.joins.com/article/view.asp?aid=2922530. For another important controversial audit of cultural institution, see Ah-young Chung, "K-Arts Protests Gov't Audit", *Korea Times*, May 27, 2009. http://www.koreatimes.co.kr/www/news/include/print.asp?newsIdx=45787. The article reports that Hwang Ji-woo, president of the Korea National University of Arts had to resign after an audit by the Ministry of Culture, Sports and Tourism in 2009.

9. Sung, "In War Over Cultural Policy, Artists Lose."

10. Soyoung Kim, "'Cinemania' or Cinephilia," 45.

11. Ibid.

12. Ibid., 44.

13. Ibid., 46.

14. Sergi Mesonero Burgos, "A Festival Epidemic in Spain," *Film International* 6, issue 4, no. 34 (2008): 13.

15. Marijke de Valck, "The Role of Film Festivals in the Age of YouTube," in *International Film Festival Development Seminar: The Status of Researches and the Role of "International Film Festivals."* (Pusan: PIFF, 2010), 71.

16. Thomas Elsaesser mentioned two important changes in the global film festival landscape: paradigm shift and empowerment of audience on October 13, 2010 in *International Film Festival Development Seminar: The Status of Researches and the Role of "International Film Festivals,"* (Pusan: PIFF, 2010).

17. For an overview of 15 years between 1996 and 2010, see Appendix 3.

Bibliography

Acharya, Amitav. "Regionalism and the Emerging World Order: Sovereignty, Autonomy, Identity," in *New Regionalisms in the Global Political Economy*, edited by Shaun Brelin, Christopher W. Hughes, Nicola Philips and Ben Rosamond, 20–32. London and New York: Routledge, 2002.

Allen, Richard. "Pesaro 1: Festival Review." *Framework*, no. 22/23 (Autumn 1983): 74.

An, Cheong-sook. "Shedding a Light on Asian Cinema: Closing the Second PIFF." *Hankyureh Shinmun*, October 18, 1997, 16.

Andrew, Dudley. "Waves of New Waves and the International Film Festival," in *Asia/Cinema/Network: Industry, Technology, and Film Culture*. The Tenth Pusan International Film Festival Symposium Program booklet, 255–65. Pusan: PIFF, 2005.

Appadurai, Arjun. *Modernity at Large: Cultural Dimensions of Globalization*. Minneapolis and London: University of Minnesota Press, 1996.

Baker, Michael. "Having It Both Ways: Korea Promotes and Censors Films." *Christian Science Monitor*, October 22, 1996, n.p.

Becker, S. Howard. *Art Worlds*. Berkeley: University of California Press, 1982.

Berry, Chris. "Introducing 'Mr. Monster': Kim Ki-Young and the Critical Economy of the Globalized Art-House Cinema," in *Post-Colonial Classics of Korean Cinema*, edited by Chungmoo Choi, 39–47. Irvine: Korean Film Festival Committee at the University of California, Irvine, 1998.

———. "'What's Big about the Big Film?': 'De-Westernizing' the Blockbuster in Korea and China," in *Movie Blockbusters*, edited by Julian Stringer, 217–29. London: Routledge, 2003a.

———. "Full Service Cinema: The South Korean Cinema Success Story (So Far)," in *Text and Context of Korean Cinema: Crossing Borders*, edited by Young-key Kim-Renaud, R. Richard Grinker and Kirk W. Larsen, Sigur Center Asia Paper, no. 17. (2003b): 7–16. www.gwu.edu/~eall/special/berry-hms02.html (accessed February 6, 2004).

———. "From National Cinema to Cinema and the National: Chinese-Language Cinema and Hou Hsiao-hsien's 'Taiwan Trilogy'," in *Theorising National Cinema*, edited by Valentina Vitali and Paul Willemen, 148–57. London: British Film Institute, 2006.

Berry, Chris, Jonathan D. Mackintosh and Nicola Liscutin, eds. *Cultural Studies and Cultural Industries in Northeast Asia: What a Difference a Region Makes.* Hong Kong: Hong Kong University Press, 2009.

Bianchini, Franco and Michael Parkinson, eds. *Cultural Policy and Urban Regeneration.* Manchester and New York: Manchester University Press, 1993.

Breslin, Shaun, Richard Higgott and Ben Rosamond. "Regions in Comparative Perspective," in *New Regionalisms in the Global Political Economy*, edited by Shaun Brelin, Christopher W. Hughes, Nicola Philips, and Ben Rosamond, 1–19. London and New York: Routledge, 2002.

Brussels, Jan. "Asian Films Getting Popular in Europe." *Kyodo News International*, January 29, 2004. http://findarticles.com/p/articles/mi_m0WDP/is_2004_Feb_2/ai_11290 2765/ (accessed August 24, 2007).

Burgos, Sergi Mesonero. "A Festival Epidemic in Spain." *Film International* 6, issue 34, no. 4 (2008): 13.

Castells, Manuel. *The Informational City: Information Technology, Economic Restructuring and the Urban Regional Process.* Oxford: Blackwell, 1989a.

————. "The Reconstruction of Social Meaning in the Space of Flows," in *The Informational City: Information Technology, Economic Restructuring and the Urban Regional Process*, 348–53. Oxford: Blackwell, 1989b.

A Century of Chinese Cinema: Look Back in Glory. Hong Kong: Hong Kong Critics Society, 2001.

Cha, Sang-keun. "Five-Star Hotels in Pusan Are Fully Booked." *Busanmaeil Shinmun*, September 23, 1998, 18.

Chang, Kyung-sup. "Compressed Modernity and Its Discontents: South Korean Society in Transition." *Economy and Society* 28, no. 1 (February 1999): 30–55.

Chen, Kuan-hsing, ed. *Trajectories: Inter-Asia Cultural Studies.* London and New York: Routledge, 1998.

Ching, Leo. "Yellow Skin, White Masks," in *Trajectories: Inter-Asia Cultural Studies*, edited by Kuan-Hsing Chen, 65–86. London and New York: Routledge, 1998.

————. "Globalizing the Regional, Regionalizing the Global: Mass Culture and Asianism in the Age of Late Capital." *Public Culture* 12, no. 1 (Winter 2000): 233–57.

Cho, Hee-moon. "Forum: PIFF's Achievement for Ten Years and Assignment for Future." *Munhwa Ilbo*, October 15, 2005, 23.

Cho, Ines. "Bright Light on for PIFF Opening." *JoongAng Daily*, October 11, 2004. http://joongangdaily.joins.com/article/view.asp?aid=2479244 (accessed September 6, 2007).

Cho Seung-hyun. "PIFF Seminar." *Kukje Shinmun*, June 7, 1996, 15.

————. "Special Programmes and Korean Retrospective." *Kookje Shinmun*, September 13, 1996, 13.

Cho, Young-jung. "Programme note of Korean Cinema Retrospective," in *The Ninth PIFF*, program booklet, 112. Pusan: PIFF, 2004.

Choe, Yong-shik. "Director to be Honored at PIFF." *Korea Herald*, November 15, 2001, 16.

Choi, Chungmoo, ed. *Post-Colonial Classics of Korean Cinema*. Irvine: Korean Film Festival Committee at the University of California, Irvine, 1998.

Christie, Ian. "Rendezvous a Bruxelles." *Framework*, no. 14 (Spring 1981): 55.

Chung, Ah-young. "K-Arts Protests Gov't Audit." *Korea Times*, May 27, 2009. http://www.koreatimes.co.kr/www/news/include/print.asp?newsIdx=45787

Ciecko, Anne, ed. *Contemporary Asian Cinema*. Oxford and New York: Berg, 2006.

Corless, Kieron and Chris Darke. *Cannes, Inside the World's Premier Film Festival*. London: Faber and Faber, 2007.

Cremin, Stephen. "Pucheon Set to Fill Regional Niche." *Hankyureh 21*, August 2, 2006. http://english.hani.co.kr/arti/english_edition/e_entertainment/146041.html (accessed October 8, 2006).

Curtin, Michael. *Playing to the World's Biggest Audience: The Globalization of Chinese Film and TV*. Berkeley: University of California Press, 2007.

Czach, Liz. "Film Festivals, Programming, and the Building of a National Cinema." *The Moving Image* 4, no. 1 (2004): 76–88. http://muse.jhu.edu/journals/the_moving_image/v004/4.1czach.html (accessed September 19, 2006).

De Valck, Marijke. "Drowning in Popcorn at the International Film Festival Rotterdam?: The Festival as a Multiplex of Cinephilia," in *Cinephilia: Movies, Love and Memory*, edited by Marijke de Valck and Malte Hagener, 97–109. Amsterdam: Amsterdam University Press, 2005a.

———. "Film Festivals: History and Theory of a European Phenomenon that Became a Global Network." Ph.D. thesis, University of Amsterdam, 2005b.

———. "The Role of Film Festivals in the Age of YouTube," in *International Film Festival Development Seminar: The Status of Researches and the Role of "International Film Festivals,"* 44–71. Pusan: PIFF, 2010.

Dirlik, Arif. "Culture against History? The Politics of East Asian Identity." *Development and Society* 28, no. 2 (December 1999): 188.

Eleftheriotis, Dimitris. "Turkish National Cinema," in *Asian Cinemas: A Reader and Guide*, edited by Dimitris Eleftheriotis and Gary Needham, 220–8. Edinburgh: Edinburgh University Press, 2006.

Elley, Derek. "Pusan Mart Hits Bull's Eye." *Variety*, Oct 5–11, 1998, 21–2.

———. "Pusan Pumps Korean Pic Profile." *Variety*, November 1–7, 1999, 19.

———. "Korean Pix Primp at Pusan Fest." *Variety*, November 20, 2001. www.variety.com/toc-archive (accessed August 11, 2006).

———. "Remake Fever Hits Pusan Festival." *Variety*, December 1, 2002. http://www.variety.com/index.asp?layout=festivals&jump=story&id=1061&articleid (accessed November 2, 2007).

———. "Korea, Beware! Ten Myths about the International Film Festival Circuit." *Cine21*, February 6, 2004. http://www.cine21.co.kr/kisa/sec-002100100/2004/02/040206163911129.html. (accessed October 10, 2006).

———. "10th PIFF." *Cine21*. October 27, 2005. http://www.cine21.com/Article/article_ view.php?mm=001001002&article_id=34493 (accessed August 25, 2007).

———. "How Things Have Changed in the World of Film Festivals during the Past 20 Years!" *Cine21*, no. 525, October 27–November 1, 2005. http://www.cine21.com/ Article/article_view.php?mm=001001002&article_id=34493 (accessed September 10, 2007).

———. "N. Korean Festival Draws Int'l Crowd." *Variety*, September 25–October 1, 2006, 7 and 12.

———. "In North Korea, Serenity Is Surreal." *Variety*, October 2–8, 2006, 10 and 16.

———. "Savvy Moves Boost Pusan Fest Fortunes." *Variety*, October 8, 2006, A1/A4.

———. "Fest's Big Ticket Thicket." *Variety Daily*, October 19, 2006, 6.

Elsaesser, Thomas. "Images for Sale: The 'New British Cinema." In *Fires Were Started: British Cinema and Thatcherism*, edited by Lester Friedman. 52–69. London: UCL Press, 1993.

———. *European Cinema: Face to Face with Hollywood*. Amsterdam: Amsterdam University Press, 2005.

———. "Film Festival Networks: The New Topographies of Cinema." Lecture presented at *International Film Festival Development Seminar: The Status of Researches and the Role of "International Film Festivals."* Pusan: PIFF, 2010.

"Exhibition of Historical Material of Korean Cinema is Empty and Quiet." *Kookje Shinmun*, September 21, 1996, 13.

"'Festival for the Public,' Korean Cinema Spotlighted: Interview with Kim Soyoung." *Kookje Shinmun*, September 23, 1996, 21.

"Film Festival Organizers Protest Planned State Funding Cut." Korea Joongang Daily, November 23, 2010. http://joongangdaily.joins.com/article/view.asp?aid=2928702 (accessed July 10, 2011).

Frater, Patrick. "Pusan Unveils Bumper Crop." *Variety*, September 9, 2005. http://www. variety.com/article/VR1117928571.html?categoryid=19&cs=1 (accessed September 9, 2005).

———. "Beyond Borders: Pusan Pumps Market Plans." *Variety*, October 11, 2006. http:// www.variety.com/article/VR1117951695.html?cs=1&s=h&p=0 (accessed July 14, 2007).

Frater, Patrick and Derek Elley. "Pusan Fest Balloons: Record Films, Attendance Marks 10th Year." *Variety*, October 3–9, 2005, B4.

Garger, Ilya. "Best Film Festival." *Time Asia*, November 15, 2004. http://www.time.com/ time/printout/0,8816,501041122–782192,00.html# (accessed September 7, 2007).

Gorenfeld, John. "Producer From Hell," *Guardian*, April 4, 2003. http://film.guardian. co.uk/print/0,,4640432–3181,00.html. (accessed December 1, 2006).

Hajer, Maarten A. "Rotterdam: Redesigning the Public Domain," in *Cultural Policy and Urban Regeneration: The West European Experience*, edited by Franco Bianchini and Michael Parkinson, 48–72. Manchester and New York: Manchester University Press, 1993.

Hall, Stuart. "The West and the Rest: Discourse and Power," in *Formations of Modernity*, edited by Stuart Hall and Bram Giebens, 276–95. Cambridge: Polity: 1992.

Han, Sang-jun. "The Cinematic World of Shin Sang-Ok," in *Shin Sang-Ok: Prince of Korean Cinema, Leading the Desire of the Masses*, edited by Sang-Jun Han and Jeong-Hwa Yang. Pusan: PIFF, 2001a.

———. "Korean Cinema Retrospective," in *The Sixth PIFF*, program booklet, 226. Pusan: PIFF, 2001b.

Han, Sang-jun and Jeong-hwa Yang, eds. *Shin Sang-Ok: Prince of Korean Cinema, Leading the Desire of the Masses*. Pusan: PIFF, 2001.

Hansen, Jeremy. "Anniversary Blues: Bureaucracy and Political Meddling Threaten Hong Kong Film Festival." *Asia Week* 27, no. 14, April 13, 2001. http://www.pathfinder.com/asiaweek/magazine/life/0,8782,105407,00.html (accessed August 15, 2007).

Harbord, Janet. *Film Cultures*. London: Sage, 2002.

Harris, Stuart. "Asian Multilateral Institutions and their Response to the Asian Economic Crisis: The Regional and Global Implications," in *New Regionalisms in the Global Political Economy*, edited by Shaun Brelin, Christopher W. Hughes, Nicola Philips and Ben Rosamond, 119–36. London and New York: Routledge, 2002.

Havis, Richard James. "A Star Is Born—Aged 78." *Moving Pictures MIFED*, 1997 Special (November 1997), n.p.

Hesmondhalgh, David. *The Cultural Industries*. London: Sage, 2002.

Hettne, Björn and Fredrik Söderbaum. "Theorising the Rise of Regionness," in *New Regionalisms in the Global Political Economy*, edited by Shaun Brelin, Christopher W. Hughes, Nicola Philips, and Ben Rosamond, 33–47. London and New York: Routledge, 2002.

Hindes, Andrew. "First Korean Pic Fest an Artistic, Popular Success." *Variety*, September 23–29, 1996, 26–9.

Huh, Moon-yung. "Opening Film," *The Seventh PIFF Catalogue*, n.p., Pusan: PIFF, 2002.

———. "For Greater and Deeper Dialogue—Reflections on the Cultural Significance of Co-Production," in *Rediscovering Asian Cinema Network: The Decades of Co-Production between Korea and Hong Kong*, edited by Lee Yong-kwan, Huh Moon-yung, Cho Young-jung, and Park Dosin, 8–13. Pusan: PIFF, 2004.

Im, Yung-ho. "The Media, Civil Society, and New Social Movements in Korea, 1985–93," in *Trajectories: Inter-Asia Cultural Studies*, edited by Chen Kuan-hsing, 330–45. London: Routledge, 1998.

"Introduction of the APEC Screening," in *The Tenth Pusan International Film Festival*, Ticket Catalogue, 126–131. Pusan: PIFF, 2005.

Iordanova, Dina. *Cinema of the Other Europe: The Industry and Artistry of East Central European Film*. London and New York: Wallflower Press, 2003.

———. "Showdown of the Festivals: Clashing Entrepreneurship and Post-Communist Management of Culture." *Film International* 4, no. 23 (October 2006): 25–37.

———. "Editorial Issue 34." *Film International* 6, no. 4 (2008), 4–7.

Iwabuchi, Koichi. *Recentering Globalization: Popular Culture and Japanese Transnationalism*. Durham and London: Duke University Press, 2002.

Jancovich, Mark, Lucy Faire, and Sarah Stubbings. *The Place of the Audience: Cultural Geographies of Film Consumption*. London: British Film Institute, 2003.

Jang, Byung-won. "Can Busan Be a Cinema City?" *Film 2.0*, November, 28, 2005. www.film2.co.kr (accessed 18 May 2005).

Jang, Ji-tae. "Asian Week and PIFF Open in the Same Day." *Busan Ilbo*, August 28, 1996, 29.

Jegal, Sooman. "Dark Clouds over PIFF." *Jeongookmael Shinmun*, October 10, 2005, 8.

Jeong, Tae-sung. *Introduction of the PPP Project*. Pusan: PIFF, 2001.

Jung, Hye-jin. "The Last Witness' Fail to Deliver." *Korea Times*, November 17, 2001, 16.

Jung, Kyung-moon. "Peppermint Syndrome Changed Cinema Culture." *Hankook Ilbo*, February 11, 2000. http://www.hankooki.com/ (accessed February 20, 2007).

Jung, Sang-do and Jin-woo Lee. "World Cinema Is the Most Popular Section at PIFF." *Kookje Shinmun*, September 21, 1996, 13.

Kang, Jin-kwon. "Pusan Film Fest to Add Los Angeles as a Venue." *Joongang Daily*, October 18, 2006. http://joongangdaily.joins.com/article/view.asp?aid=2829609 (accessed February 17, 2009).

Kang, Joon-sang. "Defending Screen Quota but Supporting APEC?" *Prometheus*, October 13, 2005. http://www.prometheus.co.kr/articles/107/20051013/20051013192600.html (accessed September 10, 2007).

Kang, Myung-goo. "Decentralisation and the Restructuring of Regionalism in Korea: Conditions and Possibilities." *Korean Journal* (Summer 2003): 81–108.

Karp, Ivan, Christine M. Kreamer, and Steven D. Lavine, eds. *Museums and Communities: The Politics of Public Culture*. Washington and London: Smithsonian Institution Press, 1992.

Katzenstein, Peter J. "Regionalism and Asia," in *New Regionalisms in the Global Political Economy*, edited by Shaun Brelin, Christopher W. Hughes, Nicola Philips and Ben Rosamond, 104–18. London and New York: Routledge, 2002.

Kim, Chang-bae. "PIFF's Economic Impact Is 5.2 Million Won." *Hankook Ilbo*, October 7, 2004. http://news.hankooki.com/lpage/society/200410/h2004100721170043400.htm (accessed on 4 June 2007).

Kim, Dong-Ho. Foreword to *The First PIFF*, program booklet, 10. Pusan: PIFF, 1996.

———. Preface, *PPP Project: Fourth PPP*, 10. Pusan: PIFF, 2001.

———. "The Past, the Present and the Future of Asian Cinema," in *FIAF 58th Congress Symposium in Seoul: Asian Cinema—Yesterday, Today and Tomorrow*, edited by KOFA, 158. Seoul: KOFA, 2002.

———. Foreword to *The Tenth PIFF*, program booklet, 5. Pusan: PIFF, 2005.

Kim, Eun-young. "PIFF Opens." *Busan Ilbo*, February 15, 1996, 1.

———. "Interview with Kim Dong-Ho." *Busan Ilbo*, August 16, 1996, 6.

———. "From Preparation to Opening." *Busan Ilbo*, September 13, 1996, 18.

Kim, Jin-kyung, and Jung-ho Lee. "PIFF Square." *Busan Ilbo*, September 21, 1996, 31.

Kim, Ji-seok. "Celebrating 20th Century Asian Cinema: 20th Century Masterpieces," in *The Fourth PIFF*, program booklet, 198. Pusan: PIFF, 1999.

———. "PIFF Family." *Cine21*, October 7, 2005. http://piff.cine21.com/2005/article_view.php?article_id=33980&mm=006005001. (accessed September 10, 2007).

Kim, Joo-young. "Festivals' Impact on Local Economy." *Maeil Kyungje Shinmun*, December 23, 1999, n.p.

Kim, Kyung-hyun. *The Remasculinization of Korean Cinema*. Durham: Duke University Press, 2004.

Kim, Myung-hwan. "PIFF Opens." *Chosun Ilbo*, May 20, 1996, 19.

Kim, Soo-kyung. "Hae-an-seon." *Dong-A Ilbo*, November 21, 2002. http://www.donga.com/fbin/output?code=Q__&n=200211210301 (accessed March 8, 2007).

Kim, Soyoung. "'Cine-mania' or Cinephilia: Film Festivals and the Identity Question." *UTS Review (Cultural Studies Review)* 4, no. 2 (1998): 174–87.

———. "Modernity in Suspense: Translation of Fetishism," in *The First Jeonju International Film Festival Symposium*, ed. Soyoung Kim, 83–90. Jeonju: JIFF, 2000.

———. "Cinemania" or Cinephilia: Film Festival and Identity Question," in *International Film Festival Development Seminar: The Status of Researches and the Role of "International Film Festivals,"* 44–60. Pusan: PIFF, 2010.

Kim, Su-yun. "British Film Critics Pleased with Improved Facilities at PIFF." *Korea Times*, October 22, 1999, 12.

Kim, Wang-bae. "Regionalism: Its Origins and Substance with Competition and Exclusion." *Korean Journal* (Summer 2003). www.ekoreanjournal.net (accessed on 3 March, 2007).

Kim, Young-jin. "Fantastic Shin Sang-Ok: A Legend in Korean Film in the '60s and '70s," in *Tenth Puchon International Fantastic Film Festival*, program booklet, 146–9. Puchon: PiFan, 2006.

Klinger, Barbara. *Beyond the Multiplex: Cinema, New Technologies, and the Home*. Berkeley: University of California Press, 2006.

KOFIC. Korean Film Database Book from 2000 To 2006. Seoul: KOFIC, 2006.

Krich, John. "Asia's Upstart Film Festival." *Asian Wall Street Journal*, April 20, 2000, 1–6.

Kwak, Han-ju. "Discourse on Modernization in 1990s Korean Cinema," in *Cinemas and Popular Media in Transcultural East Asia*, edited by Jenny Kwok Wah Lau, 90–113. Philadelphia: Temple University Press, 2003.

Lavine, Steven D. and Ivan Karp, eds. *Exhibiting Cultures: The Poetics and Politics of Museum Display*. Washington and London: Smithsonian Institution Press, 1991a.

———. "Introduction: Museums and Multiculturalism," in *Exhibiting Cultures: The Poetics and Politics of Museum Display*, edited by Ivan Karp and Steven D. Lavine. Washington and London: Smithsonian Institution Press, 1991b.

Leary, Charles, "Hustle with Speed: The 29th Hong Kong International Film Festival March 22–April 6, 2005," in *Senses of Cinema*, no. 36 (June 2005). http://archive. sensesofcinema.com/contents/festivals/05/36/hong_kong2005.html (accessed March 20, 2010).

Lee Albert. Foreword to *The Tenth Hong Kong International Film Festival*, program booklet, 8. Hong Kong: Urban Council, 1986.

Lee, Dong-jin. "Toward the New Center in Asia." *Chosun Ilbo*, November 10, 1997, 14.

———. "To Get the Innocent Dream Back, 'About-turn.'" *Chosun Ilbo*, October 15, 1999, 35.

Lee, Edmund. "Pusan Power." *Village Voice*, October 29, 1996, n.p.

Lee, Eunjung. "Selection of Opening Film." *Kookje Shinmun*, September 14, 2004, 21.

Lee, Hyangjin. "South Korea: Film on the Global Stage," in *Contemporary Asian Cinema*, edited by Anne Ciecko, 182–92. Oxford·New York: Berg, 2006.

Lee, Hyuk-sang, ed. *10 Years' PIFF History*. Pusan: PIFF, 2005.

———. ed. *10 Years' Moment*. Photo Collection, Pusan: PIFF, 2005.

Lee, Jin-woo. "PIFF Opens in September." *Kookje Shinmun*, February 2, 1996, 21.

Lee, Moon-sup. "PIFF." *Busan Ilbo*, August 13, 1996, 5.

Lee, Yong-kwan. "Opening Film," *The Fourth Pusan International Film Festival*, program booklet (Pusan: PIFF, 1999), 21.

Lee, Yong-kwan, Moon-yung Huh, Young-jung Cho, and Do-sin Park, eds. *Rediscovering Asian Cinema Network: The Decades of Co-Production Between Korean and Hong Kong*. Pusan: PIFF, 2004.

Lee, Yong-kwan and Sang-yong Lee, eds. *Kim Ki-Young: Cinema of Diabolical Desire and Reason*. Pusan: PIFF, 1997.

———. eds. *Yu Hyun-Mok: The Pathfinder of Korean Realism*. Pusan: PIFF, 1999.

Lee, Young-il. *The History of Korean Cinema: Main Current of Korean Cinema*. Translated by Richard Lynn Greever, 75–82. Seoul: Motion Picture Promotion Corporation, 1988.

Li, Cheuk-to. Foreword to *29th Hong Kong International Film Festival*. Program booklet, Hong Kong: HKIFF Society, 2005.

Martin-Jones, David. *Deleuze, Cinema and National Identity*. Edinburgh: Edinburgh University Press, 2006.

McGill, Hannah, and Andrew Pulver. "World Cinema Special—Is Nigeria the New Japan?" *Guardian*, March 30, 2007, 9–10.

McHugh, Kathleen and Nancy Abelmann, eds. *South Korean Golden Age Melodrama: Gender, Genre, and National Cinema*. Detroit: Wayne State University Press, 2005.

Min, Eung-jun. "Political and Sociocultural Implications of Hollywood Hegemony in the Korean Film Industry: Resistance, Assimilation, and Articulation," in *The Globalization of Corporate Media Hegemony*, edited by Lee Artz and Yahya R. Kamalipour, 245–64. Albany: State University of New York Press, 2003.

"Movie Lovers Get a Chance to Tour Pusan and Attend the Film Festival." *Korea Herald*, September 11, 1998, 10.

Nandy, Ashis. "A New Cosmopolitanism: Toward a Dialogue of Asian Civilizations," in *Trajectories: Inter-Asia Cultural Studies*, edited by Kuan-hsing Chen, 142–152. London and New York: Routledge, 1998.

Nichols, Bill. "Discovering Form, Inferring Meaning: New Cinemas and the Film Festival Circuit." *Film Quarterly* 47, no. 3 (Spring 1994): 16–30.

"Obituary: Shin Sang-Ok, Film Director and Abductee, Died on April 11th, Aged 79." *The Economist*, April 27, 2006. http://www.economist.com/people/displayStory.cfm?story_id=6849979 (accessed December 2, 2006).

Oh, Eun-ha, and Hong-joo Sohn. "Pleased to See Korean Film Festival." *Hankyeorye Shinmun*, September 29, 1997, 15–7.

Oh, Young-sook. "Imagination of Excess or Heresy," in *Kim Ki-young: Cinema of Diabolical Desire and Death*, edited by Yong-kwan Lee and Sang-yong Lee, 24–31. Pusan: Second Pusan International Film Festival, 1997.

Paquet, Darcy. "The Korean Film Industry: 1992 to the Present," in *New Korean Cinema*, edited by Chi-yun Shin and Julian Stringer, 32–50. Edinburgh: Edinburgh University Press, 2005.

———. "PPP Seminar: Advanced Window Marketing." Festival Report. http://www.koreanfilm.org/piff05.html (accessed November 29, 2006).

Park, Eun-ju. "The Last Witness." *Hankook Ilbo*, November 13, 2001, 36.

Park, Young-shin. "Why Bong Joon-Ho Jumped up from the Chair to Say Something." *Ohmynews*, November 18, 2006. http://www.ohmynews.com/articleview/article_view.asp?at_code=374048 (accessed November 28, 2006).

Pearson, Roberta. "A White Man's Country: Yale's Chronicles of America," in *Memory and Popular Film*, edited by Paul Grainge, 23–41. Manchester: Manchester University Press, 2003.

"PIFF Count Down." *JoongAng Ilbo*, June 6, 1996, 21.

The PIFF program booklets: First PIFF, 1996; Second PIFF, 1997; Third PIFF, 1998; Fourth PIFF, 1999; Fifth PIFF, 2000; Sixth PIFF, 2001; Seventh PIFF, 2002; Eight PIFF, 2003; Ninth PIFF, 2004; Tenth PIFF, 2005.

The PPP booklets: First PPP. Third PIFF, 1998; Second PPP. Fourth PIFF, 1999; Third PPP. Fifth PIFF, 2000; Fourth PPP. Sixth PIFF, 2001; Fifth PPP. Seventh PIFF, 2002; Sixth PPP. Eighth PIFF, 2003; Seventh PPP. Ninth PIFF, 2004; Eight PPP. Tenth PIFF, 2005.

PPP Project Guide Book, Pusan: PIFF, 2001.

"Pusan Film Fest: Huge Success With Foreign, Local Movie Fans." *Korea Herald*, October 20, 1997, 11.

Pusan Jikhalsi Sa Pyeonchan Wiwonhyoe, *History of Pusan City: Pusan-si Sa*, vol. 4. Pusan: Pusan Jikhalsi, 1991.

Ranvaud, Don. "Italian Festivals." *Framework*, no. 21 (1983): 54.

Rayns, Tony. "Korea's New Wavers." *Sight and Sound*. 4, no. 11 (1994a): 21–5.

———. *Seoul Stirring: 5 Korean Directors*, London: Institute of Contemporary Arts, 1994b.

———. "Sexual Terrorism: The Strange Case of Kim Ki-Duk." *Film Comment* (November/December 2004): 50–2.

A Report on Final Accounts. Unpublished Material. Pusan: Fifth PIFF, 2000.

———. Sixth PIFF, 2001.

———. Eighth PIFF, 2003.

"A Review of Korean Film Industry during the First Half of 2005." *Korean Film Observatory*, no. 16 (Summer 2005): 2–3.

Sassen, Saskia. *The Global City: New York, London, Tokyo*. Princeton and Oxford: Princeton University Press, 2001.

Segers, Frank. "Hae-an-seon." *Moving Pictures* (November 2002), n.p.

Shiel, Mark. "Cinema and the City in History and Theory," in *Cinema and the City*, edited by Mark Shiel and Tony Fitzmaurice, 1–18. Oxford: Blackwell, 2001.

Shiel, Mark and Tony Fitzmaurice, eds. *Cinema and the City*. Oxford: Blackwell, 2001.

Shim, Sang-kon. "Editorial: Film Festival in Pusan." *Kookje Shinmun*, February 6, 1996, 6.

Shin, Chi-yun and Julian Stringer, eds. *New Korean Cinema*. Edinburgh: Edinburgh University Press, 2005.

Shin, Jeeyoung. "Globalisation and New Korean Cinema," in *New Korean Cinema*, edited by Chi-Yun Shin and Julian Stringer, 51–62. Edinburgh: Edinburgh University Press, 2005.

Smith, Dorothy E. "Institutional Ethnography," in *Qualitative Research in Action*, edited by Tim May, 17–52. London: Sage, 2002.

Sohn, Jung-in. "Art or Law?" *Kukje Shinmum*, November 15, 2001a, 3.

———. "Runaway Was Banned." *Kukje Shinmun*, November 15, 2001b, 1.

———. "Tokyo, Hong Kong Tensed, Pusan Is Going to Be a Mecca of Cinema." *Kookje Shinmun*, October 12, 2005, 21.

Standish, Isolde. "Korean Cinema and the New Realism: Text and Context," in *Colonialism and Nationalism in Asian Cinema*, edited by Wimal Dissanayake, 65–89. Bloomington: Indiana University Press, 1994.

Stephens, Chuck. "Pusan the Envelope: Film-Festival Fever Seize South Korea's 'Hermit Kingdom.'" *LA Weekly*, November 7–13, 1997, n.p.

Stringer, Julian. "Global Cities and the International Film Festival Economy," in *Cinema and the City*, edited by Mark Shiel and Tony Fitzmaurice, 134–46. Oxford: Blackwell, 2001.

———. "Raiding the Archive: Film Festivals and the Revival of Classic Hollywood," in *Memory and Popular Film*, edited by Paul Grainge, 81–96. Manchester: Manchester University Press, 2003a.

———. "Regarding Film Festivals." Ph.D. thesis, Indiana University, 2003b.

———. Introduction to *New Korean Cinema*, edited by Chi-yun Shin and Julian Stringer, 1–12, Edinburgh: Edinburgh University Press, 2005a.

———. "Putting Korean Cinema in Its Place: Genre Classifications and the Contexts of Reception," in *New Korean Cinema*, edited by Chi-yun Shin and Julian Stringer, 95–105, Edinburgh: Edinburgh University Press, 2005b.

Sullivan, Maureen. "Pusan Focuses on Holding Back H'wood Onslaught." *Variety*, October 10–26, 1997, n.p.

Sung, So-young. "In War Over Cultural Policy, Artists Lose." *Korea Joonang Daily*, July 1, 2010. http://joongangdaily.joins.com/article/view.asp?aid=2922530.

Swann, Paul. "From Workshop to Backlot: The Greater Philadelphia Film Office," in *Cinema and the City*, edited by Mark Shiel and Tony Fitzmaurice, 88–98. Oxford: Blackwell, 2001.

The 10th Hong Kong International Film Festival, program booklet. Hong Kong: Hong Kong Urban Council. 1986.

Toh, Hai Leong. "Postwar Korean Cinema: Fractured Memories and Identity." *Kinema* (Fall 1996). http://www.kinema.uwaterloo.ca/article.php?id=296&feature (accessed June 12, 2011).

Turan, Kenneth. *Sundance to Sarajevo: Film Festivals and the World They Made*. Berkeley: University of California Press, 2002.

The 20th Anniversary of the Hong Kong International Film Festival: 1977–1996. Hong Kong: Hong Kong Urban Council. 1996.

Vasudev, Aruna. "Pusan's Enthralling Show." *The Pioneer*, October 3, 1996, 11.

Wasson, Haidee. *Museum Movies: The Museum of Modern Art and the Birth of Art Cinema*. Berkeley: University of California Press, 2005.

Watts, Jonathan. "Pusan Festival Perseveres." *The Hollywood Reporter*, October 2–4, 1998. n.p.

———. "Korea to Lift Ban on Japan." *Hollywood Reporter*, October 6–12, 1998, n.p.

———. "Japan-Korea Team at Pusan." *Hollywood Reporter*, September 17–19, 1999, 16.

"What PIFF Left Behind." *JoongAngilbo*, September 23, 1996, 6.

Willemen, Paul. "Pesaro." *Framework* 14 (Summer, 1981): 96–8.

———. "Rotterdam." *Framework*, No. 20 (1983): 41–4.

Wilson, Rob. "Melodrama of Korean National Identity: From *Mandala* to *Black Republic*," in *Colonialism and Nationalism in Asian Cinema*, edited by Wimal Dissanayake, 90–104. Cambridge: Cambridge University Press, 1994.

Woods, Peter. "Collaborating in Historical Ethnography: Researching Critical Events in Education." *International Journal of Qualitative Studies in Education* 7, no. 4 (1994): 309–21

Yang, Sung-jin. "Pusan Film Festival to Strengthen Leading Position in Asia." *Korea Herald*, September 8, 2005. www.koreaherald.co.kr/archives (accessed September 8, 2007).

———. "Quality Asian Films Await Movie Buffs." *Korea Herald*, October 1, 2005. http://www.koreaherald.co.kr/archives (accessed September 2, 2007).

Yang, Yoon-mo. "This Year's Programming." *Busan Ilbo*, November 17, 2001, 26.

Yi, Hyo-in and Chong-ha Lee, eds. *Korean New Wave: Retrospectives from 1980 to 1995*. Pusan: PIFF, 1996.

Yoo, Jae-hyuk. "PIFF Has Surpassed Thirty Years' Tokyo Film Festival in Just Ten Years." Hankook Kyungje Shinmun, September 25, 2005, 26.

Yoon, Ja-kyung. "PIFF, Looking for Sponsors." *Mael Kyungje Shinmun*, November 6, 2001, n.p.

Yoon, Lina. "On Parade at Pusan." *The Wall Street Journal*, October 1, 2005. http://online.wsj.com/article/SB112804271835656376.html (accessed September 30, 2006).

Yoshimoto, Mitsuhiro. "National/International/Transnational: The Concept of Trans-Asian Cinema and Cultural Politics of Film Criticism," in *The First Jeonju International Film Festival Symposium*, edited by Soyoung Kim, 61–9. Jeonju: JIFF, 2000.

Zhang, Yingjin. *Screening China: Critical Interventions, Cinematic Reconfigurations, and the Transnational Imaginary in Contemporary Chinese Cinema*. Michigan, Ann Arbor: Center for Chinese Studies in University of Michigan, 2002.

Websites

Asian Film Commissions Network. http://www.afcnet.org

Asia-Pacific Economic Cooperation. http://www.apecsec.org

Association of Southeast Asian Nations. http://www.aseansec.org

Berlin Film Festival. http://www.berlinale.de

Busan Film Commission. http://www.bfc.or.kr

Cannes Film Festival. http://www.festival-cannes.com

Cine21. http://www.cine21.com

CineMart. http://professionals.filmfestivalrotterdam.com/eng/cinemine/profile.aspx

European Film Promotion. http://www.efp-online.com

FIAF. http://www.fiafnet.org

Hong Kong International Film Festival. http://www.hkiff.org.hk

Gwangju Biennale. http://universes-in-universe.de/car/gwangju/english.htm

Gwangju International Film Festival. http://www.giff.org

International Film Festival Rotterdam. http://www.filmfestivalrotterdam.com

International Women's Film Festival in Seoul. http://www.wffis.or.kr

Jecheon International Film and Music Festival. http://www.jimff.org

Jeonju International Film Festival. http://www.jiff.or.kr

Korean Film Archive. http://www.koreafilm.or.kr

Korean Film Council. http://www.kofic.or.kr

Korean Film Database. http://www.koreafilm.or.kr

NETPAC. http://www.netpacasia.org

Puchon Fantastic Film Festival. http://www.pifan.com

Pusan International Film Festival. http://www.biff.kr

Seoul Net Film Festival. http://senef.net/senef

Tokyo International Film Festival. http://www.tiff-jp.net

The House of Kim Ki-Young. http://www.knua.ac.kr/cinema

Vancouver Film Festival. http://www.viff.org

Venice Film Festival. http://www.labiennale.org

Personal Interviews

Elley, Derek (senior international film critic of *Variety*, London). London, January 10, 2003.

———. Karlovy Vary, July 10 and 23, 2003.

———. London, October 6, 2006.

———. London, March 14, 2007.

———. London, September 13, 2007.

Han, Sang-jun (former Korean programmer of PIFF and former festival director of PiFan). Seoul, January 8, 2007

Han, Sun-hee (ex-online chief editor of FILM2.0, Pusan). Pusan, October 11, 2005.

Kim, Hye-joon (general secretary of KOFIC). Pusan, October 8, 2005.

———. Pusan, October 10, 2005.

Lee, Yong-kwan (PIFF co-director, ex-Korean programmer). Seoul, January 4, 2007.

Park, Kwang-su (film director/director of BFC). Seoul, January 6, 2006.

Tesson, Charles (former editor-in-chief of *Cahiers du Cinema*). Paris, June 10, 2003.

E-mail Communications

"Budget for Special Program and Retrospective (2000–2007)." Kim Ji-seok (Asian programmer of PIFF), e-mail, June 28, 2007.

Thomas Jong-suk Nam (former festival co-ordinator at PIFF 1997–2004), e-mail, August 10, 2007.

Index